What People Are Saying About *Chicken Soup for the Jewish Soul . . .*

"The people who made chicken soup a synonym for healing love now have a heartwarming book of their own. Read it and kvell!"

Rabbi Harold Kushner
author, *Living a Life That Matters*

"I defy anyone to read this book and not be moved to tears several times. This is a stunning collection of stories that will make you want to be a blessing in the lives of all the people you encounter. What more could one ask for—a book that actually makes one want to be a better person!"

Rabbi Joseph Telushkin
author, *The Book of Jewish Values: A Day-by-Day Guide to Ethical Living*

"If Jewish humor and wisdom need nourishing, *Chicken Soup for the Jewish Soul* will feed it. It is the traditional food for the soul and for the mind, whether served in a bowl or in a book."

Bonnie Lipton
national president, Hadassah—Women's Zionist Organization of America

"Wisdom, intelligence and resourcefulness, but above all, a particular sort of gentle humor, have enabled the Jewish people to survive thousands of years of adversity. These are wonderful stories, reflecting joy and sorrow and warmth, and the authors have compiled them with great sensitivity, affection and thoughtfulness."

Ronald S. Lauder
chairman, Conference of Presidents of Major American Jewish Organizations

"*Chicken Soup for the Jewish Soul* covers so many aspects of the Jewish experience, it touches us deeply. What a wonderful read for Jew and non-Jew alike."

Abraham H. Foxman
national director, Anti-Defamation League

"When the world's miseries and sheer ugliness threaten to overwhelm—as they too often do—our best defense is to recall the kindness of which we are capable. This lovely book, a collection of examples of humanity and humaneness at their most basic levels, is a valuable—and inspiring—refutation to those who think our condition hopeless. One story a day—especially on a gray day—and your spirit will be lifted."

Leonard Fein
founder, Mazon: A Jewish Response to Hunger
author, *Against the Dying of the Light*

"My family reads these stories out loud to each other. We laugh. We cry. We hug. A family that eats chicken soup together will remain culinary Jews. A family that reads *Chicken Soup* together will remain part of an enduring tradition that has transformed the world with its humor, passion and generosity of spirit."

Alan M. Dershowitz
Felix Frankfurter Professor of Law, Harvard Law School
author, *Supreme Injustice: How the High Court Hijacked Election 2000*

"*Chicken Soup for the Jewish Soul* is a book that you need to own. In the wisely chosen stories, we meet no less than ourselves at our best. It will inspire, excite and transform you. What more can a person ask for?"

Rabbi Marc Gafni
author, *Soul Prints*

"*Chicken Soup for the Jewish Soul* serves wisdom for and from the ages, informed by horror and humor, by lessons of the battlefield and of the kitchen table. It will nourish anyone's faith."

United States Senator Joseph R. Biden Jr.

"These personal stories from every corner of the world inspire us with their tales of the small everyday miracles that have nourished Jews since time immemorial. They speak to the nobility of Jewish ethics, the Jewish passion for life and the universal dignity of the human soul."

Rabbi Irving Greenberg
president, Jewish Life Network
author, *The Jewish Way* and *Living in the Image of God*

"With all the turmoil and violence in contemporary culture, here is a book that provides rest and nourishment for our souls."

Susannah Heschel
Eli Black Professor of Jewish Studies, Dartmouth College

"The Jewish soul has nourished us Christians for two thousand years. Now we get the *Chicken Soup* version. It is life-giving, edifying and graceful. All people will be enriched by these words that so beautifully capture the essence and the joy of what it means to be a Jew."

Bishop John Shelby Spong
author, *Liberating the Gospels: Reading the Bible with Jewish Eyes*

"A heartwarming and edifying work; guaranteed to make you feel better."

Gideon Patt
president and CEO, Israel Bonds
former Minister of Science and Minister of Tourism, State of Israel

"A great collection. Inspiring tales, uplifting stories and great jokes. They make us cry; they make us laugh. And if laughter is the best medicine, this book is a cure for the common cold. It's truly delightful."

Bernie Marcus
Chairman of the Board, The Home Depot

"*Chicken Soup for the Jewish Soul* not only nourishes and warms the soul, as a good bowl of chicken soup should (not too much salt please), but I found that it both inspired me and filled me with pride for the legacy given me by my fellow Jews."

Rudy Boschwitz
United States Senator 1978–1991

"This serving of Jewish soul food is a collection of poignant and touching anecdotes, true life accounts of *hashgacha pratit*—God's intervention in one's personal history. The editors are to be congratulated for their efforts in amassing these delicious morsels for the mind, tidbits of Jewish life."

Limor Livnat
Minister of Education, State of Israel

"This book is a masterpiece. I laughed and cried and wished for more. May it warm the hearts of many and serve as a living legacy for our people. Were my grown sons still small, I would read them a story from this precious book every night, over and over again. It would be a complete education in life—its joys and sorrows—and how an unseen hand with a great sense of humor works magic in our lives through our love of one another."

Joan Borysenko
author, *Inner Peace for Busy People*

"These stories are like a steaming bowl of chicken soup on a cold, rainy day—they make you feel warm inside, and you want to come back for more!"

Linda Gradstein
NPR correspondent in Jerusalem

"I had never thought of that Greco-Roman term of 'soul' as being 'Jewish,' but *Chicken Soup for the Jewish Soul* gives it the materiality it needs! These are great stories for people of every culture."

The Reverend Dr. Ross H. Trower
former Chief of Chaplains, U.S. Navy (ret.)

CHICKEN SOUP FOR THE JEWISH SOUL

Stories to Open the Heart and Rekindle the Spirit

Jack Canfield
Mark Victor Hansen
Rabbi Dov Peretz Elkins

Health Communications, Inc.
Deerfield Beach, Florida

www.bci-online.com
www.chickensoup.com

We would like to acknowledge the following publishers and individuals for permission to reprint the following material. (Note: The stories that were penned anonymously, that are public domain, or that were written by Jack Canfield, Mark Victor Hansen or Rabbi Dov Peretz Elkins are not included in this listing.)

She Didn't Pray for a Miracle. Reprinted by permission of Cynthia Mercati. ©1999 Cynthia Mercati.

The Cantor and the Klansman. Adapted from *Not by the Sword: How a Cantor and His Family Transformed a Klansman,* Boston: Northeastern University Press, 2001. ©1995 by Kathryn Watterson. Reprinted by permission of Ellen Levine Literary Agency, Inc.

Salvation in Sarajevo. Reprinted by permission of Rabbi Richard J. Plavin. ©1995 Rabbi Richard J. Plavin.

A Special Grandfather. Reprinted by permission of Bel Kaufman. ©1966 Bel Kaufman.

(Continued on page 353)

Library of Congress Cataloging-in-Publication Data

Chicken Soup for the Jewish soul : stories to open the heart and rekindle the spirit / [compiled by] Jack Canfield, Mark Victor Hansen, Dov Peretz Elkins.

p. cm.

ISBN 1-55874-899-7 (hardcover) — ISBN 1-55874-898-9 (trade paper)

1. Jewish way of life—Anecdotes. 2. Spiritual life—Judaism—Anecdotes. 3. Interpersonal relations—Religious aspects—Judaism—Anecdotes. I. Canfield, Jack, date. II. Hansen, Mark Victor. III. Elkins, Dov Peretz.

BM723 .C45 2001
296.7'2—dc21

2001024795

ISBN 1-55874-898-9 (trade paper) — ISBN 1-55874-899-7 (hardcover)

Publisher: Health Communications, Inc.
3201 S.W. 15th Street
Deerfield Beach, FL 33442-8190

Cover design and typesetting by Lawna Patterson Oldfield
Cover photos ©PhotoDisc

Dedicated
to all those who
have kept the Jewish people
alive for four thousand years by
telling stories

It is said that stories can help put you to sleep. I say stories can help wake you up!

—Rabbi Nahman of Bratslav, d. 1810

BERGMAN OF ALCATRAZ:

Reprinted by permission of Barricade Books.

Contents

2. BEING A JEW

3. ON LOVE AND KINDNESS

4. OUR COMMON HUMANITY

5. FAMILY

Acknowledgments

While it may take a village to raise a child, it took several villages of talented people to create *Chicken Soup for the Jewish Soul.* The collaboration from people around the world has made it possible to compile a book that will inspire and uplift the hearts of people of all backgrounds, faiths and nationalities.

Among the special people we want to thank most of all are our families—Maxine Elkins, Hillel and Rachel Levin Elkins, Jonathan Elkins, Shira Elkins Adatto, Jamie and Abigail Silverman Stadlin, Jeremy and Yoni Stadlin, Christopher Canfield, Oran Canfield, Kyle Canfield, Inga Mahoney Canfield, Travis and Riley Mahoney, Patty Hansen, Elizabeth Hansen and Melanie Hansen.

Maxine Elkins was a crucial gatekeeper in being the first reader of hundreds of stories that poured in from the beginning. She also helped in innumerable other ways—too many to count. At a critical point in preparation of the manuscript, Jeremy and Yoni Stadlin worked feverishly to prepare the readers' manuscript and furnished a wealth of computer expertise when the project was at a crucial stage of development. Their labor of love pushed it forward when it might have been seriously delayed.

Dinah Gornish, a very special reader and wise adviser, was of great help in locating moving stories.

Special thanks to our publisher. Peter Vegso continues to keep the now world-renowned *Chicken Soup* engine charging forward. We also acknowledge with deep gratitude Peter's former partner, Gary Seidler, who was of great encouragement at every step.

The staff at Chicken Soup Enterprises, Inc., have become not just facilitators and collaborators, but also valued and cherished friends. These include Heather McNamara, a devoted and discriminating editor and coworker; D'ette Corona, Veronica Romero, Teresa Esparza, Robin Yerian, Cindy Holland, Vince Wong, Maria Nickless, Lisa Williams, Michelle Adams, DeeDee Romanello, Trudy Marschall, Shanna Vieyra, Joy Pieterse, Kristi Knoppe, and David Coleman, who support Jack's and Mark's businesses with skill and love.

Nancy Mitchell-Autio was permissions editor when the project began, and she turned it over to her able successor, Leslie Riskin, who became almost an hourly contact person in the final stages of permissions. Leslie's cheerful attitude and detective-like skills made it possible to trace down some of the authors who have moved or changed their location, e-mail address and/or phone number.

Deborah Hatchell contributed not just administrative and managerial skill, but a sweet personality, a can-do attitude and strong support in countless ways.

Patty Aubery is a great role model to us all and the glue that holds the *Chicken Soup for the Soul* family together. We truly value and appreciate her special friendship, loving heart and brilliant business sense.

We thank Patty Hansen for her commitment to the *Chicken Soup* mission, and for her thorough and competent handling of the legal and licensing aspects of this project.

Our gratitude extends to Laurie Hartman for being such a good guardian of the *Chicken Soup* brand.

Many thanks to Mark and Chrissy Donnelly for their exceptional marketing skills and for representing *Chicken Soup for the Soul* with such style and enthusiasm.

Two experienced *Chicken Soup* story finders provided much-appreciated expertise—Beverly Merson and Bryan Aubrey. Bryan's brilliant editing skills gave many of these stories the inspirational glow that makes them ignite the reader's soul. Professor Miriyam Glazer, chairperson of the Department of Literature at the University of Judaism in Los Angeles, freely provided her editorial expertise on several stories. Special thanks to Rabbi Leonard Berkovitz and Rachel Pinhasi for their research efforts. Thanks also to Iris A. Rudin for her valuable assistance.

Veteran *Chicken Soup* coauthors Hanoch McCarty, Marci Shimoff, Martin Rutte, Raymond Aaron, Tom Lagana and Carol Kline have generously shared their own experiences in being midwife to a *Chicken Soup* masterpiece. As a long-term personal friend, Hanoch McCarty deserves special credit for his friendship, wise counsel and widely known energetic and highly skilled expertise.

Two esteemed scholars shared with us their Jewish cartoon collections, with grace and generosity—Rabbis Joel T. Klein and Mark Peilin, for which we are very grateful.

The secretaries at The Jewish Center of Princeton, New Jersey, Janice Fleming Berg and Helen Schlaffer, squeezed many special projects into their already-busy schedules for the benefit of this book, because they see in it a valuable contribution to Jewish literature. Their tears and laughter helped in the selection of many stories. Their good cheer and kindness were indispensable.

Many old and new friends were initial readers of the preliminary manuscript. Their discriminating judgment aided inestimably in the final selection. The book is infinitely richer because of their many hours of reading and offering valuable suggestions. These include: Raymond Aaron, Helene Abramson, Fred Angelis, Chana Chaya Bailey, Ann Behar, Melanie Berman, Carla Bleeker, Charlene Borsack, Kris Byron, Ellen Gilbert Castellano, Rabbi Kenneth Cohen, Leslie Cohen, C. C. Connable, D'ette Corona, Elaine Dushoff, Adele Berkowitz Elkins, Gil Gordon, Dinah Gornish, Leona Green, Ruth M. Grossberg, Nancy Richard-Guilford, Liz Howe, Lee Innocenti, Ed and Judy Kaplan, Jayne Kaplan, Heidi Keller, Howie Kirschenbaum, Kendall Leigh, Judy Slovin Levenfeld, Joan Levin, Danielle Lewis, Mike and Deanna Lissner, Rabbi Stephen Listfield, Barbara Lomonaco, Stanley and Sue Martin, Linda Mitchell, Barbara Mogelefsky, Matthew Molitch, Susan Muszynski, Sondra G. Obstein, Judith Klein Pendergast, Kim Pimley, Joy Pollock, Ellen Pristach, Ilene Putterman, Lynda Rajfer, Courtney Robart, Carol Rosenblatt, Margie Rosten, Barbara Rubin, Martin Rutte, Peninnah Schram, Gary Seidler, Audrey Katzman Seifert, Mimi Silberstein, Lori Simon, Rebecca Simon, Barbara Spack, Linda Steigman, Susan Yacker, and Malvin and Irene Weinberger.

The staff of our publisher, Health Communications, Inc., has been helpful in every way—with their prompt, eager, and energetic teams of production, marketing, and general good cheer. This is obviously more than "just another book" for them, since each and every *Chicken Soup* book is treated as an "only child." Their devotion to every aspect of the book's attractive appearance, high standard of production, vigorous promotion and loving follow-up is much appreciated by us. We especially want to thank the following people at HCI, whose special attention to this book made it the wonderful and beautiful final product that it is:

Christine Belleris, Lisa Drucker, Allison Janse and Susan Tobias, our editors at Health Communications, Inc., for their devotion to excellence. We love how easy and joyful it is to work with them.

Terry Burke, Tom Sand, Teri Peluso, Irena Xanthos, Jane Barone, Lori Golden, Kelly Johnson Maragni, Karen Bailiff Ornstein, Randee Feldman, Patricia McConnell, Kim Weiss, Maria Dinoia, Kimberley Denney, Claude Choquette, Luc Jutras, and all the other people in the marketing, sales, administration and public-relations departments at HCI, for doing such a good job supporting our books.

All the people in the art department at HCI for their talent, creativity and patience producing book covers and inside designs that capture the essence of our work: Larissa Hise Henoch, Lawna Patterson Oldfield, Andrea Perrine Brower, Lisa Camp, Anthony Clausi and Dawn Grove.

When we began this project, we had no idea how many people all over the world—Jewish, non-Jewish, American, Israeli, European, Australian and others—would hear of *Chicken Soup for the Jewish Soul,* and mail, fax or e-mail their stories to us. As the project moved forward, it became clear that selection of the stories would become the most difficult task. The Jewish experience is so personal, so emotional, so family-oriented; almost every Jew has a story. Hundreds and hundreds of stories, from people of all ages, people of all stages of personal and professional life, were delivered to us one way or another. It is not an exaggeration to say that, were it not for considerations of cost, space and practicality, this book could have contained double the number of stories it does. To all those who submitted your beautiful, touching and heartwarming stories, and would have been the next story in the book, we ask your forgiveness. As with other *Chicken Soup* books, there is always the possibility of a second volume. Perhaps some of your stories will yet see the light of day under a different cover.

To all those kind and spiritual souls who have been

asking more times than we can remember, "When is *Chicken Soup for the Jewish Soul* coming out?" we are grateful to you for your encouragement, humbled by your patience and indebted to you for your boundless and passionate love of drinking from the bottomless well of faith, courage, perseverance and wisdom contained in Jewish stories.

Introduction

The metaphor of chicken soup as a source of healing and nourishment has been a Jewish linguistic and dietary staple from time immemorial. Likewise, storytelling as an instrument of healing goes back to the earliest stories of Genesis in the Bible. The Jewish influence on the fundamentals of the *Chicken Soup* series is long and deep. While this particular collection of Jewish tales has been in the making for several years, it can be comfortably said that every Jewish story, from Adam and Eve to Natan Sharansky, is chicken soup to every human soul. Thus, the entire *Chicken Soup* series has a very Jewish as well as a universal basis.

Ever since the publication of the first *Chicken Soup* books, readers have been enthusiastically waiting for a book of *Chicken Soup* stories with Jewish content. How can there be a series of story books, after all, and not have as one of its most distinguished members a book of Jewish stories?

Many people ask the question: What is the secret of Jewish survival? What other people have been driven from their homeland, time and again, persecuted, beaten down, wandered the four corners of the earth, and yet have had an impact so far out of proportion to their still-small numbers, that it defies the imagination? Perhaps it is because when the People left the Land of their ancestors, they carried their stories with them.

No enemy could destroy an inspiring tale in the heart of a banished Jew. No ravage of disease, dislocation or disheartenment could ever rob the People of the Book of the uplifting and inspiring stories contained in their special Book.

Nobel Laureate Elie Wiesel has written that God created the human race because of God's love for stories. Without creatures on the Earth, what stories could be wrought to bring God the joy, intrigue, curiosity, celebration and sanctification that are imbedded in each and every Jewish story?

Among the stories within the covers of this volume, we have striven to select tales that reflect both the glory and the dishonor of the proud record of the Jewish people. But even in its times of blackest darkness, its deep collection of legends, anecdotes and narrative traditions of hope and future redemption kept the Jewish people from succumbing to despair or to spiritual or moral deprivation.

The Yiddishisms (who doesn't know what *chutzpah, maven* or *shlep* mean?), the universal Hebrew words (*shalom, halleluyah, amen, Sabbath,* etc.) have burrowed their way into English and other languages, along with their values, cultural norms and spiritual traditions. So have Jewish stories. Legends and tales from the Talmud, the Midrash, medieval folklore, and modern literary novels contain so much Jewish culture and values that one can say that just by reading Jewish stories one learns much of the history, ideals and sacred occasions of Jewish life.

If Jews have survived for four thousand years, from Abraham and Sarah to Ben-Gurion and Golda Meir, it is because no group of Jews has ever lived their life without carrying a chockful bag of parables, anecdotes and narratives to share with their family, neighbors and anyone who loves a good story. But Jewish stories are not simply stories—they are stories of courage, devotion to education and learning, perseverance, piety, familial love, community solidarity, heroic behavior, noble endeavors and extraordinary achievements.

It is no accident, therefore, that the two coauthors who began this popular series some seven years ago thought of calling it by a Jewish title—*Chicken Soup for the Soul.* Both *chicken soup* and *stories* are quintessentially Jewish. But, then again, most things the Jews have given the world for the last many millennia have become the cultural and spiritual baggage of all major religions, cultures and national groups.

We conclude with a story about stories. This story comes from the Hasidic tradition. Hasidism is that eighteenth-century movement that brought fire, spirit, inspiration, song, love and rich stories back to many Jews who had been bent over by the weight of prejudice and discrimination. Their stories have been resurrected and spread like magical seeds nourishing the earth's soil by Martin Buber, perhaps the best-known Jewish teacher of the last century.

In the middle eighteenth century, when Rabbi Israel Baal Shem Tov saw misfortune threatening the Jewish people, he went into a certain part of the forest. There he lit a fire and said a prayer. Then a miracle happened, and misfortune was kept at bay.

Later, when his disciple, the Maggid of Mezritch, was forced to intercede before God on behalf of the Jewish people, he went to that same place in the forest and said: "Ruler of the Universe, I do not know how to light the fire, but I can still recite the prayer." Once more a miracle occurred, and misfortune was averted.

Still later, Rabbi Moshe Leib of Sassov, in order to save his people, went to the forest and said, "I don't know how to light the fire. I don't know how to say the prayer. But I do know the place to go, and I pray that this will be sufficient." It was, and again a miracle was accomplished.

Then it fell to Rabbi Israel of Rizhin to conquer misfortune. Sitting in his easy chair, the rabbi spoke to God, "I cannot light the fire. I cannot recite the prayer. I no longer know the exact place in the forest. All I can do is tell the story, and this must be sufficient." And it was.

The story was all that was left. And it was more than enough. There are times when all we have is the story. And it must be sufficient.

Share with Us

We would love to hear your reactions to the stories in this book. Please let us know what your favorite stories were and how they affected you.

We also invite you to send us stories you would like to see published in future editions of *Chicken Soup for the Soul*. Please send submissions to:

Chicken Soup for the Soul
P.O. Box 30880
Santa Barbara, CA 93130
fax: 805-563-2945

You can also access e-mail or find a current list of planned books at the *Chicken Soup for the Soul* site at *www.chickensoup.com.*

We hope you enjoy reading this book as much as we enjoyed compiling, editing and writing it.

Dear Reader

In an attempt to assist readers who are not familiar with many of the Hebrew and Yiddish terms used in this book, we have italicized some words throughout the book and provided a glossary of terms and definitions on pages 333–334.

1

TO LIFE

I have set before you life and death, the blessing and the curse. Therefore, choose life.

Deuteronomy 30:19

She Didn't Pray for a Miracle

One who has compassion for others will receive compassion from Heaven.

Talmud, Tractate Shabbat

That morning, as every morning, Sonya awoke from a nightmare, her heart thudding. She had heard it all again so clearly—the shouts of the soldiers, the pounding on the door. Quickly she got out of bed, pressing her hands to her head. She could not, would not let the past intrude on her. After a moment, she willed herself back to calmness, and then, methodically, she began dressing for work.

Sonya had escaped from Hitler's Germany the year before. She and her family had been active in the resistance movement in their small city—and they had paid for it. Her husband had been taken away in the night. For questioning, the SS men had said. But as they led him out, he and Sonya had managed a brief embrace. They knew it was farewell. Her brother-in-law had disappeared in the same way; her sister, niece and nephew had been taken off to work as slave laborers in a weapons factory.

Last of all, the soldiers had come for Sonya's son. They had arrested him at school. That time there wasn't even the chance for a good-bye. Shortly afterwards, Sonya had been smuggled out of Germany through American intervention, and she resettled in New York City. An apartment had been found for her, and a job as well, doing alterations and fine needlework in a large department store. She had a life—but not really. To survive, Sonya had not only sealed up her past, she had closed herself off. During the day, she was as removed from the rest of the world as if she was a stone. In fact, that's how she thought of herself. As made of stone. Only at night, as she slept, would the unwanted past come creeping back.

At the store, Sonya did her work efficiently and well—and silently. She never spoke to any of the people who sat near her, and they knew better than to try and speak to her. At lunch, too, she sat alone.

Only on this day, as she sat in the store cafeteria, a voice interrupted her.

Sonya looked up, startled. "Mrs. Stein!" She gestured to the heavyset woman in the elaborate hat. "Yes, please, please sit."

Mrs. Stein was on the refugee assistance committee that had found Sonya her apartment and her job. "We have two children, from Germany," Mrs. Stein began. "They've been through so much. The girl is ten; the boy is seven. They need a home. Not just a place to live, a home. I thought maybe you needed someone, too."

Ten and seven. The exact ages her niece and nephew would have been now. Of course, she couldn't take these children. They'd be living reminders of the past. Sonya shook her head. "I cannot."

"Will you at least think about it, Sonya? I'll come back tomorrow and you can give me your answer then."

"There's no need," Sonya said stiffly. "I cannot take them."

For a few moments more, she felt Mrs. Stein's eyes on her. Kindly eyes, but eyes that saw too much. Sonya kept her head down until the woman moved away.

Sonya worked faster than usual that afternoon and left work early. She hurried home, turned off the lights and crawled into bed. That's what she did on the bad days, struggling alone in the darkness to keep the door shut on the past. But tonight it wasn't working and she knew why. The mention of those children had started up memories she couldn't stop. The ache within became an actual physical pain. The only way she could ease it was with tears. For the first time since she'd left Germany, Sonya began crying.

Sobbing, stumbling, she went to the closet and pulled out the small satchel she'd carried with her from Germany. Wrapped in heavy cloth were three photographs: her husband, her son and her sister. Tenderly, she unwrapped the picture and then she set them on the bureau. It hurt to look at them . . . but they also brought comfort. She began to remember the good times again, the happy times as well as the bad. And she knew that she had to start reaching out again, not only for herself, but for the people in the pictures. She had to carry on for all of them.

Sonya knelt by her bed. It had been a long time since she'd prayed, and the words came hard. "I want to come alive again," she whispered. "I don't know how, but I'm hoping you can help me. Amen."

It had been a very disjointed kind of prayer, but maybe God would understand.

For the first time since her husband had been taken, Sonya slept through the night. And when she awoke, it was naturally—peacefully. She knew what she had to do. She would take the children! That would be the first step in reaching out.

At noon, Sonya stood nervously at the door to the cafeteria, watching for Mrs. Stein. As soon as she saw her, she started to speak, "The children—they still need a home?"

"Yes, but—"

"Then I will take them! It will be crowded, my apartment is so tiny, but we'll manage. I want to take them!"

Mrs. Stein's face broke into a big smile. She took Sonya's hand. "Good! I'll bring them over tonight."

Right after work, Sonya began baking the traditional German pastries she hadn't made in so long. She would reach out to those children with good food—and love. They would be shy, of course. Maybe they would even be like she had been—closed off, closed in. But it didn't matter. She would keep trying.

"Sonya!" It was Mrs. Stein. Quickly, Sonya opened the door. The girl stood on one side of Mrs. Stein, the boy on the other. Sonya's heart lurched. They looked so sad. And why shouldn't they? They'd lost everything—and everyone. And there was something else, too, something strangely familiar about them that tugged at her.

"Please come in," she said. Each child carried a small satchel and wore clean clothes that didn't quite fit. *The look of a refugee,* Sonya thought. The look she herself had worn not so long ago. Was that why they seemed so familiar? Because they reminded her of the other refugee children she'd seen on the ship coming to America?

"Sonya," Mrs. Stein said, "this is Liese and Karl."

Her niece's and nephew's names. Sonya's stomach dropped away; her heart began beating hard. It couldn't be. Things like that didn't happen. It would be a miracle, and she hadn't prayed for a miracle. She'd only prayed to be able to reach out again. But still she took a step closer, searching the children's faces. It had been so long, and they would have changed in so many ways. As she had changed.

Puzzled, Mrs. Stein said, "Is something wrong, Sonya?"

Sonya shook her head, still staring. The girl lifted her eyes, wide and dark—wrenchingly familiar. It was as if she was searching Sonya's face, too. And then the boy cried out.

"Karl?" Mrs. Stein asked. "Are you all right?"

The boy pointed a trembling hand toward the three pictures Sonya had set out the night before. He ran toward the bureau, grabbed up the picture of Sonya's sister and held it to his heart.

"Mama," he whispered.

Cynthia Mercati

The Cantor and the Klansman

Hatred and bitterness can never cure the disease of fear; only love can do that. Hatred paralyzes life; love releases it. Hatred confuses life. Love harmonizes it. Hatred darkens life; love illuminates it.

Martin Luther King, Jr.

One sunny Sunday morning in June 1991, Cantor Michael Weisser and his wife, Julie, surrounded by half-unpacked boxes in the kitchen of their new home in Lincoln, Nebraska, were talking and laughing with a friend when the phone rang.

Michael, who answered with his usual warmth, heard a harsh and hateful voice say slowly and loudly: "You *will* be sorry you ever moved in [to that house], Jew boy!" Then the line went dead.

Two days later, the Weissers received a thick brown packet in the mail with a card on top that read, "The KKK is watching you, Scum." The stack of flyers and brochures included ugly caricatures of Jews, Blacks and "Race Traitors" being shot and hung, and spelled out other threatening messages, including, "Your time is up!" and "The Holohoax was nothing compared to what's going to happen to you."

The Weissers called the police, who said the hate mail looked like the work of Larry Trapp, who was the state leader, known as the "Grand Dragon" of the Ku Klux Klan. Also an avowed Nazi, Trapp was suspected of leading skinheads and Klansmen who had been terrorizing black, Vietnamese and Jewish families in Nebraska and Iowa.

"He's dangerous," the police warned. "We know he makes explosives." They advised the Weissers to keep their doors locked and call if they received any unlabeled packages—just in case Trapp sent a letter bomb.

Although Trapp, forty-four, was diabetic and in a wheelchair, he was a major Midwestern link in the national white supremacist movement. He was, in fact, responsible for the fire-bombings of several African-Americans' homes around Lincoln and for what he called "Operation Gooks," the burning of the Indochinese Refugee Assistance Center in Omaha. At the time, he was making plans to bomb B'nai Jeshuran, the synagogue where Weisser was the spiritual leader.

Trapp lived alone on the southwest side of Lincoln in a cramped one-room apartment. On one wall he kept a giant Nazi flag and a double-life-size picture of Hitler. Next to these hung his white cotton Klan robe with its red belt and hood. He kept an arsenal of assault rifles, pistols and shotguns within reach in case his perceived "enemies" came crashing through his door.

After the hate mail, Julie Weisser began to wonder about Trapp, who had gone public to recruit new members of the Klan. She was struck by how lonely he must be, how isolated in all his hatred. She found out where he lived and sometimes would drive past his apartment complex. While she felt infuriated and revolted by him, she was also intrigued by how he could become so evil. She told Michael she had an idea: She was going to send Trapp a letter every day, along with a passage from Proverbs—her favorite book of the Bible—one that talks about how to treat your fellow man and conduct your life.

Michael liked the idea, but didn't want Julie to sign her name. And friends were horrified, warning that Trapp was crazy and violent and might try to kill her.

"*He's* the one who does things anonymously," Julie responded. "I won't do that." She held off on her plan, but later on, when Trapp launched a white supremacist series on a local-access cable channel, Michael Weisser was incensed. He called the number for the hotline of the KKK—"the Vigilante Voices of Nebraska"—and listened to Trapp's harsh voice spewing out a racist diatribe on the answering machine.

Michael called several times just to keep the line busy, but then began to leave his own messages. "Larry," he said. "Why do you hate me? You don't even know me, so how can you hate me?"

Another time he said, "Larry, do you know that the first laws Hitler's Nazis passed were against people like yourself who had physical deformities, physical handicaps? Do you realize you would have been among the first to die under Hitler? Why do you love the Nazis so much?"

Whenever he thought of it, Michael called and left another message. One night, however, he asked Julie, "What will I do if the guy ever picks up the phone?"

"Tell him you want to do something nice for him," she said. "Tell him you'll take him to the grocery store or something. Anything to help him. It will catch him totally off guard."

For weeks, Michael listened to Trapp's taped invectives denouncing "niggers," "queers," "kikes" and "gooks." Each time, Weisser would reply with a message of his own.

One day, just after Michael said, "Larry, when you give up hating, a world of love is waiting for you," Trapp, who was feeling increasingly annoyed by the calls, picked up the phone and shouted, "What the - - - - do you want?"

"I just want to talk to you," said Michael.

"Why the - - - - are you harassing me? Stop harassing me!"

"I don't want to harass you, Larry," Michael said. "I just want to talk to you."

"I know your voice. You black by any chance?"

"No, I'm Jewish."

"You are harassing me," said Trapp. "What do you want? Make it quick."

Michael remembered Julie's advice. "Well, I was thinking you might need a hand with something, and I wondered if I could help," he said. "I know you're in a wheelchair and I thought maybe I could take you to the grocery store or something."

Trapp couldn't think of anything to say. Michael listened to the silence. Finally, Trapp cleared his throat and, when he spoke, his voice sounded different.

"That's okay," he said. "That's nice of you, but I've got that covered. Thanks anyway. But don't call this number anymore."

Before Trapp could hang up, Michael replied, "I'll be in touch."

Michael's calls were making Trapp feel confused. And a letter he received from a former nurse in Lincoln also affected him. If you give your love to God "like you gave yourself to the KKK," she wrote, "he'll heal you of all that bitterness, hatred and hurt . . . in ways you won't believe."

Then, at a visit to his eye doctor, Trapp felt his wheelchair moving. "I helping you on elevator," said a young female voice behind him. He asked where she was from. "I from Vietnam," she said. That evening, he found himself crying as he thought about the scent of the woman's gardenia perfume, his memories of "Operation Gooks" and his assaults on the Vietnamese community.

"I'm rethinking a few things," he told Michael in a subsequent phone call. But a few days later he was on TV, shrieking about "kikes" and "half-breeds" and "the Jews' media."

Furious, Michael called Trapp, who answered his phone. "It's clear you're not rethinking anything at all," Michael said, demanding an explanation.

In a tremulous voice, Trapp said, "I'm sorry I did that. I've been talking like that all of my life. . . . I can't help it. . . . I'll apologize."

That evening, Michael Weisser asked his congregation to include in their prayers someone "who is sick from the illness of bigotry and hatred. Pray that he can be healed, too." Across town, Lenore Letcher, an African-American woman whom Trapp had terrorized, also prayed for Trapp: "Dear God, let him find you in his heart."

That same night, the swastika rings Trapp wore on both hands began to sting and itch so much that he pulled them off—something he had never done before. All night, he tossed in his bed, restless, confused and unsettled.

Around dinnertime the next day, the Weissers' phone rang. "I want to get out," Trapp said, "but I don't know how."

Michael suggested that he and Julie go over to Trapp's apartment to talk in person and "break bread together." Trapp hesitated, then finally agreed.

As they were preparing to leave, Julie started running around, looking for a gift, and decided on a silver friendship ring of intertwined strands that Michael never wore.

"Good choice," said Michael. "I've always thought all those strands could represent all the different kinds of people on this earth." To Julie it was a symbol of how "somebody's life can be all twisted up and become very beautiful."

When the door to Trapp's apartment creaked open, Michael and Julie saw the bearded Larry Trapp in his wheelchair. An automatic weapon was slung over the doorknob and a Nazi flag hung on the wall. Michael took Trapp's hand, and Trapp winced as if hit by a jolt of electricity. Then he broke into tears.

He looked down at his two silver swastika rings. "Here," he said, yanking them off his fingers and putting them in Michael's hand. "I can't wear these anymore. Will you take them away?" Michael and Julie looked at each other in stunned silence.

"Larry, we brought you a ring, too," Julie said, kneeling beside him and sliding the ring onto his finger. Larry began to sob. "I'm so sorry for all the things I've done," he said. Michael and Julie put their arms around Larry and hugged him. Overwhelmed by emotion, they started crying, too.

On November 16, 1991, Trapp resigned from the Klan and soon quit all his other racist organizations. Later, he wrote apologies to the many people he had threatened or abused. "I wasted the first forty years of my life and caused harm to other people," Larry said. "Now I've learned we're one race and one race only."

On New Year's Eve, Trapp learned he had less than a year to live. That night, the Weissers invited him to move into their home, and he did so. They converted their living room into his bedroom. As his health deteriorated, Julie quit her job to care for him. She fed him, waited on him, sometimes all through the night, emptying pans of vomit.

Having a remorseful, dying Klansman in their home was disruptive to the whole family, which included three teenagers, a dog and a cat, but everyone pitched in. Once Trapp said to Julie, "You and Michael are doing for me what my parents should have done. You're taking care of me."

On days when Larry was well enough, he listened to

speeches by Dr. Rev. Martin Luther King and books on Gandhi and Malcolm X. He also began to listen to books on Judaism and to study the faith in earnest.

On June 5, 1992, Larry Trapp converted to Judaism in ceremonies at B'nai Jeshurun, the very synagogue that he previously had planned to blow up. Three months later, on September 6, 1992, he died in the Weisser home, with Michael and Julie beside him, holding his hands.

At Larry's funeral, Michael Weisser said, "Those of us who remain behind ask the question, 'O Lord, what is man? We are like a breath, like a shadow that passes away. . . .' And yet, somehow, we know there is more to our lives than what first meets the eye."

Kathryn Watterson
Adapted from her book, Not by the Sword: How a Cantor and His Family Transformed a Klansman, *Boston: Northeastern University Press, 2001*

Salvation in Sarajevo

I call heaven and earth to witness that whether one be Jew or gentile, man or woman, only according to their good deeds does the Divine Spirit rest upon them.

Midrash

In the autumn of 1941, most of the Jews of Sarajevo were herded onto trains and sent to concentration camps. Some managed to flee; others joined the Partisans. Josef Kabilio, a Jewish artisan, was a close family friend of Mustafa Hardaga, a wealthy Muslim merchant. Not long after the Germans occupied Sarajevo, Mustafa Hardaga went to inspect one of his properties and found Josef Kabilio hiding there. Mustafa Hardaga now faced an excruciating moral dilemma.

If he turned Josef Kabilio over to the authorities, it would be condemning him to death. Yet, if he were caught sheltering a Jew, it would mean certain death for both of them. But this was his friend for many years; what was he to do? His high principles prevailed. He took Kabilio into his home and hid him there. Kabilio made two attempts to flee Sarajevo, and both times he was caught and jailed. On both occasions, he managed to escape from jail and again Hardaga, his Muslim friend, sheltered him in his home.

Zeyneba Hardaga, the merchant's wife, also had a close relationship with Kabilio. On one occasion she spotted him in a labor brigade and risked her life by bringing food to Kabilio and his fellow prisoners. At a later date, she explained her actions. "When Josef left us for the third time, all we could do was pray and hope. Later, when my children asked why I did this, I always answered what my husband said, 'You do not abandon your friends.'"

Miraculously, Kabilio survived the war and returned to Sarajevo in 1945. Finding his home plundered, the Hardagas took him in. In 1948, he left for Israel, promising to write often, as did the Hardagas. Very soon the first letter arrived from Israel to Sarajevo, and they continued like a paper chain for decades.

Over the course of those years, Josef Kabilio married, had children and grandchildren, and became a widower. Similarly, Zeneyba Hardaga in Sarajevo became a widow and then remarried, becoming a mother and grandmother. However, with the passage of the years, in addition to losing her second husband, she also lost all her property and a good deal of her health. Ultimately, a leg had to be amputated, and she could no longer walk. Despite all these woes, she never informed her good friend and correspondent, Josef Kabilio, of her troubles.

All the while, and unbeknownst to her, Kabilio was hard at work in Jerusalem to have her recognized by *Yad Vashem,* Israel's National Holocaust Museum, as a Righteous Gentile, a non-Jew who went to extraordinary lengths during the Second World War to save Jewish lives. He went many times to the museum to speak to the office in charge of this award and learned that the necessary process of substantiation was exceptionally arduous, and furthermore, this award had never been given to a Muslim.

Kabilio persisted in the face of many obstacles, and when he turned eighty-eight, Zeyneba Hardaga received a letter from *Yad Vashem.* They informed her of her award and told her that she would be flown to Jerusalem to receive it. Seven months later, Josef Kabilio had the privilege of watching his old friend helped off the plane at Ben Gurion airport. He was shocked to see that she could not walk. His first words were, "You never told me!" With a smile, she scolded him, "You never told me what you were up to, either."

Kabilio died just four years later and never knew how valuable his work would ultimately become in having Zeyneba recognized by *Yad Vashem.* The war broke out in Sarajevo in 1992. In February 1994, Mrs. Hardaga and her family were given special preference to escape the horrors of war by leaving the city on a convoy of 294 Muslims, Jews, Serbs and Croats, organized by the Joint Jewish Distribution Committee. This Muslim family had their lives saved by a Jewish organization.

Furthermore, Kabilio's family in Israel went to the Israeli authorities and arranged for an El Al plane (Israel's national airline) to be sent to the Sarajevo area to bring Zeyneba Hardaga, her daughter and her family, to Israel. All these miraculous events occurred in large measure because of Josef Kabilio's efforts to properly recognize his friend's heroism during the war. What beautiful symmetry. The Muslim Hardagas saved Kabilio when his life was threatened, and the Jew Kabilio was instrumental in having the Hardagas saved when their lives were in danger.

Isn't this the way the world should always be?

Rabbi Richard Plavin

A Special Grandfather

When the heart is full, the eyes overflow.

Sholom Aleichem

No other grandfather was like mine. No other grandfather was so youthful, funny and full of impish pranks with us children. What other grandfather would conspire with us to mix up the guests' overshoes in the hall? Or show us how to walk on our hands when the tenant below complained of footsteps from our uncarpeted floor? Or teach us to speak in rhymes? Or invent a secret language just for us—that the world, which knows him as Sholom Aleichem, the famous writer, does not share?

My cousin Tamara and I were the only grandchildren Papa Sholom Aleichem, as we called him, had in his lifetime, and he adored us. Once, when we were very little, as we were walking with him someplace in Switzerland, each holding onto his hand, he pointed to the distance. "You see that mountain?" he asked. "I've just given it to Tamarochka (my cousin, Tamara). You see that lake? I am giving it to Belochka (to me, Bel)!"

I treasure a letter from him written a year before he died in New York to Odessa, where I lived with my parents. *"Dorogaya Belochka"*— "Dear Belochka," he wrote, "I am writing you this letter to ask you to hurry and grow up, so that you can learn to write me letters. And in order to grow up, it is necessary to drink milk, eat soup and vegetables, and fewer candies. Regards to your dolls. Your Papa, Sholom Aleichem." I did grow up, I did learn to write—but not in time.

It's difficult to know what is family legend and what is true memory, but one particular scene I remember vividly, although I couldn't have been more than three. Papa Sholom Aleichem and I are in a zoological garden, in front of a monkey. He takes a piece of paper, folds it into a cone, fills it with water from a nearby fountain and offers it to the monkey to drink. The monkey refuses. Papa bends down to me and says, in Russian, the language we always spoke: *"Isporchenaya obezyana!"* (a spoiled monkey!). He keeps refilling the paper cone with water and drinking thirstily, again and again. I learned only later that this was two years before he died, when he was plagued by an unquenchable diabetic thirst. But even about this he made a joke. He wrote to my parents: "Now I know I'll never die of hunger; I'll die of thirst."

It was more than a joke; it was the essence of his humor. Thumbing the nose at adversity, turning tables on tragedy, losing everything but winning the argument—it was laughter through tears—Jewish laughter.

Though he was loved and cherished in thousands of homes and read aloud to the sound of laughter, he suffered grave illness, excruciating pain, exile and heartbreak. Yet to the end, he wrote humor for others, from his first literary effort at the age of fourteen, when he compiled a *Glossary of Stepmother's Curses,* in which he arranged in alphabetical order the daily curses his stepmother lavished upon him; to his last work, left unfinished by his death: *Motl the Cantor's Son in America.* Of all his stories, this is my favorite. When little Motl finds himself in America, he expresses his delight at its marvels. Chewing gum, he explains, is a candy made of rubber, and teachers in America are not allowed to whip their children. "Try not to love such a country!" he exclaims.

Sholom Aleichem died on May 12A (he was superstitious and never numbered his manuscripts pages 13 but 12A), 1916, in a shabby little apartment on Kelly Street in the Bronx, at the age of fifty-seven. According to the *New York Times,* over a hundred thousand people accompanied the funeral procession, mourning their beloved writer. He lies buried in the Workmen's Circle Cemetery in Queens, New York, for in his will he asked to be buried not among the rich and famous, but among the plain people, the workers, the ordinary folk whom he loved and who had loved their folk writer in his lifetime. Also in his will, which is considered a great ethical document, he asks to be remembered on the anniversary of his death with laughter, by having family and friends gather together and read his merry stories aloud. This has been an inviolable tradition in our family, never broken to this day.

Many have seen *Fiddler on the Roof,* based on Sholom Aleichem's Tevye stories, but few know that there was a real dairyman, whose name was Tevye, who delivered dairy products to my grandfather's family. Not at all like the powerful actors who have played him, he was a small, wizened man with a funny black beard that grew out of his neck, and he had no daughters. Sholom Aleichem used to enjoy talking with him, and subsequently wrote a series of stories about Tevye the Milkman and his seven daughters (*Fiddler* subtracted two). Sholom Aleichem wrote to my parents how eager he was to have his stories translated into English and his plays produced in

America, adding: "My eyes won't see it; maybe yours will." Ours did.

It's awesome to realize that I am now, since Tamara's death, Sholom Aleichem's only living descendant who knew him, heard his voice, sat on his lap, and who—as he used to tell me when I was little—helped him write, by holding on tightly to his hand as we walked together. The tighter I held on, the better he wrote.

It was only after I grew up that I understood my grandfather's gift was a far more valuable one than a make-believe present of a lake in Switzerland. He left a legacy of love and laughter—love for the common people and laughter in the face of adversity. Try not to love such a grandfather!

Bel Kaufman

Reprinted by permission of Benita Epstein.

The Story of Mary the Maid

True humor springs not more from the head than from the heart; it is not contempt, its essence is love.

Thomas Carlyle

When I was growing up in Delaware, my dad was a Jewish communal worker, and my mom a professional Hebrew teacher. They were truly pillars of the community. Nevertheless, my mom took great pride in keeping a *balbatisch* (dignified, decorous) house, and training her daughters to do the same. It was her custom to clean windows, for example, the way most housewives did in those days. She would open the double-hung window, climb halfway out, and sit on the sill facing inward. Lowering the window onto her thighs to pin her in place, she would proceed to clean with huge sweeping motions with her arm. This meant she had to ignore the fact that she was dangling out over the street, and could fall two stories onto hard cement with one false move.

One day, my dad came home from work unexpectedly and saw her suspended in space, with her posterior hanging out. He was not amused. He thought it undignified for the wife of the executive director of the Jewish Community Center to be seen in this activity, and he considered it dangerous to boot. He really was quite upset by it, and he told Mom in no uncertain terms that she must get someone to help her. In vain, my mother protested that a maid would cost money, that no one could do the job as well as she, that she did not mind doing her own housework, and all of that. My father persisted until my mom reluctantly capitulated and agreed to hire a maid.

She was as good as her word. She told my father a week later that she had found a suitable candidate through Sylvia Rosenbaum, who lived across the street. Mary was a Polish woman with a long name consisting of a string of unpronounceable consonants. A divorced woman, she was the sole support of her two sons. The older was a no-goodnick who had a drinking problem and had recently joined the Marines, which she hoped would do him some good. The younger boy got good grades, and she was praying that he would get a college scholarship. Mother and her new assistant got along just fine from the start.

We never got to meet Mary because she came after we left for school and work, and she was gone by 3:00 P.M. Every Thursday, however, my father would leave a ten-dollar bill to pay her wages, and every Thursday night the house would sparkle, for Mary was a whirlwind with a mop and pail. Even mother admitted that her preparations for the Sabbath on Friday were much easier now that Mary was here.

All went well for the better part of the year, with Mother periodically updating us on Mary's life and activities. We felt as if we knew her and her sons, and we were liberal with our advice about how to handle them. Then one day my father came home looking glum. There had been a domestic disaster, a broken boiler, an exploded carburetor; I don't remember exactly what it was. But it was something that would be expensive to fix, and money was tight.

"How much do you need, Harry?" asked my mom.

"Four hundred dollars at least," was the reply.

My mother got a thoughtful look on her face, then excused herself from the dinner table and ran upstairs. She returned with a huge wad of ten-dollar bills that she pressed into my father's outstretched hand. "What's this?" asked my father in bewilderment, looking down at almost fifty bills. Looking like the cat that swallowed the canary, and chortling in utter triumph, my mother exclaimed, *"That's Mary the maid!!"*

We rather missed Mary, from then on, and not a peep was heard out of my father.

Naomi Bluestone

My Son the Rabbi

In a storm, it is the bamboo, the flexible tree, that can bend with the wind and survive. The rigid tree that resists the wind falls, victim of its own insistence to control.

Joan Borysenko

My mother never wanted me to be a rabbi. Her dream was that I receive a graduate degree in mathematics, learn accounting and take over my father's flourishing CPA practice. She was shocked and sad when I took her out to lunch and told her, "I am dropping out of graduate school. In the fall, I am beginning my rabbinical studies at the Jewish Theological Seminary."

My mother was deeply Jewish, but her Jewishness had nothing to do with religion. It was ethnicity, memories and a few eclectic religious observances. She had the greatest disdain for Jews who were observant. "They are more interested in the law than in people," she would say. I heard stories about the poor kids from a kosher family who had to bring their own hot dogs to neighbor kids' birthday parties because they could not eat the food.

My mother was disturbed when I began keeping kosher. "Now you won't eat in my house." When she and my dad first married, he wanted her to keep a kosher home. She said, "No, there are too many rules." Now, with her oldest son studying to be a rabbi, she bought a separate set of kosher dishes for me to use. When I told her that I would no longer drive on the Sabbath, and when I began to wear a yarmulke all the time, she became more concerned. "Why can't you be one of those liberal rabbis, who don't worry so much about the picayune laws?" That was not to be my dream.

For the first three years of rabbinical school, my mother waited for me to drop out and go into the family business. She described to me how delicious lobster was and asked me not to be too religious. One day she said, "I can live with you being a rabbi. But please don't make law more important than people."

Then one summer day, I finally convinced my mother that I would be a good rabbi. I shared with her a story of what happened to me on a cross-country drive.

During summer break from the seminary, another rabbinical student and I took off to drive across the country. As we mapped out our route, we discovered that we could reach Rapid City, South Dakota, by Shabbat. In Rapid City, there is one small synagogue that meets on an army base. It serves the few Jewish families in town, as well as those in the military. They were having Friday night services and invited my friend and me to join them.

"My friend and I would love to join you, but we do not drive on Shabbat. Is there any chance we can stay within walking distance?" The members of the Rapid City Jewish community were wonderful, arranging for us to sleep at the army base, and even getting us an invitation for a vegetarian dinner at someone's home. So began a beautiful Shabbat in South Dakota.

Friday night the lay people led the service. More people than usual attended, intrigued that two seminary students were in town. At the *Oneg* Shabbat afterwards, my friend and I led a discussion on Judaism.

Suddenly, a little boy of about nine came up to me all excited. He had some things that his grandfather had left him, and he did not know what they were. The boy proudly showed me a velvet bag and took out a pair of *tefillin.* I explained that they are phylacteries worn by Jewish men on their head and on their arm during the weekday morning prayers. They literally fulfill the commandment, "You shall bind them for a sign upon your hand, and they shall be for reminders between your eyes."

The boy was excited. "Rabbi, show me how to put them on."

"I am not yet a rabbi, only a student," I responded. And I thought about what to do. It was Friday night. The sun had gone down. On Shabbat it is forbidden by Jewish law even to handle a pair of *tefillin,* let alone put them on. I was tempted to say, "Put them away until a weekday."

On the other hand, how many observant Jews pass through this small South Dakota town each year? Who else could show the boy how to wear his grandfather's *tefillin?* The opportunity may not present itself again. I told him to roll up his sleeve. And slowly, at this Friday night *Oneg* Shabbat, I taught the boy how to wear *tefillin.* Wearing his grandfather's *tefillin* on his arm and forehead, we said the *Sh'ma* together. I could see tears in his father's eyes. There was a joy in the boy's steps as he went home that evening.

When Shabbat was over, I called my mother. She said, "Do you mean that you broke the laws of Shabbat to put *tefillin* on that little boy?"

"Yes," I replied.

"Maybe you will be a good rabbi after all."

From that moment on, my mother supported my decision to enter the rabbinate. "Now I know that for you, people are more important than laws." She cried when I received my rabbinic ordination and proudly spoke of her son the rabbi. And my mother made one more promise: "I will not eat lobster anymore. At least, when I go out with you."

Rabbi Michael Gold

The Pretzel Lady's Hanukkah

Our work brings people face to face with love. To us what matters is an individual. To get to love the person we must come in close contact with him.

Mother Teresa

Those wonderful little people who sold those huge salty pretzels near every school were very much a part of New York's long past.

I remember the lady who sold pretzels near our school in the Bronx. Regardless of the weather, this sweet little old woman stood on the corner with her basket of pretzels trying to earn her way. Our pretzel seller looked like someone's grandmother. She had the most beautiful silver-gray hair I have ever seen, and her small round face, almost like a cherub, was always a bright red in the freezing winter months.

I'll never forget the year we were finishing up school on the last day before the winter vacation. It also happened to be the first night of Hanukkah.

The air was brisk and the flakes fell, tickling our nose

and ears. As we walked toward the corner, there she was. We always saved two cents for a stop at the pretzel lady. It was almost like a ritual.

The pretzels were covered with a white sheet of paper to protect them from the weather. The old lady had a scarf covering her head with a knot tied neatly beneath her chin. She wore a heavy sweater with a shawl covering her shoulders.

On this day, we made our usual stop. She smiled warmly as we approached, and said, "I saved the warm ones for you. I have them wrapped in paper. I know you like the pretzels warm."

We felt so proud, getting this VIP treatment. After we made our purchase, she said softly, "Have a wonderful, happy Hanukkah, children. Dress warm and stay healthy. Don't get sick from the snow."

As we walked away, my little brother Berel commented sadly in between chomps on his pretzel, "She must be a pretty poor lady."

"I guess so," I added, chewing away as the snow continued to come down with full fury.

Berel was concerned. "Do you think she made enough money today selling pretzels to buy candles for a Hanukkah menorah?" he questioned.

"Gee, I dunno . . . ," I sighed, getting a little more concerned.

"Mamma's got an extra box," he volunteered. "I'll run home and get the candles; you go back and tell her to wait for me." He began to run to our house.

I ran back to the corner where she sold pretzels, but she was gone. I looked around and saw her trudging through the snow about a block away, lugging her heavy basket of unsold pretzels. She continued for about three more blocks and then turned into an alley between two old apartment houses. By the time I reached the alley she was gone, but there were fresh tracks in the snow that led to one small door in the basement section of one of the buildings.

I looked in a window and, sure enough, there she was. There was a bare wooden table on one side of the small room and two orange crates she used for chairs in another corner. Near the broken-down sink were two little gas burners. There was a coffeepot on one burner. On her table was a small, inexpensive Hanukkah menorah.

I started to walk back to the street to find Berel. By the time I reached the school, Berel was standing on the corner. "Where'd ya go?" he shouted. "I thought you ran out on me."

I explained what had happened and reassured him that I knew where she lived. We began to run back to the alley. When we got to the door we knocked, but there was no answer. We knocked a little harder, but still no answer.

Berel ran to the window, then shouted, "She's lying on the floor!" I ran to the window and could see her stretched out near the sink.

We tried to open the door, but it was locked, so we ran out to the street to get help. Just then a man was passing by. We told him what we saw, and he followed us into the alley and looked through the window. He tried the door, then with all his might he broke the door down. We ran into the apartment. Everything smelled from gas. He shouted, "Quick, open the window." He ran to the stove and shut off the gas jet. The pot of coffee she had been boiling had run over and put out the flame, but the gas continued to flow.

The man dragged the old lady toward the door for fresh air. He began slapping her face, and suddenly she started to come to. In a few minutes she was able to sit up and she asked what had happened. When the man explained, she started to smile and offered us a free pretzel. She had recognized us.

The gas fumes were cleared out, and we closed the window. Berel took out the package of Hanukkah candles and told her we had an extra box and thought she might need some.

She smiled warmly and said that she wanted to pay us for the candles, in pretzels. Berel had put away three pretzels thus far, so we politely refused.

She put two candles in the Hanukkah holder that was set on the table. She said a prayer and lit the candles.

As a warm glow filled the room, the man noticed a very old book on the shelf. He picked it up and looked at it curiously. Most of the pages were frayed and the binding was gone. It looked like junk.

As he began looking through the book, she said, "That's a very old book. Old like me. Worthless!"

The man continued to look at the book, then said, "Would you sell me this book? I'm a book dealer. I sell old books, and I would be more than happy to give you two hundred dollars for this book!"

The woman looked at him with disbelief. "It's an old book. Do you think it has any value?"

"Will you sell it to me?" the man asked again.

"Let me give it to you. After all, you saved my life," she said.

"Oh, no, that would not be fair. You would be taking away my *mitzvah*," he retorted as he put his hand in his pocket and pulled out a handful of bills. He counted out two hundred dollars, handed them to her, then gave my brother and me five dollars each. "This is my Hanukkah gift to you boys for being so alert and thoughtful."

We walked from the house together as the snow continued to fall. The man said he was late and ran ahead of us. We watched as he moved through the snow swiftly. When he reached the corner, he passed a garbage can, paused for a second, then threw the old book into the can and continued on his way.

It was then we realized that he did not want the book, but wanted to do something for that little old woman without embarrassing her.

We never did see that man again, even though we were certain he lived in the neighborhood. We never knew who he was, but he certainly made one old lady happy that Hanukkah.

Arnold Fine
Submitted by Beverly Merson

The Rebbe Said Thank You

Television has proved that people will look at anything rather than each other.

Ann Landers

When Joseph Cabiliv—today a successful real-estate developer—regained consciousness in the Rambam Hospital in Haifa, he remembered nothing of the circumstances that had brought him there. He felt an excruciating pain in his legs. The discovery that followed was far more horrendous; glancing under the sheet, he saw both legs had been amputated, the right leg above the knee, the left at mid-thigh.

The day before, Joseph, who was serving on reserve duty in the Israel Defense Forces, was patrolling the Golan Heights with several other soldiers when their Jeep hit an old Syrian land mine. Two of his comrades were killed on the spot. Another three suffered serious injury. Joseph's legs were so severely crushed that the doctors had no choice but to amputate them.

Aside from the pain and disability, Joseph was confronted with society's incapacity to deal with the handicapped. "My friends would come to visit," he recalls, "sustain fifteen minutes of artificial cheer and depart without once meeting my eye. Mother would come and cry, and it was I, who so desperately needed consolation, who had to do the consoling. Father would come and sit by my bedside in silence. I didn't know which was worse—Mother's tears or Father's silence. Returning to my civilian profession as a welder was, of course, impossible, and while people were quick to offer charity; no one had a job for a man without legs.

"When I ventured out in my wheelchair, people kept their distance, so that a large empty space opened up around me on the busiest street corner."

When Joseph met with other disabled veterans, he found that they all shared his experience; they had given their very bodies in defense of the nation, but the nation lacked the spiritual strength to confront their sacrifice.

"In the summer of 1976," Joseph tells, "the Israel Defense Forces sponsored a tour of the United States for a large group of disabled veterans. While we were in New York, a member of the Hasidic Lubavitch group came to our hotel and suggested that we meet with the Lubavitcher Rebbe. Most of us did not know what to make of the invitation, but a few members of our group had heard about the Rebbe and convinced the rest of us to accept.

"As soon as they heard we were coming, the Chabadniks, as the Lubavitch members are called, sprang into action, organizing the whole thing with the precision of a military campaign. Ten large commercial vans pulled up to our hotel to transport us and our wheelchairs to the Chabad headquarters in Brooklyn.

"Soon we found ourselves in the famous large synagogue in the basement of 770 Eastern Parkway. Ten minutes later, a white bearded man of about seventy entered the room, followed by two secretaries. As if by a common signal, absolute silence pervaded the room. There was no mistaking the authority he radiated. We had all stood in the presence of military commanders and prime ministers, but this was unlike anything we had ever encountered. This must have been what people felt in the presence of royalty. An identical thought passed through all our minds: *Here walks a leader, a prince.* He passed between us, resting his glance on each one of us and lifting his hand in greeting, and then seated himself opposite us. Again he looked at each of us in turn. Since that terrible day, when I had awakened without my legs in the Rambam Hospital, I have seen all sorts of things in the eyes of those who looked at me: pain, pity, revulsion and anger. But this was the first time in all those years that I encountered true empathy. With that glance that scarcely lasted a second and the faint smile on his lips, the Rebbe conveyed to me that he is with me utterly and exclusively."

The Rebbe began to speak, first apologizing for his Ashkenazic-accented Hebrew. "He spoke about our 'disability' saying that he objected to the use of the term. 'If a person has been deprived of a limb or a faculty,' he told us, 'this itself indicates that God has given him special powers to overcome the limitations this entails, and to surpass the achievements of ordinary people. You are not "disabled" or "handicapped," but special and unique, as you possess potentials that the rest of us do not. I therefore suggest . . . that you should no longer be called *N'hei Yisroel* ("the disabled for Israel," our designation in the IDF bureaucracy) but *Metzuyanei Yisroel* ("the special of Israel").'" The Rebbe spoke for several minutes more, and everything he said—and more importantly, the way in which he said it—addressed what had been churning within Joseph since his injury.

In parting, the Rebbe gave each veteran a dollar bill, in order, he explained, that we give it to charity in his behalf, making us partners in the fulfillment of a *mitzvah.* He walked from wheelchair to wheelchair, shaking the veterans' hands, giving each a dollar, and adding a personal word or two.

Joseph recalled, "When my turn came, I saw his face up close, and I felt like a child. He gazed deeply into my eyes, took my hand between his own, pressed it firmly, and said 'thank you,' with a slight nod of his head.

"I later learned that he had said something different to each one of us. To me he said 'thank you.' Somehow he sensed that was exactly what I needed to hear. With those two words, the Rebbe erased all the bitterness and despair that had accumulated in my heart.

"I carried the Rebbe's 'thank you' back to Israel, and I carry it with me to this very day."

Rabbi Yosef Jacobson
Submitted by Beverly Merson

A Hug in Prison

We can do no great things; only small things with great love.

Mother Teresa

About two years ago, I had the privilege of accompanying Rabbi Shlomo Carlebach to a prison in upstate New York. This time he had actually been invited by the Jewish chaplain, who asked that he perform a Hanukkah concert for the Jewish inmates there. There weren't many there, not even a minyan (quorum needed for prayer services), only about eight. No payment was involved, but Shlomo accepted the invitation without a moment's hesitation. It was a shlep, three hours each way. "No problem!" said Shlomo cheerfully.

The concert was a huge success, and Shlomo made the event into a real Hanukkah celebration, but that was only the beginning. When the Hanukkah *chagiga* (party) was over, Shlomo turned to the chaplain and said, "Please . . . I would like to visit with the rest of the inmates here. Could you get permission?"

Shlomo went into every cell, where he hugged, kissed

and talked with each inmate. Then he went into the dining room, into the recreation room, into the kitchen, into every possible nook and cranny of the prison where he was permitted to go, not satisfied until he had ferreted out every prisoner, making certain that no one had been overlooked. Finally, he was ready to leave, and we were walking down the hall when a big, burly inmate with a scarred, pitted face started running after us. "Rabbi, Rabbi," he shouted. "Please wait." We stopped immediately, and Shlomo turned to beam at him. "Yes, my holy friend?" he inquired sweetly. The man began to shift in embarrassment, almost as if he regretted his impulsive act, and then, finally gathering courage, blurted out, "I just loved that hug you gave me before! Would you mind giving me another one?" Shlomo gave him the most radiant smile in the world, and then tenderly enfolded him in his arms. They stood clasped together for a long time.

Finally, the inmate broke away and heaved the deepest sigh in the world. "Oh Rabbi," he said. "No one, no one, ever hugged me like that before." And then tears began to stream down his face.

"You know, Rabbi," he sobbed in remorse, "if only someone would have hugged me like that ten years ago, I surely wouldn't be here in this prison today."

Yitta Halberstam Mandelbaum
Previously appeared in
Chicken Soup for the Prisoner's Soul

A Ray of Peace

The Torah was given to the world in order to establish peace.

Midrash

I was talking with a young field service engineer, who I was working with on a perplexing computer-related problem. We were discussing Steven Spielberg's movie, *Saving Private Ryan,* and I mentioned that it had brought up too many real memories about battle. He agreed, and asked me, "Where did you get hurt?"

"Over there, in Israel," I said.

"Me, too."

He then revealed that he was a Palestinian. My new friend, whom I shall call "Riyadh" (not his real name) then told me how he came to be in the United States. The following story is his, as he told it to me.

Riyadh was born in the Old City of Jerusalem, one of four children. He had an older brother and two sisters. His father, a successful environmental engineer, moved his growing family out to the suburbs when Riyadh was a toddler, and he remembers his childhood in Ramallah fondly. In a very matter-of-fact way he told me that one day in 1982, while on his way home from school, he had been shot by an Israeli soldier. There had been a street demonstration going on at the time, people were running all over the place and there was a lot of confusion. Passers-by rushed the wounded youth, bleeding profusely, to his parents' home. He was seen by a local Palestinian doctor, who was unable to do more than apply a field dressing to stop the bleeding. But the doctor quickly arranged for him to be transported in a Red Cross car through the mountains to a hospital in Jordan, where he was assessed to be in critical condition. Once stabilized, Riyadh was flown out of the country secretly to a hospital in Turkey. Because of the difficult situation in his homeland, and the fact that he had departed illegally, he could not return. And so, sponsored by a Palestinian doctor in Texas, he sought political asylum and was admitted to the United States.

After recovering from his wounds, the local Palestinian community placed him in a boarding school, near a university in Texas. Now older and alone, and half a world away from home, Riyadh entered the world of American teenagers. Differences in language and customs made his first year in school difficult, but he learned very quickly.

After time in school, Riyadh faced an uncertain future. His parents urged him to stay in the United States until the situation at home calmed down. Though his visa was for only a short duration, he applied for admission to a school of engineering in Texas.

About a week after being admitted, he received a letter summoning him to a meeting with the dean of students. Riyadh was worried, wondering what the dean could possibly want with him. He was quite uncomfortable during the meeting. The dean stared at him, but also acted in a very fatherly and concerned way, inquiring whether he was happy there, and whether there was anything he could do for him.

"Well, my visa is very short," Riyadh told the dean.

"No problem, I will get it extended for the full four-year term of university," replied the dean. "Is there anything else you need?"

Riyadh alluded to his financial situation, and was then surprised by an offer of a full scholarship. After further prompting by the dean, Riyadh admitted that he didn't really have any place to live, and he had no income. On the spot, the dean offered him a position as a systems administrator, which would afford him a place to live and a small stipend.

With his college years thus assured, yet completely baffled as to how it had all happened, Riyadh began his higher education.

After two months, the dean again sent for him, making it clear that he had something he had to tell Riyadh.

Once Riyadh was in his office, the dean told him that he knew him; he knew who he was, he had recognized his name from his application to the university.

Riyadh was puzzled. The dean knew him? Recognized his name? How could that be possible?"

"Riyadh," said the dean, "I am the soldier who shot you."

As Riyadh, amazed and stunned, listened, the dean went on to relate his own story to the student. Joel (not his real name) was born in Brooklyn, and had emigrated with his parents to Israel as a child.

When he was grown, he signed up for his period of duty in the Israeli army. When he and his fellow soldiers were sent to restore order after a demonstration had turned violent, he found himself in a very dangerous situation. Rocks were being thrown, and the situation was getting out of hand. He fired his rifle in what he believed was an act of self-defense. Fate decreed that the bullet hit young Riyadh.

When Joel learned later that he had shot a young Palestinian boy, he was deeply distressed. His fellow soldiers tried to console him, saying that sometimes unfortunate things do happen in violent street confrontations, as well as in war. He should not blame himself.

But Joel needed to find out what had happened to the kid he shot. Once he learned Riyadh's name, he went straight to his parents' home to inquire about him, and to apologize. Riyadh's parents were very old-fashioned, and would not even speak to Joel; his father threw him out of the house.

Joel continued to feel personal anguish over what he had done, even though he still believed he was at the time acting in self-defense. But that didn't make any difference. After some time, he and his family decided to return to the country of his birth and make a new start.

Back in the United States, Joel went on to complete his graduate degree, and find a job with a college in Texas.

As he listened to the amazing story unfold, Riyadh felt a mixture of emotions: hate, love, loneliness. He thought of an old expression in Arabic, describing someone who slaps you with his right hand and straightens your hat with his left hand.

When Joel had finished his story, the Palestinian and the former Israeli soldier, now colleagues at an American university in Texas, looked at each other for a moment. Then they reached out, shook hands and embraced in an act of reconciliation and friendship. In an instant, that terrible moment when a stray Israeli bullet ripped into a Palestinian boy was redeemed. Time had wound its full circle, what was sundered had been united, and a ray of peace beamed out to the Holy Land from a far-off country called America.

Rabbi Harvey Abramowitz

Rosa

On a dark winter night in a Polish orphanage just after the end of World War II, children gathered around a Hanukkah candelabrum singing in Yiddish. But there was one girl who did not know what Hanukkah was. She was only five years old and had been brought to the orphanage sick and dazed. She didn't know her last name or where she was born. All she knew was that her name was Rosa, that she spoke Polish and that thunder terrified her.

The very existence of these orphaned children was a miracle. Only one in a hundred Polish Jewish children had escaped the Nazis. The children at the orphanage had one abiding hope: that someone would claim them. But no one ever came to claim Rosa.

In 1947 she was adopted by a couple who treated her like their own child. But Rosa's happiness did not last. When her new mother learned that she was pregnant, Rosa was returned to the orphanage.

A year later, an older couple adopted Rosa. They were kind, but Rosa sensed they didn't want to discuss her past. She still longed to know about her real parents.

In 1957, when Rosa was seventeen, her family got permission to leave Poland for Israel. Rosa didn't want to go.

How could her family find her if she left Poland?

In Israel Rosa studied nursing and served in the army. She met Lova, a handsome businessman and Polish survivor. He wanted to marry her. At first, Rosa refused, because, she said, she had a terrible secret—she didn't know who she was. But Lova persisted and they were married.

Now joined by her husband, Rosa searched for clues to her past, visiting government offices, questioning survivors and attending Holocaust conferences. But because Rosa knew so little about her origins, they had no starting point for their search. The orphanage had long since been closed.

As the years passed, Rosa's pain only grew worse. Every year on Holocaust Memorial Day, when the TV was filled with specials and documentaries, she watched all day, crying, hoping to learn something new. She never gave up her faith in God. Every Hanukkah she asked for a miracle.

One year, Israel Television producer Vered Berman decided to produce a special on survivors who didn't know their identity. She convinced her boss to use the station's resources to find missing links to the past. Rosa was one of fifteen survivors she tried to help.

But the paper trails led nowhere. Often the facts supplied by the children were confused with fantasy. Many of the sources had died.

Rosa's file was thin, but there was one promising clue. Rosa remembered the headmistress of the orphanage. She was a very grand woman, with a queenly manner. Rosa also remembered her name was Falkowska. What were the chances of finding a woman who had been middle-aged when Rosa was a child?

Still, Berman was optimistic. In Warsaw, the Israeli consul found the phone number of a Maria Falkowska. He called her, but her only response was, "Leave an old woman alone."

Rosa's intuition told her this had to be the only person who could provide the answer to her question. Trembling, she dialed Warsaw. The voice that answered sent her back fifty years. Rosa explained who she was, but the old lady insisted that she didn't remember her. Rosa's heart fell, but she persisted, reminding the woman of her adoption, trying to jog her memory. Finally, Maria Falkowska remembered, and told Rosa to call back in two days. She would see what she could find.

Rosa could barely eat or sleep. When she phoned again, Falkowska revealed she had kept a diary and in its yellowed pages found a note from 1952 that a couple—Amelia and Jacob Jarcyzn—was looking for their daughter, Rosa. Rosa felt as if a bolt of lightning had just passed through her.

Rosa conveyed the information to Berman, who dispatched a research team to *Yad Vashem* in Jerusalem, where millions of records are kept. Hours into the research, a researcher gave an involuntary shout. On hazy film were entries for Amelia and Jacob Jarcyzn, written in 1949 Poland. The cards didn't contain a current address, but under place of birth was Katowice, in southeast Poland.

An album had been published by the survivors of Katowice, and Berman found the Jarcyzns' story in it. Decades after the war they were still searching for their daughter. In the album was a photo of Rosa, which her parents had obtained from one of the orphanages she'd been through.

The album editor directed Berman to Doba Buchstein, a friend of Amelia's who lived in Jerusalem.

Yes, said Buchstein, who was eighty-three, she knew the family well. In 1970 they'd left Poland for Denmark. They had two sons, Sam and Henry, and an elder child, a girl named Rosa, born at the beginning of the war.

Jacob had died four years earlier. With his last breath he wept for the daughter he had never seen. Amelia, nearly eighty, was living in housing for the elderly in Denmark. She'd had a stroke but was clear-minded.

Without telling Rosa, Berman called her brothers. Henry flew from Warsaw immediately. His parents had always told him and Sam that they had a sister, but he never dared to believe that he would meet her.

Berman asked Rosa to Buchstein's home, telling her only that she'd met someone from her parents' hometown. Henry promised to wait in another room until Berman could tell Rosa the full story. But the minute he saw his sister he couldn't contain himself. He enfolded her in his arms. "He's your brother," Berman whispered. Henry phoned their mother. "I'm here with Rosa," he managed to get out.

As soon as was possible Rosa made the five-hour flight to Denmark. As she stepped over the threshold of Amelia Jarcyzn's room she was unable to swallow the lump in her throat. Sitting up in bed was a frail, dignified woman who looked like an older version of Rosa. Amelia's eyes brimmed with tears.

"My baby," she said. "I have always loved you. I have waited my whole life to hear you call me Momma."

Bittersweet emotion swept over Rosa—the joy of reunion mixed with the sorrow of fifty-five lost years. Rosa knelt by her mother's bedside and lifted her fragile hand to her lips. Tears ran down the cheeks of both women. "You must tell me everything," Amelia beseeched her.

After Rosa had told her mother the story of her life, it was her turn to listen. In fragments, over the weeks that followed, Rosa learned that her parents had fled to Russia, where they were arrested as spies. Jacob was deported to a work camp in Siberia.

Alone in a freezing prison, in February 1940, Amelia

gave birth to Rosa. She washed her beautiful baby under a prison faucet, dried the homemade diapers on her back, and slept with her child cradled in her arms, to protect her from ferocious rats.

For a year Amelia managed to keep Rosa alive despite being transferred to six different forced-labor camps. She was a nurse and when she contracted tuberculosis she feared the end was near. When Rosa took sick, Amelia smuggled her out to an orphanage run by Polish nuns, just north of the Mongolian border. When Amelia recovered, she wanted to get her child back but was conscripted into the Polish resistance army. In the upheaval of war, the orphanage was moved many times.

After the war, Amelia was reunited with Jacob, now nearly blind. They searched all over Poland. Amelia recognized Rosa in a photograph from one of the orphanages, but she had been transferred and the trail ended there.

They kept on looking, visiting Israel several times in the hope of finding her there.

After Amelia had her stroke, she was afraid that she would die without finding Rosa.

Rosa and Lova wanted to bring Amelia home to Israel, but the doctors warned that her condition was grave. Rosa's children, her brothers and their families all flew to Denmark. Eight weeks after mother and daughter were reunited, during which time they had had the chance to get to know each other, Amelia died. Rosa nursed her in her final days and she died in her daughter's loving arms.

"Don't let anyone tell you there are no miracles," Rosa says. "Even in the darkest times there's a candle of hope."

Barbara Sofer

Stranger than Fiction

In Israel, in order to be a realist, one must believe in miracles.

David Ben-Gurion

When the Old and New Cities of Jerusalem were reunited in 1967, a recently widowed Arab woman, who had been living in Old Jerusalem since 1948, wanted to see once more the house in which she formerly lived. Now that the city was one, she searched for and found her old home. She knocked on the door of the apartment, and a Jewish widow came to the door and greeted her. The Arab woman explained that she had lived there until 1948 and wanted to look around. She was invited in and offered coffee. The Arab woman said, "When I lived here, I hid some valuables. If they are still here, I will share them with you half and half."

The Jewish woman refused. "If they belonged to you and are still here, they are yours." After much discussion back and forth, they entered the bathroom, loosened the floor planks, and found a hoard of gold coins. The Jewish woman said, "I shall ask the government to let you keep them." She did and permission was granted.

The two widows visited each other again and again, and one day the Arab woman told her, "You know, in the 1948 fighting here, my husband and I were so frightened that we ran away to escape. We grabbed our belongings, took the children, and each fled separately. We had a three-month-old son. I thought my husband had taken him, and he thought I had. Imagine our grief when we were reunited in Old Jerusalem to find that neither of us had taken the child."

The Jewish woman turned pale, and asked the exact date. The Arab woman named the date and the hour, and the Jewish widow told her: "My husband was one of the Israeli troops that entered Jerusalem. He came into this house and found a baby on the floor. He asked if he could keep the house and the baby, too. Permission was granted."

At that moment, a twenty-year-old Israeli soldier in uniform walked into the room, and the Jewish woman broke down in tears. "This is your son," she cried.

This is one of those incredible tales we hear. And the aftermath? The two women liked each other so much that the Jewish widow asked the Arab mother: "Look, we are both widows living alone. Our children are grown up. This house has brought you luck. You have found your son, or our son. Why don't we live together?" And they do.

Rabbi Hillel E. Silverman

My Ideals

Faith is not a cushion for me to fall back upon; it is my working energy.

Helen Keller

That's the difficulty in these times: Ideals, dreams and cherished hopes rise within us, only to meet the horrible truth and be shattered.

It's really a wonder that I haven't dropped all my ideals, because they seem so absurd and impossible to carry out. Yet I keep them, because in spite of everything I still believe that people are really good at heart. I simply can't build up my hopes on a foundation consisting of confusion, misery and death. I see the world gradually being turned into a wilderness. I hear the ever-approaching thunder, which will destroy us, too. I can feel the sufferings of millions and yet, if I look up into the heavens, I think that it will all come right, that this cruelty too will end, and that peace and tranquility will return again.

In the meantime, I must uphold my ideals, for perhaps the time will come when I shall be able to carry them out.

Anne Frank

Choosing Life

Praised are You, Sovereign of the Universe, who has sustained us, kept us alive and brought us to this moment.

Hebrew Liturgy

Many years ago my grandfather gave me a silver wine goblet so small that it holds no more than a thimbleful of wine. Exquisitely engraved into its bowl is a bow with long ribbon streamers. It was made in Russia long ago. He gave it to me during one of the many afternoons when we sat together at the kitchen table in my parents' home memorizing phrases from his old books and discussing the nature of life. I was quite young then, no more than five or six, and when I became restless, he would revive my attention by bringing out the sacramental Concord grape wine he kept in the back of the refrigerator. He would fill my little beribboned wineglass with Manischewitz and then put a splash of wine into his own, a big silver ceremonial cup, generations old. Then we would offer a toast together. At the time, the only other celebration I knew was singing "Happy Birthday" and blowing out the candles. I loved this even better.

My grandfather had taught me the toast we used. It was a single Hebrew word, *L'Chaim* (pronounced *le CHI yeem*), which he told me meant "To life!" He always said it with great enthusiasm. "Is it to a happy life, Grandpa?" I had asked him once. He had shaken his head no. "It is just 'To life!' *Neshume-le,*" he told me.

At first, this did not make a lot of sense to me, and I struggled to understand his meaning. "Is it like a prayer?" I asked uncertainly.

"Ah no, *Neshume-le,*" he told me. "We pray for the things we don't have. We already have life."

"But then why do we say this before we drink the wine?" He smiled at me fondly. "Grandpa!" I said, suddenly suspicious. "Did you make it up?" He chuckled and assured me that he had not. For thousands of years all over the world people have said this same word to each other before drinking wine together. It was a Jewish tradition.

I puzzled about this last for some time. "Is it written in the Bible, Grandpa?" I asked at last. "No, *Neshume-le,*" he said, "it is written in people's hearts." Seeing the confusion on my face, he told me that *L'Chaim!* meant that no matter what difficulty life brings, no matter how hard or painful or unfair life is, life is holy and worthy of celebration. "Even the wine is sweet to remind us that life itself is a blessing."

It has been almost fifty-five years since I last heard my grandfather's voice, but I remember the joy with which he toasted Life and the twinkle in his eye as he said *L'Chaim!* It has always seemed remarkable to me that such a toast could be offered for generations by a people for whom life has not been easy. But perhaps it can only be said by such people, and only those who have lost and suffered can truly understand its power.

L'Chaim! is a way of living life. As I've grown older, it seems less and less about celebrating life and more about the wisdom of choosing life. In the many years that I have been counseling people with cancer, I have seen people choose life again and again, despite loss and pain and difficulty. The same immutable joy I saw in my grandfather's eyes is there in them all.

Rachel Naomi Remen, M.D.

2

BEING A JEW

A good Jew is someone who is always trying to be a better Jew.

Rabbi Louis Finkelstein

Welcome Home

A Jew, no matter how far she has strayed, is still a Jew.

Talmud

"I can't believe it!" the young woman exclaimed, with an expression of incredulity on her face. "I just can't believe that all of that happened!"

We were sitting over coffee in my dining room, and I was meeting for a study session with this lovely twenty-two-year-old, who was converting to Judaism. As a long-time Jewish educator and conversion tutor, I had seen many different kinds of students. But I had never been faced with quite this reaction to the Holocaust before. I had (incorrectly, it seemed) just assumed that nowadays everyone had learned about the Holocaust in school or had seen *Schindler's List,* or had read some of the current books about it. Somehow, it had not occurred to me that there might still be people who simply had never encountered the harsh facts of that terrible time.

For the last two hours, we had been looking at photographs, reading various accounts, comparing information, and talking about what had happened during those years and how the legacy of the Holocaust would impact upon her as a Jew. It was clear that she was visibly upset and could not really comprehend that such atrocities had happened in modern times.

"You have to remember," she told me. "Before my family moved here last year, I was raised in a very small, Midwest town. There were no Jews where we lived. There were no people to explain this history to me. My parents never talked about such things, and I never asked. In our school we hardly even talked about Victnam, much less World War II, which was like ancient history to us.

"It wasn't until I met Rick that I had ever even talked to a Jew. And I fell in love with him, not really knowing anything about his religion—or about his history. And certainly, I never knew about all of this! I can't imagine what it must be like to lose your whole family, and not to have a home."

She wiped away a tear, grieving over the immensity of the human being's capacity for hatred and cruelty.

The hour was growing late, and she had to leave. We agreed to discuss the topic further in our next study session.

"I'll call you tomorrow," she said as she left.

As I closed the door behind her, I shook my head with sadness and some concern: How, in this day and age, could someone grow up totally unaware of the enormity of the Holocaust? How would she cope with the reality of being Jewish and come to terms with Jewish history, in all its permutations? The Holocaust was not something one could wave away; she would have to confront it if she decided to continue her spiritual journey into Judaism.

Two hours later, my husband and I were about to turn out the lights and go to sleep when the phone rang. When I picked up the receiver, she was on the other end of the line, sounding very agitated.

"I must see you!" she said. "Something has happened, and I need to tell you about it!"

"Tonight?" I asked. "It's so late. Don't you want to wait until tomorrow?"

"No! No!" she insisted. "I must see you right now!"

"In that case, please do come over," I said. I couldn't imagine what had taken place, but it was clear that this was important.

Twenty minutes later the doorbell rang, and as I let her in, she seemed even more distraught than she had been earlier in the evening.

"When I left you," she began, "I couldn't get the pictures and the stories out of my mind. I didn't want to be alone at home, so I went over to my mother's house. When I got there, we sat and talked in the kitchen. I told her all about our conversation, all about the camps, the forced labor, the hatred displayed against the Jews by the Nazis, the indifference of the rest of the world. I was crying, and I felt like the ground had been pulled out from under my feet. I just couldn't understand why people didn't stop the killing, why the world let it all happen.

"I had been there for about forty-five minutes or so, and my mother listened to everything. And then she started to cry, too. At first, I couldn't get her to tell me what was wrong, and I couldn't understand why she was so upset!"

I felt my skin grow prickly and cold.

"What did she tell you?" I asked.

"She finally said that the reason I was never baptized, and the reason we lived in such a small town, and the reason that we had no relatives was because there was something she had never explained to me: My mother told me that she and my father were not born here in this country. They left Germany just after Hitler came to power. It was before I was born. She was a young bride, and my father had almost no money. But whatever they had was used to purchase tickets to leave. In the early days of the Reich people could leave if they paid a ransom. It was a lot of money—over two hundred Reichmarks. They paid, and then they left, never once looking back. They thought their parents and aunts and uncles would follow. But they were never able to do so. When they came to this country, they moved to that tiny town because they were so afraid. They wanted to get as far away from the past as they could. They never spoke German at home. They never told me anything of our history because they wanted to protect me. And they never let me think for even one moment that our family was Jewish because they were terrified that the hatred which had driven them out of Germany would stain my whole life—and then my mother held my hand and told me that I am a Jew."

I embraced her in welcome.

My immediate suggestion was that she meet with the rabbi who was overseeing her conversion. After that, we talked for another hour about the choices she would face should she decide to truly reclaim her Jewish heritage.

She called the rabbi first thing in the morning. Upon hearing her story, his response was simple and warm:

"I can't convert you. You are a Jew. Welcome home!"

Some time later, she completed her studies and formalized her Jewish status by going to the mikvah on the anniversary of her parents' immigration to the United States. Eight months after that she married her Jewish young man. She had found her way home, at last.

Patti Moskovitz

"Son, it's time you knew . . . we're not your real parents."

Reprinted by permission of Barricade Books.

The Earth's Song

The State of Israel belongs not only to its citizens, but to the Jewish people at large.

Shimon Peres, former Prime Minister of Israel

An aging Jew, Yaakov Chazan never ceased telling his favorite story about why Israel meant so much to him. In his nineties, he loved to tell and retell the story of the music of the soil.

He begins by going back almost a century, when he was a poor farmer, apprenticed to a wealthy Polish farm owner who took great pride in his land. Every once in a while the Polish farmer would bend over and cup his ear to the earth. He stood quietly, as if listening to a symphony. You could watch his eyes dance and his body swing with the soft, gentle movements of the music he heard from the land.

Naturally, Yaakov also wanted to hear this beautiful music. If such melodious and inspiring sounds can emerge from the soil, why not take advantage, and let one's soul soar from the natural rhythms of Mother Nature?

So one day, slowly and carefully, mimicking the gesticulations of his mentor, Yaakov bent over, and placed his ear exactly on the spot where he saw the Polish farmer so exhilarated one sunny afternoon. He cupped his hand to his ear and pressed it firmly against the soil.

He waited. And waited. And waited. No music. No sound. Nothing.

The farmer looked at poor Yaakov, bent over, his head burrowed into the soil, and tried to hold back a smirk on his face. Yaakov saw his teacher, turned his head upwards, trying to keep his body still, and asked: "What am I doing wrong? Why can't I hear the music? I have seen you hum, and dance, and shimmy so many times as you listen to the heavenly music you describe bursting forth from the ground. What else can I do that I have not done?"

"Yankel" (the diminutive of Yaakov), said the Polish farmer, a little bit embarrassed. "You don't hear the music, because this is not your land. You are a Jew, and this is Polish land. Only natives, only those who belong here can hear this special music."

Yaakov Chazan never forgot this incident with the Polish farmer. As one of the early pioneers of the kibbutz movement in the first decade of the twentieth century he came to the land of his ancestors to till the soil, to feel at home, to own a piece of his own land, to teach others to farm, as he was taught as a youth. He became well known as a strong advocate for settling the homeland, for Jews coming from Russia, Poland and other parts of Eastern Europe, and rebuilding the broken land, irrigating the dry soil, turning brown, crusted earth into rich, fruitful brownish-red soil.

When he told the story of his Polish farmer, he would then finish with these words.

"Now I am at home," he would say. "Now the land is my land. Now, when I cup my ear to the soil of the Land of Israel, I hear music. Oh, what music!"

"That is why I love this country," he would say. "That is why I came here. To hear the music. To dance to it, to sing to it, to be inspired by it. This is my land, and now I can hear the music. And when I listen for a while, and let myself enter its rhythms, my soul soars and my spirit rises, and I know I am at home."

Rabbi Dov Peretz Elkins

A Surprise in Jerusalem

Let all who are hungry come and eat.

Passover Seder Liturgy

Some dear friends of mine live in Jerusalem, with most of their fourteen children. Their quaint home is reminiscent of a cave, and often when I enter it, the nursery rhyme, "There was an old woman who lived in a shoe, who had so many children, she didn't know what to do," sings its way through my mind. Not that my friend Talia is old or that she doesn't or can't manage her delightful children. In fact, their home is quieter and more serene with ten or twelve children than many people's homes with one or two. It's just that their cave-home is quite small and they live by meager means.

Another friend, Ilana, was in Jerusalem when Talia had delivered her tenth child. It was a boy. In the spirit of friendship and community, friends had offered to prepare festive food for the *Brit Milah,* the circumcision ceremony that according to Jewish law is scheduled for the eighth day after a boy is born. Talia asked Ilana to do her a favor and pick up a prepared dish of food from one of her friends nearby. Talia gave Ilana directions to the friend's apartment, a few blocks away and Ilana was happy to be able to help out.

Ilana walked over to the apartment and knocked on the door. She told the woman who greeted her that she was here to pick up some food for the *Brit Milah.* The woman smiled and invited Ilana into her home, invited her to sit, then brought out some food for Ilana while she waited. The woman was most gracious as she served some delicious cake and tea. Next, she went into her refrigerator and pulled out a casserole; she then took a coffee cake out of the oven. She said she had made the cake for Shabbat, for the Sabbath meal, but now she wanted it to be part of the baby's celebration. She packaged up the food and escorted Ilana to the door. As Ilana was leaving, the woman said, "So tell me, whose *Brit Milah* is it? Which family?"

Momentarily stunned, Ilana almost dropped the shopping bag she was holding, full of food. Then she realized—she must have gone to the wrong apartment. What a mistake! Embarrassed, she began to explain to the woman what had happened and held out the shopping bag to return the food.

The woman would have none of it. She shook her head, smiled and said, "Take it—and enjoy the *Brit Milah!*"

And then Ilana realized. It didn't matter. There was no such thing as the "wrong" apartment. After all, this was Jerusalem.

Rebecca Heisler

Climbing the Mountain

The Hebrew nation compensated for the insignificance of its members and territory by its religious genius, its tenacious belief; its poems and histories cling to the soil of this globe like the primitive rocks. . . .

Ralph Waldo Emerson

I met Rabbi [David Aaron] by the Zion Gate and [we] walked through the Jewish Quarter.

I said, "Look, Rabbi, I want you to know that I am not much of a Jew. Judaism lost me at age fourteen."

What he said in response staggered me. He pointed out that no rational adult would make a business decision based on what he knew when he was fourteen. No one would decide whom to marry based on what he knew about love and relationships when he was fourteen. But lots of people seem satisfied to dismiss religion based on what they learned—or didn't learn—at fourteen.

He was right, and I was one of those that stupid.

I was stuck back at age fourteen, staring at a picture in my Hebrew book—Abraham with his long beard bent over a frightened little boy, in his hand a long knife. That boy looked a lot like me. Okay, so Isaac didn't die, but he came close. I bet he didn't go for a walk with his father after that. Tell *him* that it was only a test from God.

That's what I was remembering as Rabbi Aaron took us up to the rooftop of his school. He kept talking in a low voice as the sun continued to sink. The rays bounced off the gold of the Dome of the Rock, the icon of Islam dominating this ancient Jewish city.

As my eyes traveled around the Old City, the rabbi pointed out the Moslem Quarter, the Christian Quarter, the Armenian Quarter and the Jewish Quarter. I could feel the holiness of the city, so important to so many. All these religions were rubbing shoulders with one another and hating the friction created by such closeness.

Yet it all began with one man—Abraham, the first monotheist. The three religions that now make their home here all claim him as father. They are all based on the Torah. Jesus studied Torah; Mohammed studied Torah. But I had never studied Torah. It was about time. And it was there—as the candles of Jerusalem were lit like stars—that I made a vow to do it.

As we left the rooftop, I kept thinking: I have been a Jew for over seventy years and I know so little about Judaism. Why am I still a Jew? I pushed those thoughts out of my head as we walked through the dark alleys to the rabbi's home.

I met his young wife, a former parachutist in the Israeli army, and his five children.

We ate a delicious meal and sang songs with the rabbi beating time on the table. Through the window I could see other houses lit by the warm light of candles and could hear the same songs echoing in the night. They were happy songs. I felt good.

That night I felt that I had come home. The light of the Shabbat candles transported me back seventy years. I could see my mother's face as she lit them each Friday night. I could hear her voice, just before she died: "What day is it?"

"Friday, Mama."

"Don't forget to light the candles. . . ."

I made plans to start studying the Torah with the young rabbi the next time he came to America.

He told me that, in English translation, there are only 350 pages in the Torah. Not so many. I thought if God is a patient God, maybe he'll give me enough time to learn the things I need to know to understand this book that has made Jews the conscience of the world. Maybe I will understand why people hate us.

The next day, I took a tour through the tunnel along the foundations of the Temple. Archeologists had dug this tunnel, barely wider than a sewer pipe, to expose the entire Western Wall. . . .

The tunnel is as close as a Jew can get to the majesty and holiness of the Temple originally built by King Solomon. You feel like a rat burrowing into the history of your ancestors buried by the debris of so many conquerors.

As I walked slowly, following my guide, Tova Saul, a young religious girl who came from Pittsburgh to settle here, I let my fingers caress the huge blocks of stone.

We came to an archway, cemented in by the Arabs, where a door had once led to the top of the Temple Mount. This is how the High Priest entered the Holy of Holies. As Tova was reciting some interesting facts about the archway, suddenly all went black. And I mean pitch black. The electricity was out. I didn't know what to do. I could hear voices of people calling to each other as they groped for the exit. When the lights go out, Israelis always worry. Are the Arabs attacking again? Are Scud missiles flying? The tunnel had only one way out then, and it wasn't easy to leave the way you came.

I was standing in what, for a Jew, is the holiest spot on earth. I decided to recite the only prayer I still remembered in Hebrew: *"Shema Yisrael Adonai Elohainu Adonai Ehad."* Hear, O Israel: the Lord our God, the Lord is One!

The lights came back on. "You want to leave?" Tova asked, anxiously looking to see if the temporary blackout had frightened me.

"No," I said, "let's go on." We continued down the passageway until we came to the end.

"This is it," Tova said, pointing to an exposed piece of rough stone in front of us. The stone was no longer part of the smooth wall. This stone was something else.

"What is it?"

"This is the bedrock of Mount Moriah."

I looked at this black stone enshrouded with so much mystical meaning.

"You mean. . . ."

She finished it for me. "Yes, this is the bedrock of the mountain where Abraham took his son Isaac to be sacrificed."

The picture from my Hebrew-school book flashed into my mind. But, to my surprise, it no longer frightened me. I wasn't sure why. Something had happened to me here that I didn't quite understand.

It was very quiet in the tunnel, dimly lit, cool.

Tova's voice was barely above a whisper: "This is where it all started."

I couldn't speak. She was right.

This place represented the beginning of my doubts. And, at long last, the end of them.

Here in the dark tunnel, touching the rock of Mount Moriah, I grew up.

Kirk Douglas

An Old Woman's Warmth

Once you have lived a moment at the Wall, you never go away.

Rabbi Abraham Joshua Heschel

One evening . . . I went to the Western Wall—not for the first time. Morris and I had gone there a week or two after our arrival in Palestine. I had grown up in a Jewish home, a good traditional Jewish home, but I wasn't at all pious, and the truth is that I went to the Wall without much emotion, just as something that I knew I ought to do. Then, all of a sudden, at the end of those narrow, winding alleys in the Old City, I saw it. The Wall itself looked much smaller than it does today, after all the excavations. But for the first time I saw the Jews, men and women, praying and weeping before it and putting *kvitlach*—their scribbled petitions to the Almighty—into its crannies. *So this was what was left of a past glory,* I thought, all that has remained of Solomon's Temple. But at least it was still there. And in those Orthodox Jews with their *kvitlach,* I saw a nation's refusal to accept that only these stones were left to it and an expression of confidence in what was to come in the future. I left the Wall changed in feeling, uplifted is perhaps the word.

In 1971 I was awarded the Freedom of Jerusalem—probably the greatest tribute ever paid me—and at that ceremony I told of yet another memorable visit I had made to the Wall, this time in 1967, after the Six-Day War. For nineteen years, from 1948 to 1967, we were banned by the Arabs from going to the Old City or praying at the Wall. But on the third day of the Six-Day War, Wednesday, June 7, Israel was electrified by the news that our soldiers had liberated the Old City and that it was open to us again. I had to fly to the United States three days later, but I couldn't bring myself to leave Israel without going to the Wall again. So that Friday morning, although civilians were not yet allowed to enter the Old City because shooting was still going on there, I received permission to go to the Wall, despite the fact that I wasn't in the government then but just an ordinary citizen, like any other.

I went to the Wall together with some soldiers. There in front of it stood a plain wooden table with some submachine guns on it. Uniformed paratroopers wrapped in prayer shawls clung so tightly to the Wall that it seemed impossible to separate them from it. They and the Wall were one. Only a few hours earlier they had fought furiously for the liberation of Jerusalem and had seen their comrades fall for its sake. Now, standing before the Wall, they wrapped themselves in prayer shawls and wept, and I, too, took a sheet of paper, wrote the word *"shalom"* (peace) on it and pushed it into a cranny of the Wall, as I had seen the Jews do so long ago. As I stood there, one of the soldiers (I doubt that he knew who I was) suddenly put his arms around me, laid his head on my shoulder, and we cried together. I suppose he needed the release and the comfort of an old woman's warmth, and for me it was one of the most moving moments of my life.

Golda Meir

Hanukkah in a Soviet Prison

It was in the grim Russian winter of 1971 that I celebrated my first real Hanukkah, in prison.

I was confined in the notorious Moscow prison, Matroska Tichina, in the company of a rather large number of fellow Jews. Needless to say, a Moscow prison is not the most auspicious place to celebrate a Jewish holiday. But first, let me explain how my cellmates and I came to be in prison that Hanukkah.

In late November 1971, a group of Refuseniks staged a public hunger strike in Moscow to demand exit visas for Israel. About twenty men—most of them artists, writers and scientists—gathered in the large hall of the Central Telegraph building. It was the only public place that was open twenty-four hours a day, so it was the ideal location for them to carry out their protracted demonstration.

I was a novice Refusenik and did not take part in the strike. With some other friends, I tried to help them. It was common practice in our struggle to help our comrades when they were in trouble. It was the most potent weapon of "the weak" and "the few"—as the *Al hanissim* prayer, recited on Hanukkah, refers to the battle of the Hasmoneans' army—against the all-powerful regime, "the strong and the many." We positioned ourselves near them in the building to give them moral support. We also supplied information about the strike to foreign journalists. This demonstration became a sensation in the foreign mass media, so the Soviet authorities put a stop to it by arresting the hunger strikers. Without any trial, they were summarily sentenced to fifteen days in prison on a typical charge of the time, "petty hooliganism."

The next day, to protest against the arrest of the demonstrators, six of us went to Central Telegraph to stage another demonstration. We sent a telegram to Leonid Brezhnev, the general secretary of the Communist Party, informing him that we had begun a hunger strike to protest the arrest of our friends—Jews who wanted to go to Israel. I don't know whether they actually transmitted our telegram to Brezhnev, but within three hours, a police unit came and arrested us.

We were placed in custody overnight. The next morning, the judge sentenced us to fifteen days in prison, without benefit of counsel. We were taken to Matroska Tichina.

When we entered the cell, we almost began to dance with delight, for there were two of the hunger strikers who had been arrested the day before. It was rare in those days for them to put Jewish prisoners together, even though they were arresting Jews left and right on all kinds of trumped-up charges. Altogether, there were twenty-three of us in three neighboring cells; we kept in touch with each other by knocking on the walls and shouting. What a wonderful gift to balance out the atrocious situation of having to spend fifteen days there. This was my first incarceration, at the beginning of my career as a dissident.

In my seventeen years of refusal, I would spend a total of ten years in prison, solitary confinement and exile in Siberia. In that first arrest, I must confess that I was frightened, but at the same time, intrigued. Until that point, I had only read in the papers about dissidents and political prisoners. Now I was one myself.

Despite the appalling conditions—no beds, no blankets, vile food—we were privileged because we were together as fellow Jews. Among us was a man who knew Hebrew very well—which in those days was very rare—so we quickly established a "prison ulpan." We had engrossing discussions about subjects such as Jewish history, philosophy, and Israeli and Middle East politics. It was a kind of Jewish seminar, which provided many of us an excellent opportunity to learn more about the fascinating Jewish heritage of which we had been deprived.

Hanukkah was approaching. Getting into the spirit, we enthusiastically discussed battles and the ultimate triumph of the Maccabees. One of our more Judaically advanced cellmates gave us insightful lessons about the laws and customs of the Festival of Lights. It goes without saying that we had no prayer books or other items with which to celebrate a Jewish holiday. Hanukkah is supposed to be a holiday of gift-giving, family gatherings, *dreidels* and songs. We had no practical means of celebration, and that saddened us deeply.

Fortunately, we had among us a man who was a wizard at handicraft. Valery Krijzak—now an engineer living in Jerusalem—had truly golden hands. From the first days of our imprisonment, he amazed us with his skill. He sculpted an entire chess set out of stale prison bread. Each king, queen, rook and pawn was a little masterpiece. Someone suggested that after our release we send the set to chess champion Bobby Fischer, but the guards later confiscated it.

For Hanukkah, Krijzak made a wonderful *dreidel* out of bread, engraving the four Hebrew initials for *ness gadol haya sham* ("a great miracle happened there"). But it was the day before Hanukkah and we still didn't have any candles with which to fulfill the *mitzvah* of the Festival of Lights to commemorate the Jewish victory of over two thousand years ago. And without those lights, Hanukkah is not Hanukkah.

But then the miracle of Hanukkah took place in our days in our cell.

Without saying a word to us, Krijzak began to bang on the cell door, calling for the guard. When the small aperture was opened, he began to wail, "Call the doctor. I'm in terrible pain." Within ten minutes, the prison medic arrived. Krijzak moaned, "Doctor, I am having a terrible hemorrhoid attack. Please give me some suppositories."

Fifteen minutes later, Krijzak received several suppositories. Now we had the material from which to make candles. The rest was purely technical. We pulled out threads from our prison garb and rolled them together to make wicks. Then we placed the wax-based suppositories on our aluminum spoons and lit them with matches (prisoners were permitted to have cigarettes and matches) and melted them down. We placed the makeshift wicks into the wax, which we then shaped into candles. We stuck the candles on a plate, which we then placed on the table.

Filled with pride, we sat around our glowing table and sang *Maoz Tzur.* We sang more Hanukkah songs, talked about the Maccabees' revolt and spun the *dreidel.* We all had an immense feeling of closeness to each other and a strong sense of unity with our fellow Jews.

We may have been cut off from the rest of the world, enclosed behind thick steel doors, but we were still with our people.

Yosef Begun

Honors at the Kennedy Center

You are a holy people to the Lord your God.

Deuteronomy 7:6

[EDITORS' NOTE: *Kirk Douglas describes his emotions when receiving the award for "lifetime contributions to dramatic arts" at the John F. Kennedy Center for the Performing Arts when his son, Michael, walks onto the stage.*]

Michael began by saying warm things about me. And a funny feeling started to creep over me. *Take it easy, Kirk,* I said to myself. *Spartacus doesn't cry.* And I held it back. Michael talked about a lullaby that my mother sang to me in Yiddish, *'Rozhinkes mit Mandlen'* ("Raisins and Almonds"), a song that brings sweet dreams. I had visions of blubbering all over the First Lady's velvet gown. I was determined not to give in. But then I heard a flute playing the tune, and about fifty children walked out onstage singing. Listening to the song that I had heard so often many, many years ago, I suddenly knew the meaning of "voices of angels." Those sweet sounds seemed to fill every part of me. I closed my eyes to hold back the tears and saw visions of my mother blessing the Friday-evening Shabbat candles.

On Saturday morning, she would be so neatly dressed, her hair combed perfectly, as she'd sit in a rocking chair on the front porch with her arms folded. She looked so peaceful. It was an unusual sight. There was a holiness about my mother. And as that song about raisins and almonds floated up to me, I thought, *My God, how far away I've strayed.* Right then and there, I made a promise to start lighting candles every Friday night.

Later, my wife told me that the First Lady was carefully watching me as I tried unsuccessfully to hold back my tears. As I stood up to take a bow, I knew that TV cameras were aimed at me from somewhere. I was determined—they mustn't see me wiping my eyes. I felt my wife's reassuring clasp on my arm as I looked down into the faces of the audience and spotted [sons] Peter and Eric looking up at me.

That night, as I lay in bed, the wonderful events of the evening kept tumbling in my mind. There were so many memorable moments, but crowning them all was my grandson Cameron throwing his arms around me and whispering in my ear: "Pappy, I'm so proud that you're my grandfather."

Kirk Douglas

How Do You Talk to God?

God is near to all who call, to all who call in truth.

Psalms 145:18

When I was a little boy, I thought that my grandmother was God. You see, in Sunday school they taught us that God was very old, older than the whole world, and my grandma was the oldest person I knew. She would sit in a faded yellow, shellback chair in the corner of the room and gaze upon her visitors, and I would sit on the floor in front of her and wonder what she was thinking about up on her throne. The teacher taught us that no one knew what God looked like, but that was just because she hadn't met my grandmother. God had quiet gray hair that was set in curlers and styled every Tuesday at 9:00 A.M., and thick glasses that allowed her all-knowing eyes to focus on you, and the softest cheeks that you always wanted to nuzzle when you hugged her. God always dressed frumpy, and she wore the same orthopedic shoes forever, probably since she walked across the desert with the twelve tribes. She walked with a cane that I always assumed was the one Moses had turned into that snake that ate Pharaoh's snakes. That was Grandma's style after all. No one argued with her because she was always right.

The rabbi taught us in Sunday school that God was wise and knew everything, and that God was respected by the entire world for his wisdom. Well, my grandma knew everything and everybody, even stuff like math, and my whole family came from all over just to seek her advice. She knew what was wrong with people's marriages and the answer to every question on *Jeopardy*. No one was smarter than she was. They said God could create anything just by thinking about it. Well, every time we would visit her, I would start getting hungry for her famous meat loaf and blueberry pie. *Please,* I'd hope as the car moved along the highway, *let there be meat loaf and pie at Grandma's!* Don't you know the first thing she would say to me as I hugged her was, "Your meat loaf and blueberry pie are over on the table. Go eat it while it's hot." And I would look over and there it was, just like that! How did she know? To my child's mind, there was no doubt; Grandma had to be God.

As I got older, I began to appreciate my grandma as a person and not just as God. She was a refined Southern lady who had been one of the founders of her synagogue. She was a pillar of the community, and everyone knew her. We would go to services on Friday night, and she always walked with great dignity to her seat on the third-row aisle. We would follow her down the center of the congregation as all of the folks rose to greet her. "Good *Shabbos,* Miz Aaron!" "How ya feelin', Miz Aaron?" "Good to see your family with ya, Miz Aaron!" She would nod her head in greeting to everyone and address them by name. She was one of the oldest members of the *shul,* and she took great pride in her role there as a community matriarch. Even when she could no longer walk, I would wheel her down the aisle with her head held high and her jaw set firm. Sometimes when we followed Grandma down the big center aisle with everyone rising as we passed, I felt like I was following Moses through the Red Sea.

On one special occasion, though, I truly came to know how both holy and human my grandmother was. I was about six or seven, the age you start to learn the main Hebrew prayers in the Shabbat service. I was so excited to go to *shul* with my grandma and show her what I had learned in religious school! We took our seats in the congregation and when the services reached the *Shema* and *v'ahavta* (Deuteronomy 6:4–9), I excitedly started to sing along with everyone else. I turned to my grandma to show her what I knew and saw her smiling down at me very proudly. But then I also noticed that her lips were not moving; she was not singing along with us but rather humming!

"Grandma," I whispered, "how come you are not singing along with us?"

"I don't know the words, dear," she replied and continued to hum. I was totally amazed. *How could this be? How could my wise and all-knowing Grandma not know the words?*

"But Grandma," I said, "the words are right here on the page."

She smiled at me, one of the few times I remember her smiling. "Dear," she said, patiently, "I don't know how to read Hebrew."

Utter confusion. My little mind almost exploded as it tried to understand what she was saying. My grandma, my Jewish hero, was Jewishly illiterate?

What I did not know then was that women raised in the South in the early part of the century were often not given a Jewish education or taught any Hebrew. It was not a time where a woman's mind was valued like a man's, and this woman who founded a synagogue and kept Judaism alive in our family was never given a Jewish education. But as a kid, I couldn't comprehend any of this; all I knew was that God couldn't read Hebrew! I leaned over to her and tugged on her sleeve to interrupt her humming. "Grandma! Grandma!"

"Yes, dear?" she whispered.

"If you can't read the Hebrew in synagogue, how do you talk to God?"

She looked at me with her all-knowing eyes as she reached down to take my face gently in both of her soft, aged hands. She bent down, kissed me on the cheek and whispered into my ear, "Don't worry, sweetheart, God knows what I'm saying."

Rabbi Scott Aaron

It's Only a Matter of Time

The greatest honor I can give my children is love for our people, loyalty to self.

Theodor Herzl

Last week I ran into Uncle Yossel. Literally. I was rounding the corner at New York's Thirty-fourth and Seventh, he at Seventh and Thirty-fourth, when we collided. "Lisa, darrrling!" he screamed, rolling his Hungarian R's before planting a wet kiss on my nose, a greeting that's always been reserved for me, the youngest of his nieces. "Where are you going? You vant to come for *Shabbes* dinner?"

Uncle Yossel always had a way of reminding me that being Jewish was an active, not a passive thing. A verb rather than a noun, you might say. "I can't tonight, Yossel," I said. "I have other plans. But I'll walk with you a bit." He held a *challah* in one hand, and my hand in the other, as we strolled toward his apartment.

This time, I squeezed his palm harder than usual. I wanted to remember its texture, the roughness of a single hand that has known more of life than most. I felt his mangled thumb, severed in a pickle slicer when he was a boy in Uzhgorod; his enormous fingers, which lifted and rolled bolts of wholesale fabric along Orchard Street for half a century; his fist, which once beat a Hungarian Nazi to death and now beats his chest for forgiveness each Yom Kippur. I needed to lock his fingerprints into my memory, like jewels in a safe deposit box, so that one day I could remind myself of all that he was.

These days, I'm conscious of time. I know that the final years of all our Uncle Yossels have arrived. I know that the smell of chicken soup, wafting down the narrow hallway of an outdated, overheated, hopelessly slip-covered apartment, is in its last hour. It's only a matter of time when it all stops: the Jewish holidays, when everyone babbles at once in an animated blend of Yiddish and Hungarian, with bits of English accidentally thrown in; the blue velvet *talit* bag, lying next to a jumbo cigar on the telephone table; the bill for the kosher butcher, who still delivers from the Bronx, the ever-polished Shabbat candelabra and its endless supply of candles, hiding underneath the sink; the leather-bound *siddur*, faded and crumbling from generations of prayer, and the endless sea of *yahrzeit* candles aglow on the piano—one for each family member that died in the war. It's the end of an era. Soon we won't even have their faces to remind us that it takes more than suffering to be a good Jew.

In no time at all, we'll be left to carry on a tradition by ourselves. What will happen to us when we can no longer live our Judaism through our *bubbes*, our *zaides*, our Yossels, when the holiday tablecloths are pressed and folded away for the last time, and all that we're left with are our own reflections staring at us from a bare table? What will we do when they're not able to take our hands on a bustling New York corner, filled with the high-tech, fast-paced lure of the future, and forgive us for saying, "I have other plans," on a night that, to them, is still Shabbat?

And straightway, the answer comes. When we step into shoes bigger than our own, somehow our feet grow. When the old ones depart, the tradition passes to us and we will find the way and the will to uphold it, for it is as close to us as our own heartbeat, as much an expression of our being as our own breath. How else but by taking on the mantle of the departed have we survived all these centuries to call ourselves Jews?

Lisa Lipkin

The Power of a Blue Box

You can give without loving, but you can't love without giving.

Anonymous

When I worked in a Jewish nursing home, I learned the true meaning of the Jewish National Fund Blue Box. A Blue Box is not just a *pushke* into which coins are put. It is the repository of the dreams, prayers and efforts of generations of Jews. I learned this one day at a storytelling activity at my nursing home.

One day, to stimulate memories among the participants in my group, I brought a tray of objects. I set out a pair of small candlesticks, a couple of seashells, a lace-edged, monogrammed handkerchief, a Blue Box, and other odds and ends on the tray and passed it around. The residents would finger the objects, then pass the tray on. When their turn came, they'd share a personal anecdote that one of the objects had brought to mind.

That day, an aide had brought Clara to the group. Clara had suffered a stroke that left her paralyzed on one side and somewhat aphasic: She understood language but had trouble finding the correct words when she wanted to speak.

Clara did not take her disabilities with grace. She was angry, hostile and disruptive. Storytelling was the most inappropriate activity of all, for it focused attention on her language disability. But there she was, and I was too busy with the rest of the group to wheel Clara back into the hall. I just hoped that Clara wouldn't raise too much of a ruckus.

When the tray went around the room, Clara grabbed the Blue Box in her good hand and clasped it to her chest, refusing to relinquish it. Although no one else took an object off the tray, there were grumbles from the other participants. "Anyone can tell a story about any object—these or any others," I said. The grumbles died down. Then the stories began. One woman told how the seashells reminded her of going to the beach every summer Sunday as a child. Another described the lacy handkerchief she carried when she eloped with a soldier on the eve of World War II. The next person was Clara, but the person beyond her, knowing Clara never participated in a group, cleared her throat. Clara waved the Blue Box and said, "Mine, mine." Another old woman, a former social worker, said, "Clara wants to speak!" Clara nodded, and the room became silent.

Slowly, haltingly, Clara began her story. Often she said something that made no sense, and I would suggest words that fit better. Clara would shake her head until I hit the right word, then she'd nod. I then repeated the story up to that point, and Clara would continue. Other old ladies had told their memories in two or three sentences, but in spite of her laborious method of storytelling, Clara told her story in detail.

Her son was six, she said, when World War II was over and the news of the concentration camps became public.

Clara, a young Boston housewife, was devastated, although all her family was already in America. Her heart ached for the survivors, crammed into Displaced Persons camps, and she wanted to help. After much thought, she made a plan. Every afternoon, when her son came home from school, she would take him by one hand with her Blue Box in the other hand, and she would collect money for Israel. Clara went door to door through the Jewish neighborhoods, and everyone gave. But she couldn't just stop, so she started going through other neighborhoods. "Everyone gave," she told the group. "The Irish and the Italians and the Greeks, everyone gave.

"They said, 'I feel so bad for your people. Thank you for giving me a chance to help.'" Clara told the group that for two years, until the birth of her second child was imminent, she and her son went out almost every day to collect money for Israel, money to bring the survivors home to their new land.

When Clara finished, the room was silent. Her painfully told, detailed account had brought those days back clearly in everyone's mind. They had also peeled back the curtain of time to show this woman when she had been vitally alive. Suddenly one old woman began to clap, and then applause filled the room. Clara nodded at the group, and the side of her mouth that could move curved into a smile. Slowly the room returned to normal, and the next person told her story.

That night, Clara had another stroke, one that left her completely unable to speak. But in my eyes and those of the other people who had been in that room that day, Clara never again looked like the mere wreck of a woman. Instead, we saw past the wreckage of age to the vibrant soul of a woman who cared.

Hanna Bandes Geshelin

Four Jewish Boys in the Presbyterian Choir

The laughless people are the most dangerous.

Robert Raines

Unlike my father, my mother was a very practical lady. Nothing ever flustered her. No matter what the problem was, somehow she knew how to handle it.

A perfect example happened when I was seven years old. I was singing with three other Jewish kids from the neighborhood. We called ourselves the Peewee Quartet. Now, there was a big department store, Siegel & Cooper, that threw an annual picnic, and the highlight was an amateur contest with talent representing all the churches in New York. Right around the corner from where we lived was a little Presbyterian church. How it got in that neighborhood, I'll never know; it certainly didn't do big business.

Well, they had no one to enter in the contest, so the minister asked us four kids to represent the church. We jumped at the chance. So that Sunday, there we were, the Peewee Quartet—four Jewish boys sponsored by a

Presbyterian church—and our opening song was "When Irish Eyes Are Smiling." We followed that with "Mother Machree" and won first prize. The church got a purple velvet altar cloth, and each of us kids got an Ingersoll watch, which was worth about eighty-five cents.

Well, I was so excited I ran all the way home to tell my mother. When I got there she was on the roof hanging out the wash. I rushed up to her and said, "Mama, I don't want to be a Jew anymore!"

If this shocked her, she certainly didn't show it. She just looked at me and calmly said, "Do you mind me asking why?"

I said, "Well, I've been a Jew for seven years and never got anything. I was a Presbyterian for one day and I got a watch." And I held out my wrist and showed it to her.

She glanced at it and said, "First help me hang up the wash, then you can be a Presbyterian."

While I was hanging up the wash some water ran down my arm and got inside the watch. It stopped running, so I became a Jew again.

George Burns

"And considering all that I get out of the temple, your dues are ridiculously low!"

Reprinted by permission of Rabbi Henry Rabin.

What It Means to Be a Mensch

Jews are characterized by modesty, mercy and kindness.

Talmud

I learned this story from Rabbi Benji Levene of Gesher, who lives in Jerusalem, Israel. Benji tells of how, when he was a child, his saintly father, Rabbi Chaim Jacob Levene, tried out for a position as rabbi in Jersey City, in a synagogue where Rabbi C. Y. Bloch, of blessed memory, had served for many years. Although there were many other candidates for the position, Benji's father was chosen. When the chairman of the search committee called to tell him the news, Benji's father thanked him, but said that he would need a week before he could give his answer. The chairman was puzzled but granted the request, and at the end of the week, his father accepted the position. It was only years later that he learned the reason for his father's delay.

"It was my father's custom," Benji said, "after we had settled into the community in Jersey City, to visit the widow of Rabbi Bloch every Friday morning, and sometimes he would take me along. We would go up several flights of stairs to her modest apartment, spend a quiet hour with her, and my father would inform her of what was going on in the community. Once, my father had an errand to do, so he excused himself and left me with the widow. She gave me cookies and a soda, and then she said, 'I am going to tell you a story, which I don't want you ever to forget.

"'When your father was asked to accept the position of rabbi here, he said that he needed a few days before he could give the committee an answer. Do you know why he did that? It was because he first wanted to come to see me.

"'When he came in, he said, "I know that for many years you were the first lady of this congregation, and I understand that it will be difficult for you, after all these years, to see someone else take your husband's place. The board has offered to make me the next rabbi, but I have not given them an answer yet. I wanted to see you first, in order to ask your permission. If you want me to take the position, I will, but if in any way you feel that you don't want me to be here, I will leave right away."'

"The widow told me that at that moment she started to cry, and she said to my father, 'Now that my husband is gone, who is there who cares about me or thinks that what I feel is important? I am so touched that you came here today to ask my permission.' And then she paused, 'I told him, not only do I want you to stay and be the rabbi, but now I feel as if my own son were taking the position.'

"Then, wiping her eyes behind her round granny glasses, she continued, 'Only then did your father go back and accept the position. And for the first year, he did not sit in the rabbi's seat on the pulpit in the synagogue, in deference to my husband's memory. And he never told anyone what I have just told you.'"

Benji Levene said that this story made more of an

impression on him, and taught him more about what real piety is, than reading ten books of ethical instruction. "I learned," he said, "that sensitivity to the feelings of another human being is more important than concern for one's own status, position or power. My father's behavior in that incident remains for me the archetype of how a rabbi should act, of how a Jew should act, in fact, how all human beings should treat one another."

Rabbi Benjamin Levene
Retold by Rabbi Jack Riemer

Standing by His Word

The way to honesty in business is through the emulation of God, and the imitation of God's attribute of integrity.

Rabbi Isaiah Horowitz

In a used furniture business, unlike new, you cannot order stock from a catalogue. People call in, and you have to go out and make an offer. "You can't sell what you don't have," my father would say. So making his calls was crucial for him.

When I was age thirteen, my father lost his store manager, a one-armed guy who could do more with his one arm than many will do with two. With his one arm, he used to hook a chair on a long pole, then arc it upwards in the air where he would slide it onto ceiling hooks until someone wanted to purchase it. With his manager gone, my father came to me. Until he found the right person, would I come in while he went out to answer the day's calls?

The store has tens of thousands of items. "People like to bargain," he told me, "so I don't mark prices. You just have to know a range."

He took me around. "A quarter-horse motor you can sell for four dollars. For a refrigerator, depending on the condition, you can sell for thirty-five dollars to sixty dollars. However, if it has a freezer all the way across, sell it for eighty dollars, in excellent condition, maybe one hundred dollars. If a gasket's loose, it's garbage. Otherwise, I don't charge for scratches. Dishes come in with a houseful of furniture, and I don't even figure them in when I give a price. You can sell them for a nickel to a quarter. Something really nice."

Every day after school, I would pedal down to the store. Soon after, I was writing up a sales slip for an attractive plate when my father walked in. I had asked a dollar and the guy did not hesitate. I was very pleased. My father glanced down at what I was doing, turned to the customer and said, "You sure got a bargain today. My employee gave you the price and that's the price."

Afterward, I asked my father, "What was that all about?"

It turned out it was an antique plate, worth a few hundred dollars. I was devastated. Here I was trying to help my father in the business and instead I was losing money for him.

He said, "I could've stopped the sale if I'd wanted to. You were just writing up the slip and hadn't yet taken the money. Besides, by civil law, you're under age. But, a Jew stands by his word and the word of his agent."

Cost my father a small amount of money to teach me a lifelong lesson in integrity.

The event has a sequel. Years later, my wife and I needed to wire a large sum of money to our daughter in Israel. A bank teller advised my wife Loretta that a VISA check carried no service charge or interest unless late. When the bank statement showed considerable charges, I went in and tried to explain to the branch manager that we acted on their advice to avoid charges. To everything I said, all she could reply was, "We're sorry, but the teller made a mistake."

I then told her the story of my father standing behind the word of his employees. I finished by saying, "This was even when it didn't cause a loss to the customer, and when my father caught the error before the transaction. How much the more so afterward! I expect my bank to behave with at least as much integrity as my father."

The branch manager had not said a word during all of this, and her silence continued as I sat back in my chair. I had no idea of how she was going to react.

When she began to speak, her voice had softened, and she said in a dignified manner: "The Canadian Imperial Bank of Commerce will not be less than your father."

Then she promised that all the charges made to my account for that VISA check would be reversed.

As I thanked her and stood to leave, I was grateful that even in today's impersonal business world, a tale of integrity still had power to touch the heart and sway the conscience.

Rabbi Roy D. Tanenbaum

Aaron Feuerstein

The quality of mercy is not strained;
It droppeth, as the gentle rain from heaven
Upon the place beneath: it is twice blessed;
It blesseth him that gives, and him that takes.

William Shakespeare

Aaron Feuerstein practices his Judaism not only in his synagogue but also in his private life and in his business life, too.

However, I must admit to you that until five weeks ago when I read an article about him in the newspaper and when I saw a brief news statement about him on television, I had never even heard his name.

Let me tell you about him.

Aaron Feuerstein is the third generation of Feuersteins to run the Malden, Massachusetts, Textile Mill. Almost every other textile mill has moved out of New England to Mexico, Asia or the South—where the owners of the mills could get cheap labor.

Aaron's grandfather had started the mill ninety years ago in 1906. Aaron's father went to work in the mill when he was thirteen. Now Aaron, aged seventy, is the head of the mill.

It was obvious that Aaron was in the dusk of his career, but eighteen hundred workers were still working for him in Malden, and another fourteen hundred were working for him around the world. The company had seen its bad days but now it was producing Polartec and Polarfleece and doing about 400 million dollars in business a year.

However, on December 11, a fire spread quickly through the textile mill. Three of the nine buildings were totally destroyed. Thirty-three people were injured. Eighteen hundred workers in Malden were out of work two weeks before Christmas.

People were saying: "Feuerstein is seventy years old. He's got plenty of money. He doesn't have to work any longer. He's insured. He'll take the money and retire in Florida—and we'll all be unemployed. Some Christmas this is going to be."

However, Aaron called a meeting to be held in the gym of the Central Catholic High School. One thousand workers showed up at that meeting.

When Aaron walked in there was total silence. Then there was a murmur. And then the murmur became a roar. Finally, everyone was cheering for Aaron.

They knew that Aaron was a religious man. Every single day, he spent an hour memorizing Hebrew poets and English poets. Every week, he not only studied his Judaism, but he actually lived it. People were shouting: "Aaron, Aaron, Aaron, Aaron."

Aaron had never let them down in the past. He had always paid them the highest salaries in the textile industry. However, his mill had just gone up in flames, and they did not know what he was going to do. All their friends in the other mills were now unemployed. They wondered whether this was also going to be their fate, too.

Then Aaron Feuerstein ascended the platform and addressed the one thousand workers. He said: "We're down—but we're not out. Let me tell you what is now going to happen.

"Number one, for at least the next thirty days, and possibly longer, *all* employees will receive full salaries;

"Number two, your health insurance has already been paid for you for the next ninety days;

"Number three, in three weeks, by January 2, we will restart partial operations again;

"Number four, within ninety days we will be 100 percent operational again.

"Remember, we may be down—but we are not out. Don't stay down on the floor. Join me—and let's get up together."

For a moment, there was total silence. But then everyone began screaming and shouting, kissing each other and hugging each other.

One of the workers, Rene Gingros said: "I've been in textiles fifty-five years, so I'm at the end of the line. But I'll tell you, this is the best Christmas present I ever got—far and away."

Rabbi Jack Segal
Previously appeared in Chicken Soup for the Soul at Work

3

ON LOVE AND KINDNESS

Faith makes all things possible. Love makes all things easy.

Rabbi Sidney Greenberg

Avital

He who loves brings God and the world together.

Martin Buber

[EDITORS' NOTE: *Anatoly Sharansky was the most well-known Jewish dissident in the former USSR. The day before he was imprisoned on trumped-up charges in 1974, he married his sweetheart, Natasha, and said good-bye to her at the Moscow airport, telling her he would see her shortly—hoping that somehow he would be free and join her in Israel. He remained in prison for twelve years, and was released to Israel in 1986. In his autobiography, he describes his release from prison, through American intervention, and his reunion with his wife of twelve years. Anatoly and Natasha changed their Russian names to Hebrew names—he is now Natan, and she Avital. In 1996, he became Minister of Trade and Industry in the Israeli cabinet.*]

We drove to the American base, where American soldiers saluted us. As we sat in a small plane, the soldiers gave me the ambassador's gifts—flowers, fruit, a picture of the Glienicke Bridge and cuff links with President Reagan's signature. The plane started moving and then stopped; the brakes weren't working properly, and we had to switch to another plane.

"I thought we were already in the West," I exclaimed to the ambassador, "but it seems we're still in the Soviet Union, where something always doesn't work." I was laughing happily now, for this was one of those details that distinguish real life from dreams.

Finally we left for Frankfurt, where Avital was waiting. I divided my attention between looking out the window and carrying on an urbane conversation with the American ambassador. But the only thing on my mind was that soon I'd see Avital.

All I remember from my talk with the ambassador is how astonished I was that he was only thirty-nine. "You made your career so quickly," I said.

"Well," he replied, "you're also very young and made a career quickly."

"Yes, but in my case the KGB helped. I trust that your achievement had nothing to do with them."

In the midst of this friendly banter, the picture in front of my eyes begins to twitch, as if from a nervous tic. The world seems to lose its continuity, moving jerkily from one frozen frame to another.

We land in Frankfurt.

"Where's Avital?"

We go from a military base to a civilian airport.

"Where's Avital?"

Someone greets me in Hebrew—the Israeli consul. We hug.

"Shalom! Where's Avital?"

We walk quickly. A corridor, elevator, corridor. Faces appear and disappear.

"Hello, hello." Then, "Shalom!" "Shalom!" "Shalom!" A bearded young man with a *kippah* on his head smiles at me, "Shalom!" and points to a door. Another bearded man with a *kippah* comes out: "Shalom!"

I fly into the room—it's empty. I turn—Avital is sitting in the corner, wearing a kerchief and a dark suit. She whispers something, but I can't hear. I take a step toward her, and another, and a third. She stands up. Her lips are trembling and her eyes are filled with tears. Yes, it's really she, my Natasha—the same girl I had promised twelve years ago, at the Moscow airport, that our separation would be brief. In a desperate attempt to swallow the lump in my throat and to wipe the tears from our faces with a smile, I tell her in Hebrew: *Silchi li she'icharti k'zat* (Sorry I'm a little late).

I hold Avital's hand just as twelve years ago I had held Natasha's hand on our way to the airport. Through twelve years of struggle, longing and suffering, twelve years of desperate attempts not to lose hold of each other, I had been obsessed by the thought of how it would be when we finally met. Our separation lasted well over four thousand days, and when I concentrate I can still recall every significant moment during those years. I remember how it was when I first met Natasha outside the synagogue, and what it was like to take her to the airport and leave her there on the morning after our wedding. I recall the pain and abandonment I felt when they confiscated her photograph in Lefortovo [prison], and the joy I experienced when they finally gave it back.

But this precious and amazing moment of our reunion is somehow sealed off from me, like a black hole that pulls in the light and gives nothing back. *What was I thinking when we finally saw each other? What did I say, and what did Avital whisper to me?* Strange as it may seem, I do not know. I recall only that my head was dizzy and my knees grew weak, as it seemed that at any moment the two of us would leave the ground and start floating up into the air.

My mind now retains rapidly changing images from the next hours—how we flew over the Mediterranean on a small plane that was sent by our government; how we landed in Israel and were greeted by so many friends; how I spoke almost without understanding my own words; how we sang *"Hinei mah tov u'mah na'im shevet achim gam yachad"* (How good and pleasant it is for brothers to be together)—I had sung that song so often while I was alone in punishment cells, and now I sang it with thousands of my brothers and sisters who had gathered at the airport; how I squeezed Avital's hand tightly for fear she would slip away and the dream would end. Only at night, in the Old City of Jerusalem, did I let go of her hand when the crowd carried us to different sides and I swam on people's shoulders to the *kotel,* the Western Wall.

Holding our Psalm book in my hand, I kissed the wall and said, *"Baruch mutir asirim."* Blessed is He who liberates the imprisoned.

Natan Sharansky

The Power of Holding Hands

I was sitting on a beach one summer day, watching two children, a boy and a girl, playing in the sand. They were hard at work building an elaborate sandcastle by the water's edge, with gates and towers and moats and internal passages. Just when they had nearly finished their project, a big wave came along and knocked it down, reducing it to a heap of wet sand. I expected the children to burst into tears, devastated by what had happened to all their hard work. But they surprised me. Instead, they ran up the shore away from the water, laughing and holding hands, and sat down to build another castle. I realized that they had taught me an important lesson. All the things in our lives, all the complicated structures we spend so much time and energy creating, are built on sand. Only our relationships to other people endure. Sooner or later, the wave will come along and knock down what we have worked so hard to build up. When that happens, only the person who has somebody's hand to hold will be able to laugh.

Rabbi Harold Kushner

The Letter

The old rabbi glanced out of the window of his office at the overcast skies. It was a typical gray day in Manchester, England. As he was about to get back to work, there was a knock on the door, which then opened slowly. In walked Sue, a plain, homey lady. She hesitantly strolled over to a chair facing the rabbi and was about to sit down, when panic struck her and she said, "I'm sorry, I have made a big mistake and I should not be here." She turned around and started to walk towards the door.

"Stop! Come here, my dear, and sit down please. I welcome your company." The old rabbi smiled and carefully stroked his long gray beard. Sue came over to the rabbi's desk and slowly sat down on an old worn chair.

"Now then, why is a lovely lady so afraid to tell her rabbi what bothers her? I am here to help you, my dear, so take a deep breath and tell me your problem."

Sue stared at the rabbi, and she felt an air of serenity engulfing her very being. She took a few deep breaths and quietly said, "Thank you for seeing me. As you can see, I am a very plain-looking woman. I have a few male friends, but never have I had a close relationship with anyone. Tomorrow will be my fortieth birthday. I feel life is passing me by, and I am unfulfilled. I feel like a river run dry."

The rabbi stood up, walked around his desk and started to stroke Sue's hair. "My lovely Sue, beauty does not come from our face or physique. Beauty comes from the soul, and you are a beautiful soul."

Sue could not contain her emotions and burst into tears.

The rabbi kept stroking her hair for a few more moments then went back to his chair. He opened a drawer in his desk and pulled out a crisp, clean cotton handkerchief. "Wipe your eyes and listen to what I am about to tell you," he said. "On one side of the handkerchief is the name and address of a matchmaking agency. I want you to go home and write a letter to this agency, with all your interests and life history included. Do not read your letter over; just go out and mail it as soon as you write it."

Sue stopped crying, wiped her eyes, and read the name and address that was embroidered in the top left-hand corner of the handkerchief. She stood up, and now it was her turn to walk over to the rabbi. She threw her arms around him and kissed him on the forehead. "Thank you so much for your love and advice. I will do as you say," she said. She immediately rushed to the door and in an instant was gone from the building.

It took Sue half an hour to drive home. She ran into her house, pulled out a pen and paper, and scribbled down her interests and life history. She wondered why the rabbi did not ask her to include a photo along with the letter, but no matter. The letter was written, and she placed it in an envelope. She called to her faithful companion, Bobby, a nine-year-old collie, and put on his leash. Within a moment, she was out the door and walking the half-mile to the mailbox in town.

Everything seemed to be in a haze, and when she reached the mailbox she stood there for a minute before she decided to mail her letter. She was just about to drop it in the mailbox when she realized that she had forgotten to put a stamp on it. The shock made her drop the letter on the ground. She bent down to pick it up. Within a moment another letter fell on top of hers, and without looking up she lifted them both from the ground. As she stood up, her eyes opened wide in amazement for there stood a man, and he was smiling kindly. "I'm sorry," he said. "I dropped my letter."

"It's quite okay. Here it is," said Sue. As she gave it back to him, they both noticed his letter had no stamp on it either. They burst into laughter.

"My name is Bob, and I would like to take you for a cup of tea to the little café across the street."

Overcoming her surprise, Sue replied, "That would be delightful."

No sooner had they had sat down and ordered a pot of tea than Bob started to explain the reason for his letter. "I'd seen an advertisement in the local paper by a matchmaking service, and I thought to myself, 'I'm forty-five years old and have never been married. What do I have to lose by sending in a letter about myself?'"

Sue's heart was beating so strongly that it was shaking her body. Her face began to go bright red. "I was about to mail out a letter to that same agency, Bob," she managed to say.

Their eyes locked in an angelic stare, and there was silence for many moments.

"Here is your tea," the waitress said. Neither Sue nor Bob even heard her. "Your tea," the waitress repeated. "Here is your tea, and would you like some biscuits?"

"Oh, yes . . . thank you," said Bob, without taking his eyes off Sue.

At that moment, Sue's dog, which had been quietly sitting at Sue's feet, put a paw on Bob's lap. "I forgot all about your dog," said Bob. "What is his name?"

"Bobby," replied Sue.

"How fantastic," replied Bob. "I have a collie named Suzy."

They both laughed.

After a year of courting, Sue and Bob were married. The old rabbi officiated at the wedding. As Bob placed the ring on Sue's finger, the rabbi said it was a match made in heaven—two souls, united as one, were soul mates forever, sealed by the letters L.O.V.E.

Sue smiled at the mention of sealing letters. She still had the letter she had written and forgotten to stamp. It hadn't mattered. God had put the stamp on and also made the delivery—a lot faster than the post office could ever have done!

Michael Levy
Submitted by Tom Lagana

Lovers . . . Still

Love, that you may be loved.

Moses Mendelssohn

My mother and father observed an unusual ritual throughout their nearly forty-nine years of marriage. Whenever they left home together, just before walking through the door, they would kiss each other. Usually it was a perfunctory kiss, a force of habit kind of thing, but without question it was mandatory for them, almost like paying homage to a superstition, which it was not.

Apparently they had kissed at the door ever since they were newlyweds, and the custom held. Even if they were in the midst of a quarrel (and their arguments were always civil), there would be that brief pause, the kiss, and the discussion would continue as they walked outside. As a kid, I thought all couples kissed whenever they left their home.

Certain memories surrounding my father's death remain especially clear in my mind. The phone call, the funeral, the hundreds of people offering consolation, my teenage son's arm around my shoulders, and reciting

Kaddish, the mourner's prayer I had led thousands of times, now as a mourner myself.

But most of all, I remember watching my mother leaving the apartment on the way to the funeral. When she reached the front door she paused for a moment, only a moment, and sighed. Then she squeezed my hand hard, and walked out into the hallway.

I wouldn't dare try to characterize my parents' marriage. After all, what does a child, even a grown child, really know about his parents' relationship? But there is history that I experienced along with them, and themes in their lives to which I was privy. Lots of heartache and hard times, but also a good deal of joy and pride and a more comfortable life towards the end.

My mother and father often joked facetiously that theirs was an intermarriage, and perhaps in 1940 they did qualify somewhat, Mom as the granddaughter of German-Jewish immigrants and Dad as the grandson of Russian-Jewish immigrants. Her ancestry was of the punctual, exacting variety, and his of a more relaxed, quixotic nature. Their two backgrounds occasionally clashed, as at the conclusion of a Thanksgiving visit to our home in Philadelphia.

Always one of my favorite holidays, we had enjoyed a large, festive celebration on Thursday, and now it was Friday afternoon with just Sherri, our kids and my parents sitting around the dining room table picking through leftovers. Everyone was feeling relaxed and full. My mother excused herself from the table, announcing that she was going upstairs to pack so that she and my father could get back home to Baltimore in plenty of time to attend Sabbath evening services. A few minutes later, the predictable call from on high. "Norman, are you coming up to help?"

My father, who in his later years had developed grousing

into an art form, was annoyed. Not only was he annoyed, but this day he had an audience to whom he could ruefully complain, "Punctual. Always punctual. She has to be on time. Everything done on schedule. Very precise." (The final syllable emphasized through clenched teeth.) He was enjoying himself as he rehearsed the old theme. Mom called again, and Dad continued to expound on the qualities of persons afflicted with a German-Jewish heritage. The kids fell silent. Sherri and I became increasingly uncomfortable.

For one of the first times in my life, for I was still their child—I decided to intervene, and the device I chose was humor. I took a big breath, then looked at my father with raised eyebrows and suggested, "Yeah, Dad. She's a real pain. Why don't you dump her?"

Sherri and the kids did double-takes, then began to laugh hysterically. My father, caught off-guard, smiled, pretended to agree that it was not a half-bad idea and joined in the laughter. Even my mother thought it was funny, once we let her in on the joke.

In the final years of their marriage my parents experienced an increase in tension, sniping, impatience and anger. I stood to the side, sad, hoping the same would not happen between Sherri and me, and wondering if what I was witnessing was unique to Mom and Dad or a natural by-product of the frustrations of aging.

Still, the Psalmist wrote how in God's sight a thousand years are like one day. In human experience I learned that sometimes one brief moment can outweigh decades. One brief moment can become more significant than all the events and feelings of the years that surround it. A moment in a cold, formal hospital room, for example.

A few months after that Thanksgiving encounter, my father entered the hospital for prostate surgery, a common operation for men his age, but scary nevertheless.

On the morning of the surgery he was slightly groggy but still cavalier when my mother and I kissed him good-bye. We ate a little breakfast and passed the time as people do in hospitals until the doctor arrived with a good report and the promise that Dad would be returned to his room within an hour.

We awaited him. Finally a squad of orderlies and nurses wheeled him into the room and carefully transferred him from litter to bed. When the people cleared away I looked down to see a much older-looking Norman Alper, his hair matted, his mouth shriveled, a red mark across the bridge of his nose and saliva sliding down his chin. He slept fitfully.

But soon he awoke, and looked at us, and smiled. And then one of the most wonderful scenes I have ever witnessed took place. Carefully, lovingly, Mom handed Dad his dentures which, in his vanity, he had never before been without. He fitted them into his mouth, and his face brightened. Almost ritualistically, she returned his glasses. His hearing aid. She dabbed his cheek and combed his hair. And at the last, she replaced his wedding ring on his finger.

Step by step, she brought him back to her. Step by step, he returned to her. Pure joy. Pure, sweet joy passing back and forth between them.

I stood nearby but, to them, not present. They were alone with each other.

I watched my elderly parents. Lovers. Still.

Rabbi Robert A. Alper

I Married Her Sunshine

There is a comfort in the strength of love; t'will make a thing endurable, which else would overset the brain or break the heart.

William Wordsworth

Like many young newlyweds, I often found myself verbally sparring with my mother-in-law.

My own willingness to argue with her disturbed me. I had been raised from infancy to be respectful of my elders, so why was I behaving so differently now? It was a worrisome situation.

But one Passover night, everything changed. All the men had gone to synagogue, and she and I were left alone for a very long while. I will remember for a lifetime what she said to me that night. It was as if a floodgate had opened up inside her, and a torrent of words came pouring out.

She began by describing the beautiful life she led before World War II. Raised in affluence by loving parents, she was surrounded by an enormous extended family who doted on her, the "baby" of the clan. "They were hard-working, kind, generous and exalted," she said of her family. The smile on her face as she told of this wonderful time in her life made me realize that at that moment she was back in their comforting embrace.

As she continued her story, her serene appearance began to change and was replaced by a look of great pain. She became detached and remote, as if she was recounting the events of someone else's life rather than her own.

The little girl she was all but disappeared when the German tanks came rolling through Poland in 1939. "My grandmother, after watching her beloved husband and eldest daughter being dragged away in the middle of the night, was determined to save what remained of their family. For six long years 'Mama' used her considerable wealth to 'rent' space under a barn from a kind, Gentile farmer, who was an old family friend."

These were the six years of life when a young girl should have blossomed into womanhood. Yet, she explained, she spent those six years in total darkness and in near silence. At a time when the giggles of school friends sharing secrets were the only hushed words she should have heard, the fear of being discovered was so crippling that she and her mother could not speak above a whisper. The only companions she had were the field mice who came in at night, and as she listened to the chickens above her head being fed their daily fare, she wondered why her food rations were so meager. And like a flower robbed of the nurturing sunlight and water she began to wither away.

And then finally liberation. As she emerged from the cave that had become her home the brightness was blinding, and yet she drank it all in as a parched desert traveler would absorb the waters of a running brook. But, just as the bud began to blossom again, the clouds rolled in once again, robbing it of the precious sunshine.

You see, the peasants who had been occupying her

home during the war were not pleased to discover that the former tenants had miraculously survived. Angry at the prospect of having to leave their lush surroundings, they became increasingly hostile.

One evening, as her mother peeked out of the window, she saw an angry mob heading towards the house. Quickly she pushed her daughter into the cold pot-bellied stove to spare her from whatever was to come. As the crowd gathered, the young girl watched through the window of the oven as her mother argued for her property, and then, as she begged for her life. But her words were to no avail, and as her young daughter looked on, she was shot, along with her sons, in cold blood.

When the group dispersed she quietly emerged from her hiding place. Although her mother had meant to spare her certain death, the young girl wished in her despair and heartbreak that she, too, had met her mother's fate. At that moment, she swore to leave behind the land of her birth forever.

Somehow she was placed in a foundling home and eventually found her way to America to live with a distant relative. From the outside, she looked like any young girl, energetic, vivacious, attractive. But on the inside something had died. Something that she thought would never live again.

Then one day she met a handsome young man, who swept her off her feet. And once again she began to experience love. What had died on that horrible day in Europe just a few years before was reborn on the sidewalks of New York. She and her Prince Charming married and after one year they were blessed with a beautiful son.

And then she turned to me and in broken English spoke the most eloquent sentence I have ever heard. "From the moment the war began, until the moment I gave birth to your husband, the sun did not shine for me."

And at that moment I understood. I understood why she was obsessed with her children. I understood why her children were the "most" beautiful and brilliant. I understood why her children could do no wrong. I even understood why she constantly pushed them to eat.

Strong feelings of shame began to overwhelm me. How could I not have accorded the proper respect to a woman who had endured unspeakable hardships, and yet had the courage and the faith in God to rebuild her own life, and bring a new one into the world? How could I have not seen the signs of a woman so deeply scarred that the only joy she derived from life involved her family? Why had I silently ridiculed her when her overprotective tendencies appeared? How could I have been so blind?

Then and there, I resolved to change the way I looked at her. Never again could I peer into her face and not see the little girl hiding in an oven. Never again could I stare into her eyes and not see the vision of death and destruction that she so vividly described. Never again could I eat at her table and not imagine the pangs of hunger that must have enveloped her. And never again could I hear her voice and not think of the hushed whispers of her lost youth.

Now, when I see a woman who thinks her children are the "most" everything, I ask myself, *Why shouldn't she think so?* Now, when I see a woman who loves so unconditionally that in her eyes her children can do no wrong, I admire her conviction. I no longer see a woman who is pushy at mealtime, but a generous and giving human being. And now I can even see why I seemed unworthy of her son's hand in marriage. For after all, who would be worthy of marrying her "sunshine"?

Miriam Goldbrenner

3423215785

READER/CUSTOMER CARE SURVEY

CA7

We care about your opinions. Please take a moment to fill out this Reader Survey card and mail it back to us.
As a special **"thank you"** we'll send you exciting news about interesting books and a valuable **Gift Certificate**

Please PRINT using ALL CAPITALS

First Name ____________ MI. __ Last Name ____________

Address ____________

City ____________ ST ____ Zip ______ - ____

Phone # (___) ___ - ____ Fax # (___) ___ - ____

Email ____________

(1) Gender:
- ○ Female
- ○ Male

(2) Age:
- ○ 13-19
- ○ 20-29
- ○ 30-39
- ○ 40-49
- ○ 50-59
- ○ 60+

(3) Your children's age(s): *Please fill in all that apply.*
- ○ 6 or Under
- ○ 7-10
- ○ 11-14
- ○ 15-18
- ○ 19+

(8) Marital Status:
- ○ Married
- ○ Single
- ○ Divorced / Widowed

(9) Was this book:
- ○ Purchased For Yourself?
- ○ Received As a Gift?

(10) How many Chicken Soup books have you bought or read?
- ○ 1
- ○ 3
- ○ 2
- ○ 4+

(11) Did you enjoy the stories in this book?
- ○ Almost All
- ○ Some
- ○ No

(12) How did you find out about this book? *Please fill in ONE.*
- ○ Personal Recommendation
- ○ Store Display
- ○ TV/Radio Program
- ○ Bestseller List
- ○ Website
- ○ Advertisement/Article or Book
- ○ Catalog or Mailing
- ○ Synagogue
- ○ Other ____________

(13) What FIVE subject areas do you enjoy reading about most? *Rank only FIVE.*
Choose 1 for your favorite, 2 for second favorite, etc.

	1	2	3	4	5
Self Development	○	○	○	○	○
Parenting	○	○	○	○	○
Spirituality/Inspiration	○	○	○	○	○
Family and Relationships	○	○	○	○	○
Health and Nutrition	○	○	○	○	○
Religion	○	○	○	○	○
Business/Professional	○	○	○	○	○
Entertainment	○	○	○	○	○
Teen Issues	○	○	○	○	○
Computers	○	○	○	○	○
Pets	○	○	○	○	○

TAPE IN MIDDLE; DO NOT STAPLE

NO POSTAGE NECESSARY IF MAILED IN THE UNITED STATES

BUSINESS REPLY MAIL

FIRST-CLASS MAIL PERMIT NO 45 DEERFIELD BEACH, FL

POSTAGE WILL BE PAID BY ADDRESSEE

CHICKEN SOUP FOR THE JEWISH SOUL
HEALTH COMMUNICATIONS, INC.
3201 SW 15TH STREET
DEERFIELD BEACH FL 33442-9875

FOLD HERE

9383215786

(18) Where do you purchase most of your books?
Please fill in your top ***TWO*** *choices only.*

- ○ General Bookstore
- ○ Religious Bookstore
- ○ Warehouse / Price Club
- ○ Discount or Other Retail Store
- ○ Website
- ○ Book Club / Mail Order

(20) What type(s) of magazines do you SUBSCRIBE to?
Fill in up to ***FIVE*** *categories.*

- ○ Parenting
- ○ General Inspiration
- ○ Religious / Devotional
- ○ Business / Professional
- ○ World News / Current Events
- ○ General Entertainment
- ○ Homemaking, Cooking, Crafts
- ○ Women's Issues
- ○ Other (please specify) ____________

(25) Are you:

- ○ A Parent?
- ○ A Grandparent

Do you have your own Chicken Soup story that you would like to send us?
Please submit separately to: Chicken Soup for the Soul, P.O. Box 30880, Santa Barbara, CA 93130

CA7

Unspoken Blessings

Encouraging words are as honey,
Sweet to the soul and health to the being.

Proverbs 16:24

On Friday afternoons when I would arrive at my grandfather's house after school, the tea would already be set on the kitchen table. My grandfather had his own way of serving tea. There were no teacups and saucers or bowls of granulated sugar or honey. Instead, he would pour the tea directly from the silver *samovar* into a drinking glass. There had to be a teaspoon in the glass first, otherwise the glass, being thin, might break.

My grandfather did not drink his tea in the same way that the parents of my friends did either. He would put a cube of sugar between his teeth and then drink the hot tea straight from his glass. So would I. I much preferred drinking tea this way to the way I had to drink tea at home.

After we had finished our tea my grandfather would set two candles on the table and light them. Then he would have a word with God in Hebrew. Sometimes he would speak out loud, but often he would close his eyes and be quiet. I knew then that he was talking to God in his heart. I would sit and wait patiently because the best part of the week was coming.

When Grandpa finished talking to God, he would turn to me and say, "Come, *Neshume-le.*" Then I would stand in front of him and he would rest his hands lightly on the top of my head. He would begin by thanking God for me and for making him my grandpa. He would specifically mention my struggles during that week and tell God something about me that was true. Each week I would wait to find out what that was. If I had made mistakes during the week, he would mention my honesty in telling the truth. If I had failed, he would appreciate how hard I had tried. If I had taken even a short nap without my nightlight, he would celebrate my bravery in sleeping in the dark. Then he would give me his blessing and ask the long-ago women I knew from his many stories—Sarah, Rachel, Rebekah, and Leah—to watch over me.

These few moments were the only time in my week when I felt completely safe and at rest. My family of physicians and health professionals were always struggling to learn more and to be more. It seemed there was always more to know. It was never enough. If I brought home a 98 on a test from school, my father would ask, "And what happened to the other two points?" I pursued those two points relentlessly throughout my childhood. But my grandfather did not care about such things. For him, I was already enough. And somehow when I was with him, I knew with absolute certainty that this was so.

My grandfather died when I was seven years old. I had never lived in a world without him in it before, and it was hard for me. He had looked at me as no one else had and called me by a special name, "*Neshume-le*" which means "beloved little soul." There was no one left to call me this anymore. At first I was afraid that without him to see me and tell God who I was, I might disappear. But slowly over time I came to understand that in some mysterious way, I had learned to see myself through his eyes. And that once blessed, we are blessed forever.

Many years later when, in her extreme old age, my mother surprisingly began to light candles and talk to God herself, I told her about these blessings and what they had meant to me. She smiled at me sadly. "I have blessed you every day of your life, Rachel," she told me. "I just never had the wisdom to do it out loud."

Rachel Naomi Remen, M.D.

With Faith, Back into Life

The sudden death of my father changed every aspect of our lives. My mother, a widow at thirty-four, had to plunge into the working world to provide us with basic needs. As caterer and waitress, her hours were long and exhausting. Our paths crossed from moment to moment as each one rushed on to the next assignment. At the age of eleven, I had to make my own contributions of time and supportive tasks. There was little time to express the pain and fear at the loss of a beloved, funny and sympathetic companion-father. I missed him every moment of the day and night, but I had to mask the tears and sorrow for my mother's sake. She was carrying her own burdens and I found I could not add to her grief by sharing my sense of loss.

My day began as a ritual. Mother worked into the late hours, so she was asleep when I began my school day. New England mornings can be cold, and I can still feel the chill of my clothes as I moved quietly from bedroom to bathroom to kitchen. There was always a note from her with a coin that would allow me to buy my lunch at school. The note was encouraging, but an underlying sadness reflected her loneliness and her fatigue.

Classes began at 8:30 A.M., but my day began at 5:30 A.M.

It was a long walk to school, and there was a ritual that preceded my arrival at the Theodore Roosevelt Junior High School. Each morning I would walk to the morning service at Temple Mishkan Tefila, which was halfway to school. Every morning, as an only child, I would be part of the morning service and recite the *Kaddish,* the mourner's prayer. It was my tribute to my father and, as I later recognized, a major aid in dealing with a devastating loss. There was no one else to recite the *Kaddish,* so the fact that I was not yet a Bar Mitzvah (age thirteen, and eligible to recite *Kaddish*) was overlooked by the doting and protective members of the minyan.

After the first week of this schedule, something quite unusual happened. Mr. Einstein, the *Shamash* (the sexton) of the synagogue appeared at my front door each morning just as I left the house for my trek to the synagogue. He was not a young man, and on the first week I noticed that he arrived for the minyan in an automobile driven by a congregant. Now, each morning he seemed to be passing my home just as I began my walk to synagogue and school.

He explained, "Your home is on the way to the synagogue. I have to go this way and I thought it might be fun to have some company. That way, I don't have to walk alone."

Each morning he was there. We trekked through snow, pelting rain, the exquisite New England fall, the hopeful days of spring, the stifling humidity of summer. We walked, and he taught. Each morning there was another story about the Jewish people, the prayer book, the questions of faith. He listened to my expressions of grief and quietly reflected the tradition that deals with sorrow as with joy. He held my hand as we crossed busy intersections and, after some weeks, he held my hand throughout the journey. I sat next to him in the synagogue, and he listened and he taught and he hugged . . . and he moved into a void that was tearing at my heart and soul.

Years went by, and we spoke by phone and letters. I had entered the seminary, and the day of my ordination as rabbi was my present to him.

Mr. Einstein was in his nineties when I visited Boston with my wife and six-month-old child. I wanted him to see my baby so I phoned and asked him to come to the home he had passed so often. He agreed but said that it was impossible for him to walk, would I please come to get him by automobile. I realized that I had never known where he lived so I asked for directions and set out to meet him.

The journey was long and complicated. His home, by car, was fully twenty minutes away. I drove in tears as I realized what he had done. He had walked for an hour to my home so that I would not have to be alone each morning. My home was not on the path to the synagogue; it was completely out of his way. He had made me feel that I was helping him with companionship; the opposite was true. He knew my loneliness, and he did not want my day to begin without him. He met my son and held him. Members of the family stood by and watched; there was not a dry eye. Each one knew our story and the sight of the next generation nestled in the arms of a beloved teacher and friend required no words. It is a picture that is etched in my heart. When I took him to his home and embraced him, we both wept. We knew it was the last time we would see and touch each other.

My life has been blessed with personal and professional success. Yet, wherever I went, in soft moments and in moments of exultant triumph, Mr. Einstein was holding my hand. By the simplest of gestures, the act of caring, he took a frightened child by the hand and he led him with confidence and with faith back into life.

Rabbi Gerald I. Wolpe

The Laundry Bag

The highest form of wisdom is kindness.

Talmud

The Israel Defense Forces is known to be keenly attentive to keeping pace with new technologies to maintain its military edge. One unclassified secret is that most army bases lack one critical bit of low-tech machinery: washing machines. Young recruits in Israel's army (which still observes a nearly universal draft) pile up their soiled uniforms for the much-awaited weekend furlough, when they pack their dirty laundry into one of their overstuffed duffel bags to bring home. Although the world has changed in many respects, it's still a fair bet to say that, in most cases, Mom does the wash.

Every Friday, Israel's main roads and highways are packed with streams of young men and women soldiers seeking transport home, huge duffel bags in tow. Many key intersections have soldiers' hitchhiking posts, called *trampiadas* in Hebrew slang, alongside the bus routes.

One Friday afternoon, a young soldier fortunate enough to get a ride home was unfortunate enough to forget his duffel bag in the trunk of the car that had given him a lift. Luckily, the next day, he received a call from the driver, who had traced his home number through the tags on his duffel bag.

The driver offered to meet him at the hitchhiking station where he had dropped him off. They met, as planned, and the young soldier thanked the good Samaritan. He was relieved to retake possession of his duffel bag, though disappointed to have to return to the base with the same dirty laundry he had taken home.

Back on base, the soldier unzipped what he anticipated to be a malodorous duffel bag, but was taken aback to find freshly laundered and folded uniforms, underwear and socks. He also found a note, attached to a bag of cookies. The note, unsigned, was from someone's mom, telling him that she had done his uniforms along with her son's. "I hope you like these cookies," read the unsigned note. "Take care of yourself and be careful."

Chava Weiss

The First Media Fundraiser

In 1932, in 1936, in 1940 and in 1944, Franklin D. Roosevelt was elected president of the United States, and throughout those years "birthday balls" in his honor were held in major cities across the country to raise money for research into poliomyelitis, a disease that had left the man crippled. At that time, scientists of the day knew little about the virus and could do little to help afflicted adults and children. There was a desperate need for a safe, effective vaccine, as well as for funds to construct a hospital and therapy center in Warm Springs, Georgia.

At these lavish affairs, contributors paid handsomely for the privilege of mingling with the celebrities of the day, Hollywood personalities like Jean Harlow, Jeanette MacDonald, Frederic March and many others, but the proceeds were never enough. Then, as time went on, and FDR's political positions led to controversy, criticism of his political positions began to spill over onto the foundation. His name was no longer the great asset it had once been, and the planning committees became desperate for ideas. At one of their meetings, Eddie Cantor was present, invited perhaps because of his known admiration for FDR and his reputation as a great fundraiser for charity.

Like Roosevelt, Eddie was a January baby, but unlike the president, he did not come from power and privilege. He was not a graduate of Groton or Harvard; in fact, he had barely finished grammar school. Like many of the sons and daughters of Jewish immigrants crowded into the East Side of New York City, Eddie was a child of the slums.

Born Itzak Iskowitz, Eddie never knew his parents. When he was a year old, his mother died giving birth to a stillborn child, and a year later, his father succumbed to pneumonia. Then, his Grandma Esther took on the job of raising the two-year-old. Her basement flat on Henry Street became his home, and she ordered him around in Polish and Russian and Yiddish. Toiling long hours to keep bread on the table and a roof over their heads, she peddled notions, lugging her heavy basket up the endless flights of tenement stairs. She worked as a matchmaker; she cooked and cleaned and mended for other people, and she did her best to watch over this skinny kid who spent his time playing hooky from school, hanging around pool halls, snitching fruit from pushcarts and singing for pennies on street corners. But somehow she managed to scrape together a dollar and a half to pay the rabbi to teach him Hebrew, and every Friday evening, she and the boy sat down together for a *Shabbos* meal prepared with love.

She wanted Eddie to have an education, and when he turned six, she dragged him off to Public School 136. When asked for a name, poor Grandma, who spoke no English, stuttered her own—Kantrowitz. The registrar put down what she thought she heard—Kantor. The "Eddie" came later when a sweet dark-haired girl name Ida Tobias, who became his wife, didn't think that Itzak was American enough.

But Eddie's talent for singing and dancing took him from the street corners to neighborhood theater amateur hours, then to jobs as a singing waiter and finally into vaudeville. By the time he was twenty, he was starring in the famed Zeigfield Follies on Broadway, and then moved on to Hollywood. But even with his hectic schedule and his devotion to his wife and five daughters, he was never too busy to work for charitable causes.

"Eddie," said President Roosevelt, "do you think that we could we get a million people to give us a dollar apiece?"

Eddie shook his head. "Times are hard, Mr. President, and a dollar is a lot of money, but most people can still give you ten cents. Let me broadcast on my radio show, and I can get ten million dimes quicker than one million dollars. We can ask the American people to send them directly to your office." Then he added, "We'll call it the March of Dimes."

When Cantor's suggestion was put to the administrative White House staff, there were negative reactions. However, the president was adamant, and Eddie put his appeal on the air.

The first response was a complete disappointment—$17.50—and the staff was too embarrassed to issue a statement to the press. However, the next morning, a postal truck delivered twenty-three sacks of mail, creating chaos in the White House office. The high total for a normal day was about 5,000 letters, but secretaries were now dealing with 150,000 by the end of the first week. Dimes came in every possible form, glued to cards, baked in cakes, pasted into collages, etc., and in four months amounted to a total of 2,680,000 coins—the first March of Dimes.

Eddie had always been a fundraiser. In 1917, when America entered World War I, Eddie was selling Liberty Bonds and entertaining the troops. When the war ended, he continued to visit veterans' hospitals. Then, in the 1930s, as the horrible news of happenings in Germany began to filter back to the United States, Eddie Cantor went into action. At one gathering in the Grand Ballroom of the luxurious Waldorf Astoria Hotel in New York City, over one thousand women gathered to listen to the little man at the microphone. To all of them, the voice and the face of one of the most popular comedians of the era were familiar, but he had not come to entertain. That night, he had come to make a plea for funds to rescue Europe's Jewish children from the Nazi terror. He opened by saying, "The message I give to you I want you to take home to your husband. If your husband believes in insurance, tell him that if we fail those on the other side, God knows what will happen here. They are waiting for us, these anti-Semitic groups here and all over the world, to see whether or not we fail here. I have had organizations threaten me, threaten my family, call up the people for whom I work. They intend to annihilate our people and I know that we must unite for our own survival."

Then he continued, "There is no reason on earth why every woman in this room cannot give $360 within the next year to take a child out of Germany. If every woman in this room would take out one child, you can save a thousand children. Will you help me, please?" There was applause and one woman called out, "How about a song, Eddie?"

"Make it $500, and I'll sing all night."

There was applause; there were donations. Then the little man was on his way to make the same plea at gatherings in twenty other cities in the United States and then on to Europe. He met with anyone who would make a contribution to the immigration program of Youth Aliyah. As Hitler moved across Europe, Eddie stepped up his schedule.

When Eddie was warned that he was doing too much, he cut his workload to do benefits. "No one is too busy to help children," he would say, and the youngsters appreciated his efforts. In 1938, the children of a cooperative village near Hedera, in what was then Palestine, presented him with a proclamation naming their new home Kibbutz Aryeh (their translation of Eddie) in his honor. They were evidently unaware that they could have used his Hebrew name, Itzak, which means "one who smiles."

At a time when most Americans were silent, Eddie spoke out against native Nazi sympathizers, men like Father Coughlin, the radio evangelist, and industrialist Henry Ford I. He even accused certain U.S. State Department officials of being Nazi sympathizers, maintaining that he could not ignore history even if it cost his job. The result was that he was blacklisted for three years, until his friend Jack Benny arranged to have him rehired.

During World War II, Eddie was at it again, selling U.S. Treasury Bonds, aiding in Red Cross blood drives and performing in military and naval hospitals and on the front lines. After the war, he turned his attention to the new State of Israel, raising over sixty million dollars in various bond drives.

On September 10, 1952, as Eddie was preparing his first TV show of the season, he was stricken with a heart attack. Hospitalized for six weeks, he received letters from servicemen and ex-servicemen wishing him well. And there were donations given in his name to the many causes he supported. Even at that time, he remarked, "It's hard to worry about your health when you're worried about the State of Israel."

Today many think of media fundraisers in terms of Jerry Lewis and his muscular dystrophy campaign or Marlo Thomas and her pleas for St. Jude's, or any of the many others that air on TV and radio. They aren't old enough to remember the little guy who started it all.

Miriam Biskin

4

OUR COMMON HUMANITY

Seek for your neighbor what you would seek for yourself.

Hasdai, 1230 C.E.

Stranger on the Bus

Man becomes truly human only at the time of decision.

Paul Tillich

A light snow was falling and the streets were crowded with people. It was Munich in Nazi Germany. One of my rabbinic students, Shifra Penzias, told me her great-aunt, Sussie, had been riding a city bus home from work when SS storm troopers suddenly stopped the coach and began examining the identification papers of the passengers. Most were annoyed, but a few were terrified. Jews were being told to leave the bus and get into a truck around the corner.

My student's great-aunt watched from her seat in the rear as the soldiers systematically worked their way down the aisle. She began to tremble, tears streaming down her face. When the man next to her noticed that she was crying, he politely asked her why.

"I don't have the papers you have. I am a Jew. They're going to take me."

The man exploded with disgust. He began to curse and scream at her. "You stupid bitch," he roared. "I can't stand being near you!" The SS men asked what all the yelling was about.

"Damn her," the man shouted angrily. "My wife has forgotten her papers again! I'm so fed up. She always does this!"

The soldiers laughed and moved on.

My student said that her great-aunt never saw the man again. She never even knew his name.

Rabbi Lawrence Kushner

The Merit of a Young Priest

It was June 1942. The Murder of Jews in the Cracow ghetto was at its height. About five thousand victims were deported to the Belzec death camp. Hundreds were being murdered in the ghetto itself, shot on its streets on the way to deportation. Among them were Dr. Arthur Rosenzweig, head of the Judenrat, the famous Yiddish poet Mordechai Gebirtig, and the distinguished old artist Abraham Neumann.

The Hiller family realized that their days in the Cracow ghetto were numbered; they, too, would soon be swept away in one of the frequent *Aktions.* Yet there was still a glimmer of hope. They were young and skilled laborers; if they were deported to a labor camp, perhaps they would still have a chance of survival. But the fate of their little son Shachne was a different matter. Small children had become a rare sight in the ghetto; starvation, disease and the ever-increasing selections took their constant toll. Helen and Moses Hiller began feverishly to plan the rescue of their little Shachne. After considering various possibilities they decided to contact family friends on the Aryan side in the small town of Dombrowa, childless Gentile people named Yachowitch.

Helen Hiller, with the help of the Jewish underground, made her way to Dombrowa. She went to Mr. and Mrs. Joseph Yachowitch and begged them to take care of her little son. Although they could do so only at great risk to their own lives, the Christian friends agreed to take the child.

Despite the ever-increasing dangers of the ghetto, the young parents could not bring themselves to part from their only child. Only after the large *Aktion* of October 28, 1942 when six thousand additional Jews were shipped to Belzac and the patients at the Jewish hospital, the residents of the old-age home, and three hundred children at the orphanage were murdered on the spot, did the Hiller family decide to act.

On November 15, 1942, Helen Hiller smuggled her little boy out of the ghetto. Along with her son, she gave her Christian friends two large envelopes. One envelope contained all the Hillers' precious valuables; the other, letters and a will. One of the letters was addressed to Mr. and Mrs. Yachowitch, entrusting them with little Shachne, and asking them to bring up the child as a Jew and to return him to his people in case of his parents' deaths. The Hillers thanked the Yachowitch family for their humanitarian act and promised to reward them for their goodness. The letter also included the names and addresses of relatives in Montreal and Washington, D.C.

The second letter was addressed to Shachne himself, telling him how much his parents loved him, that it was this love that had prompted them to leave him alone with strangers, good and noble people. They told him of his Jewishness and how they hoped that he would grow up to be a man proud of his Jewish heritage.

The third letter contained a will written by Helen's mother, Mrs. Reizel Wurtzel. It was addressed to her sister-in-law Jenny Berger in Washington. She wrote to her of the horrible conditions in the ghetto, the deportations, the death of family members and of the impending doom. She wrote: "Our grandson, by the name of Shachne Hiller, born on the 18th day of Av, August 22, 1940, was given to good people. I beg you, if none of us will return, take the child to you; bring him up righteously. Reward the good people for their efforts and may God grant life to the parents of the child. Regards and kisses, your sister, Reizel Wurtzel."

As Helen was handing the letters to Mrs. Yachowitch, she once more stated her instructions: "If I or my husband do not return when this madness is over, please mail this letter to America to our relatives. They will surely respond and take the child. Regardless of the fates of my husband or myself, I want my son to grow up as a Jew." The two women embraced and Mrs. Yachowitch promised that she would do her best. The young mother hurriedly kissed her little child and left, fearing that her emotions would betray her and she would not be able to leave her little son behind in this strange house, but instead, would take him back with her to the ghetto.

It was a beautiful autumn day. The Vistula's waters reflected the foliage of a Polish autumn. The Wavel, the ancient castle of the Polish kings, looked as majestic as ever. Mothers strolled with their children and she, the young Jewish mother, was trying to hold back her tears. She slowed her hasty, nervous steps so as not to betray herself and changed her hurried pace to a leisurely stroll, as if she, too, were out to enjoy the sights of ancient Cracow. To thwart all suspicion, Helen displayed a huge cross hanging around her neck and stepped in for a moment to the Holy Virgin Church in the Old Square.

Smuggling little Shachne out from the ghetto to the Aryan side was indeed timely. In March 1943, the Cracow ghetto was liquidated. People in the work camp adjacent to the ghetto were transferred to nearby Plaszow and to the more distant Auschwitz. Anyone found hiding was shot on the spot. Cracow, the first Jewish settlement on Polish soil, dating back to the thirteenth century, was *Judenrein* [Nazi expression denoting "empty of Jews"]!

Mr. and Mrs. Joseph Yachowitch constantly inquired about the boy's young parents. Eventually they learned that the Hillers had shared the fate of most of Cracow's Jews. Both of them were consumed by the flames of the Holocaust.

The Yachowitches, too, faced many perilous days. They moved to a new home in a different town. From time to time, they had to hide in barns and haystacks. When little Shachne suffered from one of his crying spells, calling for his mother and father, they feared that unfriendly, suspicious neighbors would betray them to the Gestapo. But time is the greatest healer. Little Shachne stopped crying. Mrs. Yachowitch became very attached to the child and loved him like her own. She took great pride in her "son" and loved him dearly. His big, bright, wise eyes were always alert and inquiring. She and little Shachne never missed a Sunday service and he soon knew by heart all the church hymns. A devout Catholic herself, Mrs. Yachowitch decided to baptize the child and indeed, make him into a full-fledged Catholic.

She went to see a young, newly ordained parish priest who had a reputation for being wise and trustworthy. Mrs. Yachowitch revealed to him her secret about the true identity of the little boy who was entrusted to her and her husband Joseph, and told him of her wish to have him baptized so that he might become a true Christian and a devout Catholic like herself. The young priest listened intently to the woman's story. When she finished her tale, he asked, "And what was the parents' wish when they entrusted their only child to you and your husband?" Mrs. Yachowitch told the priest about the letters and the mother's last request that the child be told of his Jewish origins and returned to his people in the event of the parents' death.

The young priest explained to Mrs. Yachowitch that it would be unfair to baptize the child while there was still hope that the relatives of the child might take him. He did not perform the ceremony. This was in 1946.

Some time later, Mr. Yachowitch mailed the letters to the United States and Canada. Both Jenny Berger, from Washington, D.C., and Mr. and Mrs. H. Aron from Montreal responded, stating their readiness to bring the child to the U.S.A. and Canada immediately. But then a legal battle began on both sides of the Atlantic that was to last for four years! Polish law forbade Polish orphan children to leave the country. The immigration laws of the United States and Canada were strict, and no visa was issued to little Shachne. Finally, in 1949, the Canadian Jewish Congress obtained permission from the Canadian government to bring 1,210 orphans to the country. It was arranged for Shachne to be included in this group, the only one in the group to come directly from Poland. Meantime a court action was instituted in Cracow, and Shachne was awarded by a judge in Poland to the representatives of the Canadian-American relatives.

In June 1949, Shachne Hiller boarded the Polish liner MS Batory. The parting from Mrs. Yachowitch was a painful one. Both cried, but Mrs. Yachowitch comforted little Shachne that it was the will of his real mother that one day he should be returned to his own people.

On July 3, 1949, the Batory arrived at Pier 88 at the foot of West Forty-eighth Street in New York City. Aboard was little Shachne, first-class passenger of cabin No. 228. He was met by his relatives, Mrs. Berger and Mrs. Aron. For the next year, Shachne lived in Montreal. On December 19,

1950, after two years of lobbying by Jenny Berger, President Harry S. Truman signed a bill into law making Shachne Hiller a ward of the Berger family. When Schachne arrived at the Bergers' home on Friday, February 9, 1951, there was a front-page story in the *Washington Post*.

It was more than eight years since Shachne's maternal grandmother Reizel Wurtzel, in the ghetto of Cracow, had written the letter to her sister-in-law (his great-aunt) Jenny Berger, asking her to take her little grandson to her home and heart. Her will and testament were finally carried out.

Years passed. Young Shachne was educated in American universities and grew up to be a successful man, vice president of a company, as well as an observant Jew. The bond between him and Mrs. Yachowitch was a lasting one. They corresponded, and both Shachne and his great-aunt Jenny Berger continually sent her parcels and money, and tried as much as possible to comfort her in her old age. He preferred not to discuss the Holocaust with his wife, twin sons, family or friends. Yet all of them knew about the wonderful Mr. and Mrs. Joseph Yachowitch who saved the life of a Jewish child and made sure to return him to his people.

In October 1978, Shachne, now Stanley, received a letter from Mrs. Yachowitch. In it she revealed to him, for the first time, her inclination to baptize him and raise him as a Catholic. She also went on to describe, at length, her meeting with the young parish priest on that fateful day. Indeed, that young parish priest was none other than the man who became Cardinal Karol Wojtyla of Cracow, and on October 16, 1978, was elected by the College of Cardinals as Pope—Pope John Paul II!

Yaffa Eliach

By Might or Spirit?

Breathing the air of the Land of Israel makes one wise.

Talmud

I had a revelation about the limits and possibilities of human power, as a soldier in the Israeli Army, at the height of basic training.

My unit had spent the entire day out in the Judean wilderness practicing maneuvers and shooting drills. Man, were we fierce. Between the bunch of us, we must have blown apart every target in sight. We were just tearing into them, pumping out huge quantities of lead from our automatic M-16s. Flinging our grenades, we blew the daylights out of makeshift enemy bunkers, creamed their positions with our mortars. Nothing seemed safe from us.

By the time we got back to the base, we were practically quivering with the rush of all that storming, crawling, perching, shooting and pulverizing, of annihilating everything in sight, of the rich power of destruction. We were intoxicated with our ability to undo just about anything we could lay our eyes on, drunk with our sense of invulnerability, swelled with the knowledge that anyone or anything that came in our paths would pay the price, the beautifully awful price.

We walked towards our base with the setting of the brutal sun, our faces and nostrils still covered with the fine soil of the mean terrain and with the smell of gunshot.

Twenty yards from our base, we passed by an old Arab house, home to two large extended families. We must have been quite a sight to these Arab clans, with our heavy backpacks, our muddy stubble and our big fat guns. As we passed, four little children ran fiercely out of the front door as they did almost every time we marched back from the fields. They were all barefoot and blue-eyed with chestnut hair and ginger-colored skin. The oldest was a boy of around seven, the two younger ones, a boy and a girl around five who looked like they might have been twins, and the last, a cute little three-year-old with badly cut bangs who dragged along a tattered doll behind her.

Apparently these children had learned a little something about how to relate to Israeli soldiers from the older kids in the neighborhood. Each one of them, including the one with the doll, bent down and chose three smooth pebbles to throw at us, absurd little Davids going up against our marching Goliaths. They knew there was nothing we could do, so they flung those stones as best they could and cursed at us in Arabic. The pebbles didn't hurt, not like the heavy rocks our boys would sometimes take back in the days of the Intifada, but we certainly couldn't let these kids get the idea that it was okay to chuck stones at Israeli soldiers. So we played our part in this macabre drama, reaching back for our guns, rapping the heel of our hands on our rifle-butts, while they ran away squealing, back into the safety of their awning.

We continued our march back past the guard tower and into our base as dusk painted the Judean Hills with its fluorescent palette. That evening, some of my religious buddies from the unit asked me if I would join them at the base's synagogue for the *Ma'ariv* (evening) service, to help them make a *minyan.*

We walked into the chapel with our guns slung back on our backs, the barrels still sizzling. And as I sidestepped past the other soldiers to my place on the bench, I noticed that on the *Aron HaKodesh,* someone had embroidered a passage from the Bible. Wiping the dust from my eyelashes, I discovered that they were the words of the prophet Zechariah, and they were well chosen. Here, in the synagogue on the base of what is perhaps the most potent fighting force in the world, this is what they said:

"Not by might, and not by power, but by My spirit—said the Lord of Hosts," and those words, well, they put it all into perspective.

I decided to put the words to work when those kids confronted us again. So the next time we trudged back from the fields and the kids charged at us with their harmless pebbles, I wedged my gun behind my back, crouched down like a catcher and gestured to the oldest boy to show me his best pitch. He wound up like Tom Seaver and gave me the finest fastball he could muster. He whipped the second one in the strike-zone as well, but before he could get off the third, I stood up and motioned him to toss it underhand. When the third stone reached me, I threw the first pair into the air as well and started to juggle all three. I proceeded to show off a trick or two I had learned when I first taught myself to juggle way back in high school. The kids just stood there with these big old smiles on their faces, as did the other guys in my platoon. They still ran away squealing, but not before letting off a laugh or two.

I was convinced that my new "spiritual" approach had altered the way those kids looked at us, the way they might have perceived Israeli soldiers for years to follow, and I felt pretty good about it. But the next time we marched past their home, those kids still ran out at us just as fiercely as the last time, but this time, instead of picking up three stones, the oldest boy picked up an extra stone for good measure.

My heart sank.

I had never juggled four stones before.

Jonathan Elkins

A Simple Blessing

When we recognize where our power truly comes from, we become blessed.

Ben Vereen

Sherman, Texas, was a long way from the *yeshiva.* But that's where they told me my student pulpit was, so that's where I was going. Student pulpit duty is a rabbinical school requirement intended to help you learn the ropes by serving a weekend a month in a small community that can't support a full-time rabbi but still has enough left in it to keep the synagogue doors open.

Congregation Beth Emeth with its twenty-five Jewish families hunkered down just south of the Oklahoma border, was my rabbinical boot camp. Other than the occasional High Holy Day when a retired rabbi from Dallas conducted services in the one-room synagogue, I was the first rabbi or student rabbi to visit Sherman on a regular basis since Jews arrived there in the early twentieth century. The notion of a rabbi was so new to the community that I was often referred to by non-Jews in town as "Rabbi Steven Leder, the pastor from the Hebrew church."

On my first visit I pressed on doing all of the things an energetic, idealistic student rabbi was supposed to do: services, tutoring the few children, teaching adult education, visiting the Jewish businesses on Main Street, drinking iced tea with the temple president at the diner next to the pawnshop and the VFW post.

Whenever I had some extra time on Saturday afternoon, I would visit the few elderly Jews in town who were too frail or sick to come to services on Friday night. Bill was one of those Jews.

Bill had a bad heart—so bad the doctors in Dallas told him he was best off at home, close to his oxygen and the telephone. His wife, Betti, was a practicing Baptist who had driven him to synagogue and had sat with him every High Holy Day for forty-five years. But now her eyes were bad, and even if Bill could go to synagogue, she couldn't drive him and be by his side.

It was my first visit to Bill and Betti's house. I imagined that I would chat a little about their lives, when they came to Sherman and why, maybe tell them a bit about myself, then wish them well and be on my way. At least that's what I had planned as I stepped up on to the porch past the rusted chairs and knocked on the screen door.

The house looked as though it hadn't changed much inside for a long time, with its faded pictures, black-and-white TV, an ashtray from a cruise to Mexico in 1973. Bill was in the kitchen fixing us some iced tea and cutting the sponge cake Betti had made the night before. The three of us sat around the speckled Formica table, ate our white cake on orange plastic dishes, and chatted about this and that just as I'd imagined it. Life seemed hard for them, yet neither seemed to mind too terribly much.

After an hour or so, my rabbinical duty done, I glanced at my watch, mentioned my next appointment and stood up to leave. Just as I was thanking them and promising to

ext month, Betti clutched my hand, quick and
aps you'd like to bless us, Rabbi," she said.

Bill, weak and awkward, nodded and whispered, "Yes. Bless us, Rabbi," as he held Betti's hand and reached for my own.

There we stood, grasping hands in that little Texas kitchen, in that little Texas town—the blind Baptist woman, the old Jew and the bewildered rabbinical student who had only come for conversation. *A blessing?* I thought to myself, convinced that this was neither the time nor the place. *What am I supposed to say?*

But there they stood, eyes closed, hands held tight, fervent, expecting. And to my lips came the words of a three-thousand-year-old blessing spoken originally by the High Priest and used today by rabbis in sanctuaries of marble and glass: "May the Lord bless you and keep you." There in that Texas kitchen: "May the Lord illumine your life and be gracious unto you." Behind the tattered screen door: "May the Lord's spirit be upon you and grant you peace."

"Amen," said Bill and Betti as they opened their eyes, visibly moved. "Amen."

I've never forgotten that afternoon or that kitchen, because I learned an important lesson there. We can all bring blessings to people who need them. Blessings require no great sanctuary, no marble, no golden ark, no microphone. All a blessing takes—all seeing God takes—is a little time; a few words with two people locked in the silent struggles of life, seeking meaning and recognition amid their faded pictures. That's all it took, just a little time and a few kind words to say I wished them well and "God bless."

"Amen," said Bill and Betti as they opened their eyes. "Amen."

Rabbi Steven Z. Leder

We Are All Jews Now

The highest flights of charity, devotion, trust, patience, bravery, to which the wings of human nature have spread themselves have been flown for religious ideas.

William James

Viewed from high on the Rimrock cliffs that run along the northern edge of Billings, Montana, the city presents an attractive sight, a thriving metropolis nestling within the great open spaces of the American West. Citizens of Billings say it's a good, civilized place to live. They pride themselves on the quality of their schools and their strong family values.

So it came as a shock to many when in November 1995, a series of hate crimes took place against minority groups in the city.

Whoever was responsible for these acts must have thought that their victims would be easy targets. Billings is predominantly white; Native Americans, African Americans and Jews make up only a small percentage of the population. But there are just enough of them to frighten and harass—or so the haters must have thought.

They mounted a series of nasty attacks. Graves were overturned in a Jewish cemetery. Offensive words and a swastika were scrawled on the house of a Native American woman. People worshipping at a black church were intimidated. A brick was heaved through the window of a Jewish child who displayed a menorah there.

But the white supremacists, or whoever they were, had reckoned without the citizens of Billings, who had an answer for them—and it wasn't what the hate-mongers were expecting. An alliance quickly emerged, spearheaded by churches, labor unions, the media and hundreds of local citizens.

The results were dramatic. Attendance at the black church rose steadily. People of many different ethnic backgrounds and faiths began to attend services there. Their message was clear: "We may be all different, but we are one also. Threaten any one of us and you threaten us all."

A similar spirit propelled volunteers to come together and repaint the house of Dawn Fast Horse, the Native American woman. This happened at amazing speed. Dawn had awoken one morning to see that her house had been defaced. By the evening, after two hundred people showed up to help, the house had been repainted.

When it came to the incident of the brick being thrown through the window of the Jewish child, an interfaith group quickly had a creative idea. They recalled the example of the Danes during World War II. When the Nazis tried to round up Danish Jews into concentration camps for subsequent extermination, the Danish people worked quickly, within a two-week period, to transport almost every Danish Jew to safety in Sweden until the end of the war.

So the people of Billings organized, and a campaign began. Everyone pitched in, including the local newspaper, which printed a Hanukkah page, including a full-color representation of a menorah. Thousands of Billings residents cut the paper menorah out and displayed it in their windows. By late December, driving around Billings was a remarkable experience. Nearly ten thousand people were displaying those paper menorahs in their windows, and the menorahs remained in place throughout the eight days of Hanukkah. It was a brilliant answer to the hate-mongers: A town that had few Jews was saying with one collective voice, "We are all Jews now."

The story of what happened in Billings quickly spread, inspiring a national movement called "Not in Our Town." That Jewish child who had so innocently displayed her menorah in the window helped set in motion a chain of events that affirmed all over America the liberating principle of unity in diversity.

Not for nothing does a menorah have many candles flickering on a single stand.

Bryan Aubrey

The Temples Are Burning

Always come to the aid of those who are being oppressed.

Rabbi Nahman of Bratslav

In June 1999, I was vacationing on a quiet little island in Croatia with a former college roommate. It was the first vacation I had taken since my ordination and appointment as assistant rabbi at Congregation B'nai Israel in Sacramento.

For *Shabbat,* my Catholic friend and I did candles, *kiddush* and *motzi* over dinner, and we were going to spend the rest of *Shabbat* sitting on the beach. (There are very few synagogues in Croatia.)

At midnight, I decided to call a congregant of mine in California, where it was three o'clock in the afternoon. She was ill, and I wanted to check on her welfare. But the conversation we had that night was not what I had been expecting.

"The temple's been firebombed," she said.

"What?"

"Ours and two others—Beth Shalom and Kenesset Israel.

I don't know any more yet. It happened in the middle of the night. My husband's at the congregation now trying to find out more."

Shock hit me like a tidal wave. Three synagogues firebombed? In America? I couldn't believe it!

Early the following morning, I learned that the attacks had not been by firebombs, but by arson. The first fire had been set at about 3:00 A.M. at Congregation B'nai Israel in Land Park. This was followed within forty-five minutes by fires set at Congregation Beth Shalom and Kenesset Israel Torah Center.

In addition to the damage to the temples, the seven-thousand-volume library at B'nai Israel had been utterly destroyed. Many of the books were rare and irreplaceable.

I was devastated, even more so when I was told that my own office had been burned down. I had a small collection of prayerbooks from pre–World War II Germany and Hungary, some of which were given to me by a former landlord who was a Holocaust survivor. I also had my grandparents' Judaica library in my office. I was horrified that books given to me to protect had been destroyed in a hate crime.

It was horrible to hear all this news when I was sitting on an island in the middle of the Adriatic, so far from home. I felt lonely and desolate, and I could hardly imagine what everyone at home was experiencing.

I made immediate plans to return. During the long, lonely journey from Europe I learned more—that the damage to all three synagogues was estimated at around two and a half million dollars, with two million of that damage having been done to B'nai Israel alone. I also learned that while the FBI was investigating, at that time there were still no suspects.

There was one moment of elation: I learned that my office had not in fact been burned down, although it had suffered severe smoke damage. Another piece of news that cheered me was that in spite of the devastation, not a single Torah in any of the three temples was destroyed. The Aron Hakodesh, the Ark of the Covenant, the chest that holds the scrolls, had held firm.

Three days later I arrived home, exhausted, in Sacramento. It felt good to be back with my own community in this time of heartbreak and outrage. I knew I would be doing much comforting in the days that lay ahead.

I arrived only half an hour before a community service was due to begin. I'd just gone twenty-eight hours without sleep, but nothing would stop me from attending.

I entered the Sacramento Community Theatre having no idea what to expect. When I walked out onto the stage, what I saw took my breath away. Over 200 people sat on the stage. It was like a Who's Who of Sacramento and beyond: there were state officials and legislators, city council members, the chief of police, representatives from the ATF and the fire department, people from the governor's office, and clergy from every faith and ethnic background in the entire Sacramento community.

Then the curtain opened, and I was even more astonished. The theatre was packed! About 4,500 people were in attendance, including those who crowded into overflow rooms, where they watched on a big screen.

In the crowd were Hispanic Americans, Asian Americans and African Americans; Muslims, Catholics and Protestants from many different denominations; Buddhists and more, as well as people who might have called themselves nonbelievers, but who believed that victims of cowardly attacks in the night should not suffer in isolation.

It was the most inspiring program I have ever experienced. The outpouring of love and support was overwhelming. Speaker after speaker rose to express their concern, their sorrow and their hope. Each was met with thunderous applause and a standing ovation. Everyone in that theater that night was standing shoulder to shoulder with the Jews of Sacramento, and saying, each in his or her own way, "You are not alone."

That night when I came home, I saw signs in my neighbors' windows that said, "United We Stand." That gesture touched me deeply. As I thanked each of them, I found out that up to then they hadn't even known I was a rabbi. It was a small sign of how the community was coming together in new, positive ways as a result of the tragedy.

When I was finally able to get into my office, I broke down and cried for the first time. The smell was suffocating. Everything was covered with a thick layer of smoke and ash.

But I was deeply moved that people drove in from as far away as Tahoe, the San Francisco Bay Area and Bakersfield to deliver donations and books and to express sympathy.

Although the work has been endless, our congregation and community are optimistic. Money and offers of help have poured in from all across the country. When the Secretary of Housing, Andrew Cuomo, came to visit, he urged us to rebuild bigger and better. And that is what we intend to do. We will not hide. We will continue to teach, to worship and celebrate our Jewish heritage. It was because of these great waves of support that I and my congregants soon came to see the frightening attacks as an isolated event and not reflective of the larger community. Whoever had perpetrated them had zero support in the community. And the attacks weren't like so much of the anti-Semitism of the past. Following this incident, the U.S. government was quick to help. Congress unanimously passed a resolution condemning the attacks; the government promised low-interest loans, and money was promised for programs in

Sacramento that would build understanding between different faiths and ethnic groups.

It may sound corny, but because of what happened, I feel proud to live in America. I am deeply grateful for the astonishing outpouring of support from non-Jews. It is overwhelming to me that so many would care, and so deeply. I am grateful also to be a rabbi. You get to see the best in people—my congregation, and the entire Sacramento community, has been so wonderful, jumping in to rebuild and do whatever else they can.

In quiet moments now, I reflect that although people who are filled with hatred may burn down temples and libraries, the human heart, in its capacity to love and to reach out to others in distress, will always endure. As I was taught as a child, love is a more powerful weapon than hate.

Rabbi Mona Alfi
As told to Bryan Aubrey

Let Freedom Ring in Iowa City

The essence of religion is the human quest for salvation.

Mordecai M. Kaplan

"It's about freedom," my daughter Nicole explained to each of almost twenty non-Jewish guests she was inviting to her Passover Seder. "Therefore, you should bring something that represents freedom to you. It can be an object, a song, dance, poem, quotation—anything that you want. Sometime during the evening, I'll ask you to share what you brought and what it means to you."

Unusual Seders such as this one were a fixture in our lives. They began the year Nicole shared an apartment with four other young female students at the University of Iowa. None were Jewish, and two were fundamentalist Christians. But Nicole was eager to share her roots with her many friends from various ethnic backgrounds, including Loyal, her new African American boyfriend. So "Shlep-a-Seder" began in 1992 with my loading boxes of matzahs, Passover staples, dishes, tablecloths and Haggadahs into my car and driving five hundred miles from Southfield,

Michigan, to Iowa City. Wine was the only item well-stocked in the college town—even Mogen David wine—and all of the guests were happy to contribute some.

There were nine of us that first year. By 1995, the Seder participants expanded to twenty-three. To accommodate them, we put all the living room furniture in the outer hallway—it looked like a doctor's waiting room—and rented some tables and chairs and set them up in a U-shape, with chairs on the outside and inside. We squeezed together joyfully.

Nicole made a supplemental Haggadah with many meaningful excerpts to add to the New Model Seder book. People of Chinese, Mexican, Tanzanian, Egyptian, African-American and corn-bred Iowa backgrounds, all wearing yarmulkes, sang choruses of *Dayanu.* They ate *haroset,* and bitter herbs, and dipped parsley and eggs in salt water. Ahead of them would be other strange delicacies like gefilte fish, carrot kugel, matzah stuffing and flourless cakes buoyed up by egg whites.

I was stirring the soup in the kitchen as the youngest at the table, Scott, my apostate son, struggled with the four questions in Hebrew. Nicole, his older sister valiantly tried helping. I kept thinking, *Why don't they fake it? No one at the table would know.* Then, soup ladle in hand, I entered and announced, "Not one of you can appreciate how much time and money went into Scott and Nicole's being able to recite those questions in Hebrew."

Nicole decided it was time to intervene. "This would be a good time for someone to share a freedom idea with us," she declared. And, good students and professors that they were, most had completed the assignment. Throughout the evening, we witnessed a delightful parade of cherished items. There was Sarah's paintbrush that allowed her to express who she really is; Derrick's meaningful quotations about freedom, including some from Ralph Waldo Emerson. Then there was Scott, playing Bob Marley's "Redemption Song," and Blandina, talking about her husband's love and friendship as the ultimate source of freedom. My own contribution was to tell the story of "The Golem of Prague."

"And now we open the door for Elijah," Nicole announced. Before anyone got up, the door opened and twenty-three of us stared as a petite, blonde, young woman entered. She was either ditzy, dizzy or drunk—she had no idea where she was but that didn't seem to faze her. She just smiled and wandered out again.

While we all suppressed laughter, I thought: *Why not?*

We had assembled such an unusual population, a patchwork quilt, for a Seder, why couldn't Elijah, the one who heralds an age of peace and proclaims the Messiah, be a tipsy sprite from Iowa? What is this Seder all about, anyway?

I spent the rest of the Seder answering my own question. In part, it was about blonde Kiki from Iowa, majoring in African-American studies, leaning over and saying to me, "I think that Nicole's lucky to have a mother who goes to all this trouble to bring everything here year after year so that we can learn about her heritage."

I replied, "I think Nicole's lucky to have so many friends who want to share her tradition."

In part it was about the love and warmth extending from tiny Blandina, Loyal's effusive Swahili professor, as her strong fingers massaged my aching neck and shoulders. It was about AJ's Oriental features relaxing and smiling. It was about Darcey bringing a piñata she had made to brighten the room, and Hanley struggling on braces up three flights of steep stairs. In part it was about Bassel bringing more than his share of wine and holding his infant daughter, Rakaya, during a story of Jewish bondage in his ancient Egypt.

But it was more than all these things. Before we closed with a tape of Martin Luther King's inspiring "I Have a Dream" speech, Andrea said, "I didn't know what to bring. I told my father about my Jewish friend Nicole, how I was going to her Seder not knowing what to expect, and I was supposed to bring something that represented freedom to me.

"My dad said, 'Andrea, a Seder is something I've never experienced. And the one you're going to would never have happened when I was your age. That Seder *itself* is what real freedom is about!'"

Let freedom ring.

Corinne Stavish

". . . But we'll get our sandals all muddy."

Fighting for Freedom

Be isolated, be ignored, be attacked, be in doubt, be frightened, but do not be silenced.

Bertrand Russell

Boris Nadgorny was a promising young physics student in Moscow in the 1980s. But this was a time when the Soviet Union had a policy of intense oppression of their Jewish citizens, and Boris could never achieve his full potential as long as he remained in the shadowy halls of Soviet academia. But Soviet officialdom wouldn't let him leave the country.

Jewish activists around the world tried everything they could to help Soviet Jews. When the case of Boris became known in England in 1987, he was "adopted" by the students at Oxford University. Jews and non-Jews at Oxford worked very hard to bring his case to the attention of the world.

Boris's name soon became well known among the entire Oxford student body. Among their many action programs was a telephone campaign to the Soviet Embassy in London. On a daily basis, students would call and ask why Boris Nadgorny was not permitted to emigrate. They wore badges all over the campus that read, "I phoned the Embassy twice today, have you?" All eight thousand students, Jewish and non-Jewish, participated in this remarkable daily phone-athon.

Besides all the normal procedures for political action, Oxford students came up with an ingenious plan. The student body invited a Soviet official to the Oxford campus to report on *glasnost,* the new spirit of freedom brought to the Soviet Union by Mikhail Gorbachev, who had recently come to power. The official was Sergei Shilov, the cultural attache of the Soviet Embassy in London. Shilov did not realize that the real aim of the students was to ask him during the question-and-answer period about Boris.

Five hundred students attended the meeting in a large hall and listened as Shilov was asked about Soviet Jewish "Refuseniks." Then he was asked specifically about Boris Nadgorny—why had he not been permitted to leave the country?

"No," Shilov replied, "Boris was not refused, it is not true, and he can go any time he wants."

At that point an Oxford student, Irina Brailovsky, stood up and said that she was a former Soviet Refusenik, and that she had accurate information that Boris had just recently been refused permission to emigrate.

Next came the big surprise, which had taken careful behind-the-scenes management by the organizers of the meeting. The meeting chairman entered the room and announced that Boris Nadgorny was at that very moment on the telephone to Oxford, and a loudspeaker had been set up so that he could speak to the gathered group.

A buzz of excitement went around the hall, which was hushed immediately as the sound of Boris's voice came loud and clear over the loudspeaker.

"Yes, I was refused just two weeks ago," he said in heavily accented English.

Someone at the meeting then asked Shilov about his own statement, made only minutes earlier, that Boris was in fact allowed to leave the Soviet Union.

With Boris still waiting on the telephone, it was impossible for a Soviet official to continue to lie so blatantly in front of a large group of people. This was a time when the Soviets were earnestly seeking warmer relations with the West, and Shilov could not risk having his Oxford debacle spread across the pages of the British press the next day.

"Will you speak directly to Boris and tell him that he may leave?" asked the chairman of the meeting.

Shilov had no option but to do so. "You are free to leave," he said to Boris, as the hundreds of students listened, ecstatic about the success of their audacious plan.

Boris Nadgorny was out of the Soviet Union within four months of that telephone call. He has since received his Ph.D. in physics from Princeton University, and now holds a prominent place in his field in the world of American academia.

Rabbi Dov Peretz Elkins
(Reported to me by Boris's parents, Eduard and Nina Nadgorny, during my visit to the USSR in October 1988)

Cardinal Bernardin

Every human being has the freedom to change at any instant. . . . A human being is a self-transcending being.

Viktor Frankl

In March of 1995, Cardinal Bernardin traveled to Israel with a group of Christians and Jews. The trip was coordinated by The American Jewish Committee, the Archdiocese of Chicago and The Jewish Federation with the cooperation of the Chicago Board of Rabbis and The Spertus Institute. While he was there, the Cardinal delivered a speech at Hebrew University, for which he received the university's Honorary Fellowship.

In his speech, the Cardinal detailed years of Christian theology regarding anti-Semitism. He said that the Catholic Church must acknowledge guilt for that terrible legacy which resulted in hatred, bigotry and ultimately, the Holocaust. He repudiated any remaining anti-Semitic practices or teachings in Catholicism, calling them "sinful," and asked all Christians and Jews to recommit to fighting anti-Semitism in all forms and at all levels.

Finally, the Cardinal suggested ways that Christians and Jews could, together and separately, further the cause of positive relations. He called upon Christians to teach about anti-Semitism, increasing awareness of Vatican II's rejection of anti-Judaic theology. And he asked Jews to reconsider the way they thought about Christians and the Church. He asked that Christian-Jewish dialogue be made a vibrant reality with the goal being to ensure peace among all peoples.

The speech was a watershed. As a result, the archdiocese and the Jewish organizations that worked together on the Cardinal's trip decided to sponsor a lecture every year commemorating Cardinal Bernardin's speech on Mt. Scopus.

I attended the first lecture in March 1996. An incident that occurred there at the Palmer House between Cardinal Bernardin and me changed the way I thought about him forever.

In my job at The American Jewish Committee, I handle interreligious affairs. So I had had some correspondence with the Cardinal and been involved in some planning sessions with him. He knew my name but not much else about me. Or so I thought.

When a friend of mine, Rabbi James Gordon of Congregation B'nai Sholom in Buffalo Grove, asked me to introduce him to the Cardinal at that lecture, I agreed. We both had a lot of respect for Cardinal Bernardin, and as he had just completed a round of treatment for his cancer, we approached to offer our good wishes.

As I introduced Rabbi Gordon, I mentioned that we had been praying for the Cardinal's continued good health and that he looked well. He took my arm as he answered me, looking into my eyes to thank me for my good wishes. I noticed that a line had formed behind me to speak to the Cardinal so I tried to extricate myself and by way of excusing myself, I said something I'm in the habit of saying, "Good-bye, be well, Rab . . . ."

Then I looked around for the floor to open to swallow me up. I had just called the Catholic Archbishop, "Rabbi."

But he only smiled and said, "That's okay, Marsha. You can think of me as a Catholic rabbi."

Later, at the reception following the speech, Cardinal Bernardin sought me out. I had spent most of my time there hiding behind potted plants trying to avoid his gaze because I was still embarrassed. But I couldn't escape him because he had something to say to me.

"I know you are an observant Jew," he told me. "And I know that 'Rabbi' was just the most reverent, respectful thing you could think of to say to me. Thank you."

There wasn't anything I could think of to say, then. I have no idea how he knew that I was an observant Jew. Somehow, he had made it his business to find out.

The cardinal was the kind of man who cared less about how others viewed him than how they viewed themselves as a result of anything he might have said or done. He was respected and respectful, and while all cardinals are due the deference that goes with the job, he earned it.

There are some traits that some people possess that blur the lines that traditionally divide people—the lines of religion or ethnicity. Kindness of heart and generosity of spirit are two of those traits and Cardinal Bernardin embodied both. As a result, his life touched us all. So did his death.

He laid the groundwork for the Catholic Church to accept complicity for the Holocaust, insisting that it be taught in every possible Catholic venue—in schools and from the pulpits. He preached "courageous honesty"—that anti-Jewish theology must be acknowledged and atoned for, that anti-Semitism was a sin.

As the Archbishop of Chicago, he accomplished a lot. He affected the lives of millions of people, influencing how they think, pray and act. As a man, the kind, caring human being that he was, Cardinal Bernardin affected the life of at least one observant Jew.

The word "rabbi" means teacher. And as Henry Adams said, "A teacher affects eternity; he never knows where his influence ends." I called him "rabbi." And so he was.

Marsha Arons

A Jewish Christmas Story

I will do more than live and let live—I will live and help live.

Walter W. Van Kirk

Every year, after Thanksgiving, I long for the first signs of Christmas. I delight in the appearance of the green twigs, red ribbons and silver balls, sprinkled with artificial snow. The fat Santa amusing children in department stores and the big tree at Rockefeller Center fill me with excitement. Yet, I am Jewish, and in my own home Hanukkah is celebrated. So why does Christmas mean so much to me? I would like to tell you my own "Jewish" Christmas story.

It is Christmas Eve, 1942. I am eleven years old. I live in Poland, a predominantly Catholic country where Christmas is widely celebrated. I am fascinated by the Christmas atmosphere. I am also cold, hungry, tired and very much afraid.

For the entire month of December, German soldiers have searched the Jewish quarter of our small town, looking for children and old people. Since they cannot work or bring any benefit to the Third Reich, they are to be "eliminated." The victims are rounded up, assembled in an old courthouse and taken to be killed in a small forest at the outskirts of town. Most of my friends are not here anymore.

I have been hiding with my mother, who is not old but whose hair turned prematurely gray at the beginning of the war. We have changed our hiding place several times. Once, we were caught and then miraculously set free. We have hidden in cellars, attics, barns and other improbable places. We do not bathe or eat hot meals. We live like hunted animals, just escaping our predators, always on the run. We have finally run out of hiding places and returned to the ghetto.

My parents know that my chances of surviving are nil, so as a last resort they contact Frania, the woman who worked for us as a housekeeper before the war. She is a deeply religious Catholic woman and was with our family since before I was born.

Frania comes to our small, shabby apartment on Christmas Eve. She figures that on that night, the guards at the entrance of the ghetto will be drunk and more lenient. Her estimation proves to be correct. She has no trouble entering the forbidden area. She is appalled by our living conditions. She remembers our affluent, prewar lifestyle.

She does not take long to make up her mind. She has nothing to gain and everything to lose. If she is caught hiding me, she will be tortured and hanged in the middle of town, as a warning to others. We have all witnessed such scenes. Yet without hesitation, she tells me to get ready. She promises my parents that she will take good care of me and after the war raise me as her own daughter. There is almost no chance that my parents will survive. Frania is a plain woman. She never went to school and she cannot read or write. She is not a woman of big words, but her heart is very big—made of gold.

It takes me no time to prepare. I am always ready to run. In the preceding four weeks, I have never taken off my clothing. I wear my entire wardrobe: two dresses, a sweater, some underwear and an old coat that belonged to my late brother. Because I am skinny, I fit easily into all these clothes. By wearing everything I own, I stay warmer and nothing can be stolen. Frania covers my black hair with a woolen cap. My pale, starved face is bundled with a big scarf. I am protected against the cold and my non-Slavic looks are camouflaged. I realize that I will never see my family again, yet I do not cry. I do not know how to cry. I hug my parents. Frania takes my hand and tells me not to be afraid. She calls me by my old pet name and we go.

Nobody stops us as we leave the ghetto. We are accompanied by the stars shining in the dark sky as the white snow crunches under our feet. We meet people going to the midnight Mass. We greet them with "Merry Christmas" and Frania starts singing carols. After a while, I join her in singing, and suddenly I am one of the many people in the street singing.

We reach Frania's small apartment. During the day, she works and I hide under a bed. I miss my mother, and I am very sad, yet I do not complain. After several months, Frania realizes that she cannot take the place of my mother and my older sister, so they come, too. We all hide under beds. I do not know how we manage. All the while, Frania's deep faith helps us survive.

We remain with Frania through two more Christmases. Each of them is filled with careful preparations. We make Christmas decorations out of scraps of paper, small gifts from old boxes and pieces of fabric. We sit at a festive table and try to bake and cook. The cakes are made of inferior black flour and artificial sweetener. They look sad and lie flat like mud pies.

After two and a half years, the Russians liberate our town and we are freed. Eventually, we are reunited with my father, who returns from a concentration camp. In December 1949, we leave Poland for good. With heavy hearts, we part from Frania. We believe we will never see her again. As the train leaves the station, the last thing I see is her face full of tears. It is heartbreaking, and I have begun to cry again.

Twenty-five years later, I was fortunate enough to see Frania again. She came to visit us in the United States. I did not recognize her at the airport. She was very worn. Her face looked like plowed earth. When we both got over the initial shock—after all, she last saw me as an eighteen-year-old—we resumed our loving relationship. She was the same person I remembered: generous and full of common sense. She spent several weeks with us, cooking my favorite dishes and spoiling my children. She remained modest and never considered herself a hero. According to her, everything happened on Christmas Eve, when people are supposed to love each other and she only did what she had to do.

Irene Frisch

"All I do is shlep, shlep, shlep."

Reprinted by permission of Benita Epstein.

Go in Good Health

No one ever becomes poor through the giving of charity.

Maimonides

Even in the 1930s when the Great Depression left no family untouched, *tzedakah* and tolerance were twin morals in our home. Alongside the candlesticks my mother had brought from Europe stood the Jewish National Fund box, into which my mother dropped her weekly spare change, and spare it was.

We lived in a middle-sized city in Western Canada. In our home, we lived in a world of Judaism and Orthodoxy. Outside, everyone, no matter what their heritage, was labeled "English." At home, observance of the Sabbath and the Jewish holidays dominated our lives. My father attended synagogue services daily, and several times a week a teacher came in to give Hebrew lessons to us five children. At school and on the playground we mixed, sang Christmas carols and ended the day with the Lord's Prayer.

The outside world to us also consisted of many churches. My own firsthand experience with churches began when we were very young and my parents bought a home across the street from a Roman Catholic church and parochial school. We used to hear the church bells ring all day, and we learned to set our clocks by them. From our screened verandah we would see the nuns and priests walk from building to building, their hands tucked into their long gowns. In the summer, we would hear the bells ring out their glad tidings on Saturday afternoons, when young happy couples would park their Model Ts in front of their church, and with their huge families, would gather for their weddings. With my "English" friends I would run to the open church door in time to see a bride and groom walk up the long aisle to the altar. After the guests were seated we would steal quietly into the last pew. There, before the crucifix of Christ, their Lord, the couple would kneel and promise never to break their solemn vows. To a young child, the organ, the choir, the stained glass windows (no-no's in our little clapboard synagogue), plus the candles burning in the little red glasses and the lavishly embroidered robes made a lasting impression.

Later I would watch the hooded sisters and the long-robed brothers stand in the doorway to greet and give their blessings to the newlyweds. I saw in these devout faces a radiant love that only they knew, and I wondered how being married to God could fill their lives so well.

Living on the same street and watching them go by daily, they became to me something mysterious, a mystique that I could feel and yet not touch, that I could see and yet not know. They were different, and they lived in a world very alien to my very orthodox home; and yet their constant smiles as they passed our house gave me a feeling of kinship. I used to walk by their residence and wonder about them as I gazed childlike at the black shades in their windows, wishing I could know more about how they lived and felt and worshipped their God.

One winter, when I was ten, was a particularly cold one. It seemed as if the snow would never stop falling and the wind would never stop blowing. Christmas drew near, and the Depression seemed endless. We began to feel the tightness of money all around us. There were large heating bills, warmer clothing to buy for five children, and more and more food seemed to disappear from our table. But, one by one, the Christmas lights began to glitter in our neighbor's windows, and the fortunate Gentiles who had evergreens in their front yards shook off the snow and put up a few lights to welcome the holiday.

In our home, Hanukkah came and went. We lit the candles, one more every nightfall. Uncles came and gave us Hanukkah *gelt* [money]. My father taught us *"Oi Hanukkah, Oi Hanukkah, a yontif a shaineh"* (a holiday, a pretty one) and then we ate Hanukkah-latkes and dreamed of better times next year.

One evening, a week before Christmas, the doorbell rang. When I opened it, two nuns stood on our front porch. "Merry Christmas!" they exclaimed.

I stared at them in wonder. Never before had I been so close to nuns. Their white stiffly starched bibs and cowls looked like the icicles that hung from our eaves. One rang a small bell, and the other held a brass plate.

"Mama," I called breathless. "There is someone here!"

My mother came from the kitchen, her hands covered with flour. She was in the midst of making apple strudel. A wisp of hair was falling over her face, and as she came to the door she moved the back of her hand slowly over her forehead. Then she noticed the visitors, and in Yiddish said to me, "Tell them to come in. It's cold out there."

I looked again at the callers and then at my mother, and was not quite sure I had heard right. Then my mother opened the door with her floured hand and said, *"Kimt aran. Sis kolt."* (Come in. It's cold.)

The nuns pushed the storm door open and entered. "Merry Christmas," they said again. "We are collecting for the poor. Would you like to donate?"

My mother could speak very little English, and understood less, but the plate spoke for itself. "Go," she said to me in Yiddish. "Get me my purse."

Still stunned by the strangeness of the presence of nuns in our home, I dashed upstairs. From under the corner of my mother's mattress, I brought out the little black leather pouch that held the precious and very scarce money that had to clothe and feed seven people. Then I stood on the bottom step and leaned over the banister and watched as my mother dropped two dimes and a nickel into the plate. Twenty-five cents! It was a fortune to me. It could then buy two quarts of milk, two loaves of bread and a whole bagful of rock candy.

The nuns, their faces devoid of makeup but wreathed in smiles, were profuse in their thanks. "Thank you, and God bless you!" they repeated several times.

"Geht gezinter hait" (Go in good health) my mother told them. As she opened the door and said again how cold it was, her voice showed real concern. The sisters seemed to understand her. "Oh, that's all right," they said, their voices quiet and peaceful. "God takes care of His children." Then they were gone.

My mother closed the door and went back to her baking. I followed her into the kitchen, wanting to ask a million questions, but all I managed was, "Why?"

"They're good people," my mother told me, rolling her dough. "Very good. They do good things for others. It's their holiday, but we must help."

"What do they do?"

"I don't know all they do. But they have hospitals, and children's homes, and help the poor, and we should help them. Some day you will understand."

As the years went by we continued to set our clocks by the church bells. The sisters came each Christmas to collect alms for the poor. My mother continued to drop change into the brass plates. My sisters and brother married and moved away.

During most of those years my father was very ill and was in and out of hospitals many times. During his last illness he was in a Catholic hospital.

One morning my mother received a call that my father was in critical condition and that she was to come at once. I received a message at work that I was to come immediately and I rushed to the hospital. When I arrived there a sister met me at the door of my father's room. "Your father passed away ten minutes ago," she told me.

My concern now was for my mother. She had been all alone with my father at his death, with no one to comfort her. The sister led me to another room, where she had given my mother a sedative. I was amazed to find my mother so calm in her grief, and I kept repeating, "You were all alone! If only I had gotten here on time!'

My mother shook her head. "I wasn't alone," she assured me. "The sister was with me."

"But someone in the family should have been with you," I cried.

"No one is ever alone in this world," my mother told me. "I said the prayer for the dying person, and when the sister heard me she put her arm around me and said the prayer with me." Then, as my mother and I wept together in our grief, the sister put her arms around both of us, and as we all prayed together, I recalled my mother's words of long ago, "They do good, and we must help them."

Lottie Robins

Upstairs at the Rialto

Prejudice is the reason of fools.

Voltaire

Lucille came to work for us when we moved from an apartment to the house my father built in 1950. There was more to care for in a house, and with help, my mother could still work in my father's haberdashery. It seemed a long way from the store to home. At first, we took the bus, which cost a nickel, but when we got tired of waiting for it we just walked. Lucille always used the bus because she lived "on the other side of the tracks" and that was much too far for walking.

All the "colored" people in our town lived "on the other side of the tracks" as if that was why it was there. The railroad was our Mason-Dixon line. Once or twice, when I went with my father to drop off ironing at Lucille's house, I remembered movies I'd seen of poor "colored" people in the South, and I felt sad that Lucille had to live in almost as bad a way. All the tiny frame houses needed painting and some had rusty gas tanks at the side. The yards were full of old cars and stoves and broken-down chairs. The first time I went there, I felt embarrassed for Lucille because I thought she must feel that way. Then, I was vaguely bewildered. I couldn't understand why the difference between the way we lived and the way "colored" people lived was so stark, so absolute, one side of the tracks from the other. One time I asked my father about this. He said, "That's just the way it is."

My parents were not overtly racist, especially not my mother. She loved everyone. But she and my father were products of their time, so my mother, like all the other Jewish women in town who had maids, referred to Lucille as her *schvartza* (black). "She's such a wonderful *schvartza!*" she would say of Lucille. "She's like a member of the family."

Lucille was tolerant of such insults, not that my mother called her that directly. Once, when I was eating lunch with her, I blurted, "My sister says I shouldn't eat with you 'cause you're colored!" Lucille smiled and kept on munching her peanut butter and jelly sandwich. Another time, I asked why her hands, which fascinated me, were brown on one side and pink on the other. She laughed and said, "'Cause that's how God made 'em!"

I loved the touch of those hands when they wiped my mouth clean or caught me when I slipped from the jungle gym. I felt secure with my hand in Lucille's. For all her slightness of frame, she had a power and authority that made me feel safe.

So one day when my mother said I could go to the movies with Lucille, I was wildly happy because there was something I wanted to do very badly, and I couldn't do it without her. I wanted to sit in the balcony at the Rialto Theater.

The balcony was the forbidden fruit to me. I wanted to know what went on up there that made it off limits if you were white. *Why did an usher stand at the stairs to ensure that only "colored" kids went upstairs? Why should they get special seats up high and not the rest of us?*

I don't know if it crossed my mother's mind that Lucille and I would be sent upstairs, but looking back on it I suspect it made little difference to her. Lucille, on the other hand, hoped for once in her life, by virtue of my presence, to sit downstairs where it was quieter and cleaner.

"I'm with her," she said to the usher, grasping me resolutely, and raising our clasped hands in solidarity as we entered the theater.

"Upstairs!" he answered, jerking his head toward the balcony.

"Yes, Lucille!" I pleaded. "Upstairs! Please! Please?"

Lucille looked at me, stunned. "Honey, you sure?" she asked, shaking her head from side to side. "My, my," she murmured, smiling, as I pulled on her arm.

I headed straight for the center of the first row. So high up and no one's head in front of you! I hardly noticed that my seat was broken and that there was no carpet on the popcorn-strewn floor. Once the previews started, everyone quieted down, the children only screaming and throwing popcorn when the Marx Brothers did something hilarious.

When the movie ended, Lucille and I made our way down from the balcony jostled by woolly-headed boys taking three steps at a time, jackets flying behind them. Converging with everyone else in the lobby, I suddenly heard hoots and hollers from a gaggle of white boys.

"Hey, looky there! A nigger lover!"

"Eeny, meeny, miney, moe, caught a nigger by the toe!"

"Y'all want some chitlins?"

I realized they were laughing at me. The feeling that rose in my stomach made me want to vomit. I was terrified, sickened, ashamed, guilty, enraged and sad. I clung to Lucille, who put her arm around me and guided me outside into the cold air.

"Don't pay them no mind," she said, going down on her knee to button my jacket. But the tears had started down my cheeks. I wasn't sure if I was crying for Lucille or for myself. I just knew I felt miserable, sullied, as if I'd lost something I hadn't even known was mine. Lucille took her handkerchief and gently wiped my eyes with her lovely, long fingers. "They don't know 'bout you and me bein' friends. They're just a bunch of stupid boys." She hugged me and took my hand in hers. We walked home in silence.

I never told my mother or anyone else what had happened. It felt too big, too important. It was mine and Lucille's secret; only she would understand. But I made a point of eating lunch with Lucille every day after that when she came to our house, and when I heard my mother use the word *schvartza* I told her it was no different than saying "nigger." Whenever my father went to pick up the laundry at Lucille's, I insisted on going along, climbing the broken steps and giving Lucille a fierce hug. I liked the feel of her bony arms around me, and most of all, I liked that nobody who saw us like that in *her* neighborhood ever said a thing.

Elayne Clift

The Story of Raoul Wallenberg

God helps the brave.

J. C. F. von Schiller

I'm a professional photographer. My offices in New York are only three blocks from the United Nations, where signs designate "Raoul Wallenberg Walk." Those who know of Wallenberg think of him as someone who saved nearly 100,000 lives in Budapest, Hungary, in the last, fierce days of World War II. To me, Raoul Wallenberg not only saved lives, he also left a mark on those he saved. I know. He left a deep mark engraved in my heart and mind, one that has shaped my thoughts and actions ever since.

I first met Wallenberg on October 17, 1944, when I was a young man. By then, the Nazis had "cleansed" the Hungarian countryside of Jewish people; more than 430,000 men, women and children had vanished, at the rate of 12,000 a day, never to be seen again. Now, in the closing days of the war, the Nazis prepared to exterminate the last large population of Jews alive in Europe, those in Budapest.

Raoul Wallenberg, a young Swedish architect, had been sent to Budapest in July for the sole purpose of saving lives. He worked through the Swedish Legation, although he'd never been trained as a diplomat. He'd been in the import-export business and knew his way around Europe. His weapons were his wits, determination and a belief in the worth of each human life to the point of risking his own in exchange.

I'd grown up learning photography from my father. He was the court-appointed photographer to the Hapsburgs, the personal photographer of the Hungarian regent, Admiral Miklos Horthy, and the top society photographer in Budapest. Admiral Horthy gave us a personal exemption from the existing laws imposed on the Jews. On October 15, when the Arrow Cross—the Hungarian Nazis—took over the government, all exemptions were canceled. Through my father I knew one of the Swedish diplomats, Per Anger. Knowing my life was in immediate danger, I headed for the Swedish Legation. Against all odds, I made it through the crowds of people seeking help, and was admitted.

I told Per the bind I was in. "Let me introduce you to someone," he said. He leaned out the door. "Raoul?"

Raoul Wallenberg came in, a young man, early thirties, slim with brown hair. His air was down-to-earth, a center of calm in a world gone mad. Per said, "This is Tom Veres, a photographer, a friend of mine. He could be useful."

Wallenberg said, "Good. You'll be my photographer. You will document the work we are doing. You'll report directly to me." They made out official papers on the spot.

Much of my time was spent taking pictures for *schutzpasses* (passports) that Wallenberg then issued by the thousands. They stated that the bearer was approved to move to Sweden after the war, and was already under the protection of the Swedish government.

But the day I found out what it really meant to be Wallenberg's photographer was a month later, on November 28, when his secretary handed me a piece of paper with his instructions: "Meet me at Jozsefvarosi Station. Bring your camera."

The Jozsefvarosi train station was a freight depot on the outskirts of town. I took my Leica and got on the tram, not knowing what to expect. To tell you the truth, everybody, especially those on the Nazis' hit list, thought lying low was the best plan. Keep quiet, keep out of sight. Don't get involved. Yet here I was, on a raw November morning, heading for Jozsefvarosi Station.

I found the station surrounded by Hungarian Nazis and gendarmes from the countryside. Anyone in his right mind was trying to get out. Wallenberg expected me to find a way in. I shoved my camera into my pocket and went to one of the gendarmes. Using the world's phoniest Swedish accent, I spoke in a mixture of broken Hungarian and German. "I'm a Swedish diplomat! I must go in to meet Raoul Wallenberg!"

The gendarme stared at me incredulously but let me in. The scene inside the station was harrowing. Thousands of men were being loaded onto cattle cars. Wallenberg was there, as were his Studebaker and his driver, Vilmos Langfelder. When Raoul saw me, he walked over and whispered slowly, "Take as many pictures as you can."

Pictures? Here? If I were caught, I'd be on that train myself, legation or no legation. I climbed into the backseat of the car and took out my pocketknife. I cut a small slit in my scarf and positioned the camera inside it. I got out and walked through the train yard as calmly as possible, snapping pictures.

Wallenberg had his black ledger out. "All my people get in line here!" he called. "All you need to do is show me your *schutzpass!*"

He approached the line of "passengers." "You, yes, I have your name here. Where is your paper?" The startled man emptied his pockets, looking for a paper he never had. He pulled out a letter. "Fine. Next!"

Men caught on at once. Letters, eyeglass prescriptions, even deportation notices became passports to freedom. In his ledger, Raoul and his assistants carefully checked off, or added, each name in the book. I tried to become invisible, snapping away, trying to catch the atrocity of what was going on.

"Tommy! Tommy!"

I heard my name and turned around. Had I been recognized?

"Tommy!" In line, almost on the train, was my best friend, George. George and I had known each other for years. We'd been assigned a seat together in first grade and had sat together by choice every year since. He was brilliant academically, the valedictorian of our gymnasium. Now he was in line to die. I had only a split second to think.

I walked over to him, grabbed him by the collar and said, "You dirty Jew, get over there!" I pointed toward Wallenberg's line. "I said go! Are you deaf?" I kicked his backside. He understood and got in line.

Wallenberg had pulled hundreds of men out of line when he sensed the Nazis losing patience. "Now back to Budapest, all of you!" he said.

The new "Swedes" walked out of the station to freedom. Wallenberg turned back to the captors. He began to lecture them in measured tones about health conditions, crowding on trains, anything to take their attention off the departing men.

As soon as they had a good head start, Raoul and I got back into the car where Vilmos waited. The danger we'd been in didn't hit me until then. This man, a Swede, who could have waited out the war in safety, was marching into train yards—and asking others to do the same!

When we got back to town, I found George, took him to one of Wallenberg's protected houses and took his picture for a *schutzpass*. "Now stay here until I get your papers!" I said.

The next day, word came: more deportations from Jazsefvarosi Station. Again I was asked to come. It was a ghastly repeat. Gendarmes with machine guns, thousands of men being herded onto trains. Wallenberg with his table and his black "book of life."

This time my Leica was already hidden in the folds of my scarf. As Wallenberg started calling off common names that many men might answer to, I started snapping photos.

That day, my cousin Joseph was among those marked for death, as was one of Hungary's great actors. I pulled them out of line to join Wallenberg's hundreds.

It was then I saw my chance. I walked around the train, inches from the armed guards. On the other side, the side away from the station, I climbed onto the already filled car. The train hadn't yet been padlocked from the side. I jumped, pushing all my weight onto the bolt that held the door shut. The spring clicked. The long door slid back in its tracks.

The men inside, who a moment ago had stood prisoner in the darkness, now blinked in the November sky. "Move, quickly!" I said. Men started jumping off the back of the train, running to the line where Wallenberg continued to give out passes.

Inside the station Wallenberg clearly saw that his time was up. "All of you released by the Hungarian government back to town! March!" At the same time a Hungarian police officer saw what I was doing. He pointed his revolver at me. "You! Stop what you're doing!"

Raoul and his driver got into their Studebaker, and they drove around to my side of the train. Raoul opened the door and leaned out. "Tom! Jump!"

I didn't have a moment to think. I made the longest jump of my life.

Raoul pulled me inside and Vilmos stepped on the gas. Raoul smiled and looked back at the train station. "I don't think we'll come back here for a while!" he said.

A couple of days later, at Wallenberg's Ulloi Street offices, George's mother came to see me. She was crying. George had tried to slip out to see his fiancée in a house two corners away. Two Arrow Cross thugs arrested him within those two blocks. I never saw my best friend again.

By January the Soviet Army was pressing close to the city, but the Nazis and Arrow Cross still ran Budapest. Wallenberg was in a pitched battle to keep the thirty thousand people in protected houses from being added to the seventy thousand people already locked in the Central Ghetto. He was doing everything he could to stop the pogrom to finish the ghetto off.

By now there was constant bombing day and night, so hundreds of us lived in the Ulloi Street offices. On the night of Monday, January 8, a pounding came at the legation door. Within moments, the Arrow Cross burst in, shining blinding flashlights from face to face.

The Arrow Cross didn't know that Edith Wohl was at the telephone switchboard upstairs and that she made a quick call. "Everybody line up!" the officer yelled at us. "At once! Or we'll shoot you on the spot!"

It was finally happening. I was standing under guard in line, about to be marched to my death.

"All right, everyone. It's time for a walk to the river!" one soldier spat. He turned to a couple of his buddies sitting nearby. "It's your turn to take them."

"We just got back from taking the last group!" one of them complained. "There's still snow on our boots!"

Just then the door burst open. There stood Wallenberg. "What are you doing? These are Swedes! You've made a very serious mistake! Let them go!"

The Arrow Cross turned, stunned, to find a truckload of Budapest police filling the room, guns drawn.

Raoul Wallenberg stared down the Nazi captain. "You heard me. Let them go. Now!"

The captain stared at the machine guns surrounding him. He stared at the Swede. The captain let us go.

The war was within days of being over when the bad news came. Everyone, Jews and Christians alike, who lived in my family's apartment house had been marched away by the Arrow Cross because they'd found the huge hidden food stocks kept by the well-known Zserbo Confectionery stored in the building's basement. My parents were taken as well; they were taken straight to the Danube and shot, their bodies thrown into the river. It was too late for Raoul to save them.

But it wasn't too late for thousands of people whom Raoul had pulled out of trains or off marches. It wasn't too late for the people in the ghetto whom Wallenberg and his accomplices had saved from the final pogrom, even as the firing squads were assembling.

The last time I saw Raoul Wallenberg, he and his driver, Vilmos Langfelder, were getting ready to leave for Debrecen to meet with the newly established provisional government about setting up reconstruction programs. He asked me if I wanted to come, but I had yet to find out the whereabouts of my parents. The two men left on January 17 with a Soviet escort. Before reaching Debrecen, they were taken into custody by the NKVD, a precursor of the KGB. Neither man has been seen outside Soviet prisons since.

I've thought often about how the timing of my parents' tragic deaths kept me from disappearing along with Wallenberg. Sometimes I think my life was spared so that I could tell his story.

What happened to Wallenberg is shrouded in mystery to this day, but what he did for thousands of men and women and children will always be bright and clear. The people whose lives Wallenberg saved, they were simply his fellow human beings, and as such, he felt responsible for them. He wasn't some superhuman, although his actions were heroic. He was an ordinary person who dared other ordinary people to do what he did.

So here, I tell his story.

Tom Veres

The Compassion of a King

There could be no greater calamity than a permanent discord between us and the Arab people . . . we must strive for a just and lasting compromise with the Arab people.

Albert Einstein, 1939

During the early months of 1997, the Mideast peace process was on the rocks. Violent incidents on both sides had soured the political atmosphere, and there were fears of more violence to come. The fears were justified.

On March 13, 1997, a Jordanian soldier went out of control and shot and killed seven Israeli schoolgirls, aged between thirteen and fifteen, during their field trip to the Jordan River's "Island of Peace," near the northern border between Israel and Jordan.

One of the girls, Adi Malka, knew sign language, and her deaf parents relied almost entirely on her as their link to the world.

Thousands of Israelis attended the funerals. Grief and outrage swept the land, and relations between Israel and Jordan seemed about to plunge to a new low.

But the day following the funerals, one man resolved to do what he could to comfort and heal.

An American woman visiting Israel with her family takes up the story.

"Grief was overwhelming. The girls' pictures covered the front page of the paper. I couldn't bear to watch TV or read the stories at first. It was just too much. I felt overwhelmed. How do people live here year in and year out with tragedies like this?

"But then, in the midst of our grief, King Hussein came. It was the most remarkable thing I have ever seen. All of Israel was glued to the television. His humility, his sincerity, his ability to say 'I'm sorry' was a true gift to this country. To see this king, on his *knees,* in the homes of these Jewish families—listening, comforting, apologizing on behalf of his people—was absolutely unbelievable. The whole country was in tears watching this. 'I feel as if I have lost a child of my own,' Hussein said. 'If there is any purpose in life it will be to make sure that all the children no longer suffer the way our generation did.'

"And he really did comfort this country in a way that nobody could have imagined possible. He won the hearts of this country. He could have easily remained aloof and discounted this crazy soldier as unstable and unrepresentative of the Jordanian army. He would have had every reason to do that. Instead, he came here and expressed his deep compassion."

The American visitor was not alone in her feelings. Yehezkel Cohen, whose daughter Nurit was killed in the shootings, said of Hussein, "I really love him. Despite the sorrow, I say this: I hope and believe in King Hussein and a real peace."

Beth Huppin

[EDITORS' NOTE: *King Hussein died of cancer in February 1999, two years after this incident. Just after his death, two years after their daughter was killed and King Hussein came to visit them, Shimon and Ruhama Cohen had a baby girl on February 6, 1999. They named the baby girl "Jordan," as a "gesture to the king," who showed so much warmth and compassion to their family after his subject's bloody act. The late king maintained contact with the family following the incident in 1997, even during his final illness. The family wanted to honor him, and their new daughter, writes* The Jerusalem Report *(3-1-99), is "a gift after a tragedy" to maintain their connection with the late king and his kind act.*]

Jerusalem Encounter

Jerusalem: the city which miraculously transforms man into pilgrim; no one can enter it and go away unchanged.

Elie Wiesel, *A Beggar in Jerusalem*

As a member of a kibbutz bent upon building a Jewish homeland, I left my entire family in Poland and arrived in Palestine in the spring of 1936. Before settling in, I wanted to see the country. My first destination was Jerusalem, city of my dreams. For days, I walked the narrow streets of the Old City, fascinated by the pageantry of its people, the cacophony of languages, the fragrant, spiced air.

On one of my journeys I ventured out of the city and into the nearby Judean hills, where I stumbled upon an Arab café in an unlikely setting—the rooftop of a Russian convent. The tiny café was hemmed in by a sun-baked clay balustrade with garlands of grapevines running along its edge. Customers sat at low, brass tables, sipping coffee and talking in subdued tones.

The sun was glinting on the sparkling brass of the table where I sat down. When I lifted my eyes to look beyond the balustrade, Jerusalem lay stretched out beneath me, from the rectangular buildings, broad boulevards and blooming gardens of Rehavia, the modern section, to the Old City with its shadowed streets winding in and out of ancient gates.

I could hardly believe my eyes. There in the distance rose the stone walls of the Tower of David. Down to the left stood the Wailing Wall, its stones polished by tears. The Wailing Wall, whose fissures hid a people's heart wrapped in a prayer, held a two-thousand-year history of longing for self-determination. Out of the ruins of the last Temple, out of that Wailing Wall, grew the Mosque of Omar, its graceful splendor consecrated to the worship of Allah. The golden dome shimmered in the sun as my eyes wandered from its mosaic gateway to fall on the Via Dolorosa.

I closed my eyes and let my thoughts sink into the past. The memory of thousands of years of suffering swelled into a sea, engulfing me. When I turned to the present, Nazism and Communism were competing with each other for the degradation of humanity. The world was far from being at peace on that beautiful spring afternoon.

The sun was beginning to set behind the stark hills, and a golden haze embraced Jerusalem. A bell chimed, another answered in a deeper tone and a third rang out on a higher pitch. The bells intertwined, their silvery tones brushing against the hills and returning in muted echoes. I had the sensation of being suspended between the ages.

Twilight is short in Palestine, and the scenery was changing rapidly. Lights began to glow on the horizon. Up on a minaret balcony, a white figure appeared, turning slowly in all directions. The *muezzin* was calling his people to worship. Wherever they stood, Moslems rolled out their prayer rugs and knelt, joining the caller in the evening prayer.

The lights went on in a nearby synagogue. The rabbi and a group of students were walking up the steps into the house of prayer.

The Franciscan Brothers turned on the lights in their house of worship, preparing for vespers.

A sweet voice emerged from the Yemenite synagogue. It was the song of the *hakam,* chanting a prayer.

A lilting soprano floated out of the English church, not far in the distance, and was soon joined by others.

Prayers rang out in Hebrew, Latin, Russian, English, Arabic. The earth stood still in deep meditation. Then, like a whisper, I felt my heart stir. Adding my voice to the chorus, I began to chant my prayer.

"And they shall beat their swords into ploughshares and their spears into pruning hooks. Nation shall not lift up sword against nation, and they shall not learn war any more."

A great calm began to envelop me, and all my bitterness melted away. A new love was being born in me. I could see the oneness of all people and all religions. I was at peace.

That encounter with Jerusalem sustains my hope for universal peace to this day. Whenever the world is in turmoil, whenever I am about to lose my faith in humanity, I summon the memory of Jerusalem's evening prayer.

Bronia Galmitz Gallon

5

FAMILY

It is far better to establish a home than an opinion.

Edmond Cahn

A Shabbat Miracle

There is no Judaism without the Sabbath.

Rabbi Leo Baeck

Living ten thousand miles away from my parents, we always looked forward to their yearly visits to Israel. Whenever they visited my family, we always got along wonderfully. That is, until Shabbat.

Long ago, my great-grandparents had decided to stop observing Shabbat, and my grandparents and parents had followed in their footsteps. We had grown up with very little awareness of or interest in Jewish rituals. After college, I became more interested in Judaism and gradually began to learn Hebrew, study Jewish sources and practice a more observant lifestyle. This process culminated with my moving to Israel. Though my parents were always very proud of being Jews, my choices were alien to them. They felt that I had rejected the way they had raised me, and could not understand why what had been acceptable for three generations had to be changed. Endless talks had not been able to change these feelings that the unity of our family had been shattered.

We were often able to camouflage these feelings of loss during the week. But then Shabbat inevitably arrived. All the rituals of Shabbat represented the change from how my parents had raised me to how I lived my life today. Starting with the Thursday night cooking, through the Friday cleaning, showering and getting into Shabbat clothes, the tension in the air would become more palpable with every passing moment.

By the time we sat down to eat, we could hardly look into each others' faces. My wife and I sat in our special Shabbat clothes, the kids all cleaned up, with white shirts and freshly scrubbed faces, opposite my parents, sitting in their regular clothes, looking excessively uncomfortable.

We would sing *Shalom Aleikhem* and then *Eshet Hayil* while my parents, knowing no Hebrew, would sit in painful silence. Then the children would come to my wife and me for the moving traditional Shabbat parent's blessing, and we would proceed with *Kiddush, Hamotzi* and the meal, all the while trying to make conversation in attempts to cover up the true feelings of discomfort.

We proceeded like this for years, always dreading the approaching of Shabbat. Then, inexplicably, everything changed.

One Shabbat, after singing the seemingly interminably long songs of *Shalom Aleikhem* and *Eshet Hayil,* I sat waiting for the children to come for their blessings. Then, utterly unplanned and unanticipated, an uncontrollable force came over me. Without any awareness of what I was doing, I rose from my chair and took several steps to where my father was sitting.

For a moment I just stood next to him, in a daze, not really understanding what I had done. He looked at me and asked what I was doing. I looked at him and said, "Dad, give me a *brakhah,* a blessing." Bewildered, he said, "I don't know any Hebrew."

"So say whatever you want to."

He paused, then placed both hands on my head, paused for another moment, and then whispered, "I love you, son."

At this point, the children were all asking, "Why is Grammi crying?" I walked over to my mother, and amidst her tears of joy, I bent down for her to give me her blessing.

Then I returned to my seat and gave the kids their blessings. The tensions had all disappeared. The Shabbat experience that had once separated us, the Shabbat that had once shown how different we were, had now become the Shabbat of expressing our love for each other. It had become our Shabbat, for all of us. No longer was there a break in the generations.

Now, though still completely different in our lifestyles, we all look forward to sharing Shabbat together. Come Thursday nights, the excitement grows as we anticipate the moment of sharing our three generations of blessings.

Rabbi Aryeh ben David
(formerly Andrew Nemlich)

Grandmother's Candlesticks

Mighty is the force of motherhood! It transforms all things by its vital heat.

George Eliot

I awoke from a sound sleep and bolted upright in the dark room. The digital clock read 6:01 A.M., and the birds had already begun their morning song. I sat very still, my breathing shallow; my heart raced as thoughts and feelings overwhelmed me. I knew that she had been here, that she had stood over me while I slept, that she had come to kiss me good-bye. I still felt her warmth on my lips, and her undeniable scent permeated the room.

"Grandma," I whispered. "Grandma, where are you?" I wanted so desperately to talk to her, to hold her one more time.

My husband, still asleep, moved closer to me. I touched him lightly on the shoulder. "Ray, wake up, honey," I whispered as I felt the hot tears roll down onto my cheeks. As if in a dream I heard myself say with absolute certainty, "Grandma Edna just died."

Afraid of my intuition, I reached over to turn on the

light, which was next to my bed. On my nightstand is a picture of Grandma and me, which was taken the last time I was with her. She is holding my daughter Lauren, who was two and a half years old at the time. There is a faraway look in Grandma's smiling eyes, betraying the cataracts that plagued her for so many years. Looking at the photograph, I can see our similarities so clearly now that she is gone. Our faces contain the same history, they read like maps of the same territory traveled over different periods of time. Small, pert Russian noses, fair, freckled skin and shining, mischievous eyes. We loved each other without question or hesitation and while the meaning of her world shrunk as the opportunities in mine grew, she never failed to tell me what to do and how to do it.

Born in the small Russian town of Lutsk in 1887, Edna Wolfe left Russia at eighteen months and sailed to America with her two older sisters, her brother and her father. Her mother was forced to stay behind because she could not leave her own blind mother alone. When she was finally able to come to America, she traveled with nothing but the clothes on her back. "But she tricked them," Grandma would tell me with a twinkle in her eye. "She hid our *Shabbas* candlesticks in the lining of her winter coat and never took that coat off until she landed in New York."

Those candlesticks were a testimony to a way of life; they were the triumph of a broken family fighting to find their way back to one another in a land that promised everything.

Grandma lit those candlesticks every holiday and each Shabbat. She would close her eyes and mumble while swaying back and forth in front of the dancing flames. As a young girl, I thought she knew everything, that the power of the world rested in those small, freckled fingertips that spread the warmth of the candle's light. I saw her as the source of our family tradition, the ultimate word on what we should all do and be.

Some things are easy to remember, like the smell of her kitchen when she was cooking, or the red leather pocketbook she brought me from Mexico for my fifth birthday, or the soft, brown leather recliner in her den, which smelled like rosewater and my grandpa's aftershave.

Some things I never understood, like her stiffness when Grandpa hugged her or why she never seemed satisfied with her life. I realize now that what she loved best was people. As was common for women of her generation, she had only a fifth-grade education and never felt comfortable in the world of books. Instead, she read people's faces and studied the fine print of their expressions; what they said, what they left out. She defined herself through her children but desperately resented them when they didn't need her anymore.

I asked her one day when I was in high school if she ever wanted to do something, have a career, write a book. She answered without hesitation, "What would I do with all of that? I did what I knew. I cooked, I cleaned, I raised my children. And now they're gone, off with their busy lives, always so busy. I never thought . . ." Her words trailed off and a distant look crossed her face. In her memories, she found not comfort but abandonment and betrayal.

After I graduated college, I would visit her whenever I could. She couldn't understand my need to go, to see the world. In her opinion, I was missing the point. "Raise a family," she would tell me, "and your heart will never be the same."

It was getting harder for me to share my world of politics, feminism and adventure with her, and I would leave feeling frustrated at how little I was able to communicate. As we both got older, however, it became less important for me to make her understand my life because I realized that she still had so much to tell me about hers. She was becoming more afraid of death, and she needed to talk about her world in order to make sense of it before she died. Why did she feel so discarded, so useless after all the years of being the central force behind her family? Why did not one of her children ask her to come and live with her?

I will never forget the day I visited her in the nursing home just a few months before she died. She had become diminished, not so much by age but by the bitter ironies of her life. She seemed happy when I told her about my two children, my home, my husband. But my law career and the many aspirations I had were of no real interest to her. She held my hand on the small sofa, and I stared at the big, brown freckles that covered her skin. She needed so much reassurance now, to know that her life had been meaningful.

I painted her fingernails while we talked, and she reminisced about the old days. Of her sisters and the hours they spent laughing together in the kitchen, sharing secrets, when they all lived together in the house on Fair Street. Of my father and what a "prince" he had been but how he never understood her anymore. I sensed in her ramblings that she was in another time and place entirely.

As I got ready to leave, she slowly got up from her chair. She walked towards me and then, changing her mind, headed directly towards the hutch that contained the few remaining items she kept from the old days. She took down the beautiful brass candlesticks that I had loved since I was a little girl. "My darling girl," she said with tears in her eyes, "you have always been filled with the love of your Jewishness. May you find joy and meaning in whatever you choose to do with your life. But remember, nothing you do will be more important than your family." She handed me the candlesticks and said, "It is only right that these should belong to you now."

It has been almost four years now since my grandma died. It seems that all I need is the scent of cinnamon or a jar of Ponds Cold Cream to bring her back to me. But I know that as time passes she will become harder to recall. I am certain this is why she gave me her candlesticks. For each time I light the candles, I feel her love for me gently burning in the flames and bestowing upon me the power and inner-strength to create a life of meaning and purpose. And in doing so, I have come to understand the legacy of her life and the meaning of her blessing.

Amy Hirshberg Lederman

Connecting the Generations

A cold drizzle was creating puddles around my feet as I made my way home from the Seattle Public Library. It was an afternoon in December 1940, soon after my arrival in the United States. Under my coat I was protecting a copy of *Anne of Green Gables,* which I had just checked out for the third time. Despite my limited English, I was determined to discover how Anne met the challenge of adapting to an unfamiliar environment, mirroring my own new life in America.

The dim, gloomy street reflected my mood as the faint lights from Christmas trees, already visible behind the windows, reminded me that tonight was the first night of Hanukkah. I stopped and leaned against a wet lamppost recalling images of past Hanukkah nights and of my now fragmented family.

I was back in our Vienna apartment. My parents, Grandfather Mendel with his dignified beard, Grandmother Tova in her blue silk dress and pearl necklace, and Cousin Bertha, her raven hair pulled into a bun, were all gathered around our silver Hanukkah *menorah.* My great-grandfather, a silversmith in Poland, had crafted it for the marriage of his eldest daughter. In every generation since, it had brightened my family's Hanukkah celebrations. It symbolized not only the victory of the Maccabees, but also the invincible spirit of Judaism and the continuity of our family.

A hundred years later and six thousand miles away, I still delighted in the thought of its rich silver patina, with lovely rosebuds and exquisite leaves and stems engraved on its nine branches.

A dump truck pulled up and splashed me from the feet up, shattering my reverie. "Where did everything go?" I mumbled to myself.

But I knew where everything had gone. Grandfather had been arrested on *Kristallnacht* and taken to Dachau, where he was killed. Grandmother died of a heart attack soon after the Nazis had looted their apartment and destroyed their stationery store. Bertha, arrested by the British trying to escape to Palestine on an illegal boat, was interned in a detention camp. But the Hanukkah *menorah?* Since it was forbidden to take any valuable artifacts out of the country, its fate was a mystery.

It was dark by the time I arrived home. My father was already back from the synagogue, and my mother was peeling potatoes. She laid aside one large potato and began to grind the others for latkes. When I asked her what the extra potato was for, she answered, "That will be our Hanukkah *menorah.*"

I shook my head in sorrow. With so many people and things vanished from my life, was our precious heirloom to be replaced by a potato? Was that to be another new custom in our new country? Mother hollowed out two shallow grooves on opposite ends of the potato and pressed a small candle into one. Father was about to light the second candle when there was a knock on the front door. When he opened it, a mailman thrust a package into Father's hand. "Special delivery," he said. "Sign here."

The package was covered with foreign stamps, which turned out to be from Palestine. There was no return name or address anywhere on the box. We were dumbfounded. Who could have sent us a package from the Holy Land? With unsteady hands, we tore away the paper. The first thing we saw was a sealed envelope addressed to my parents. Father opened it and read the letter aloud in German.

Dear Cantor and Mrs. Schiffman,

After the Nazis looted Mrs. Schiffman's mother's apartment, she died from a heart attack. The concierge went into her apartment and found a package hidden in the closet. The concierge was a Christian woman who knew the family. She took the package to Bertha just before she left for Palestine. On the boat to Haifa, Bertha told me the story. She said if the British catch one of us, the other must mail the package to the address inside. I was lucky to escape after we landed, helped by the Hagganah. I had plenty of trouble in the beginning and I am sorry to say, I forgot about the package. Yesterday, I found it. Please excuse me for this long wait.

Respectfully,
Bertha's Chavarah

The three of us pried open the box. Inside, wrapped in torn tissue paper, lay a black and white horsehair cushion. As Mother lifted it out of the box, we all wondered, *What was so important about this cushion that Bertha had risked so much to ensure its safety?* Father examined it from all angles, even sniffed it, and pressed his hands into the bristly cloth. He stopped suddenly.

"Quick, Marta. Get me some scissors." Mother found her sewing basket and handed him her small scissors.

Father carefully began to snip open the stitches along one side of the cushion. With a mass of straw littering the floor, he reached in and pulled out the still shining, so familiar, silver Hanukkah *menorah!*

I could barely contain myself. Our beautiful *menorah* had returned just in time for the first night of Hanukkah in our new home. For a moment, we were stunned, and then we all started talking at once. How did it get out of Austria? Who would have risked smuggling it out of the country? We assumed Bertha had hidden it in the cushion, taken it on the train across the border and onto the boat. Then she made sure that, in the event she could not carry out her intentions, someone else would.

Father put the *menorah* on the table and transferred the candle from the potato into its rightful place. He lit the *shammas,* which he held up high, and recited the *b'rakhah* over the Hanukkah candles. When he began to sing *Sheheheyanu* in honor of the first night, mother and I joined in with fervor. For me, the blessing that night applied to more than just the beginning of Hanukkah. It also acknowledged the miracle that had reconnected me with my roots. I felt a surge of hope and optimism. For the first time in a long time, things did not look quite so bleak; something precious had come back to me. The fact that it had arrived when it did was a special omen.

Today, the silver Hanukkah *menorah* stands on the sideboard in our dining room. My older son, David, knows that one day it will stand in his home, and later, in that of his daughter, Anna, and then in that of one of her children, and down the generations. Its flickering candles will symbolize the continuity of our family, as well as the inextinguishable flame of Judaism.

Gina Klonoff

The Rimonim

The Torah is a Tree of Life to those who grasp her,
Whoever keeps her is content.

Proverbs 3:18

Wintertime in Old Jaffa, Israel, is sometimes quite cold. It was early evening when a man in his fifties came into my gallery, the Antiquarium. Among the items of silver that he offered for sale was one big *rimon,* a decorative silver Torah ornament. Only one? Every Torah Scroll needs two, one for each side. They always come in pairs.

"You see, I don't want much for it. I kept it for so many years . . . since I was a child. I was born in Germany. It was *Kristallnacht,* and we all had to run to the synagogue in order to save something. I was a little boy then. An old man opened the Torah shrine and handed to me this *rimon* and said to me, 'Run!' So I did. Then I was taken by a Christian family. I did not see my family again. Then we passed to the east, to Romania. That's where I come from now. I am a newcomer to Israel, and I need the money. I still remember our synagogue in Germany, it was beautiful. . . . You see, the Jews managed to remove and bury many Jewish objects, and that was before the Nazis bombed down and destroyed our beautiful synagogue."

I had to be insane to buy only one *rimon.* It was of no use to a synagogue or to a collector of Judaica; the transaction was insane. But I did it, although I did not know why.

It was a beautiful silver *rimon,* decorated with crowns and bells and lions on top. Two-story towers with alternating pierced windows and arches with bells. This *rimon* was made by a master, in the city of Fuerth, Germany, in the eighteenth century. So I had that *rimon,* I polished it and put it on display. Months passed, and the *rimon* moved from one place to another. Again polishing, and again and again.

Years passed, and this *rimon* always changed places. Here and there I had a collector who would ask about it and admire it. But always the same question: Where is its pair?

One morning, after many years, I had a visit from a lady who wanted to sell antique silver objects. She opened her bag, and I could not believe what my eyes saw. It was a dream. She had there the second *rimon.* I asked her where she got it, and she replied, "I am a new immigrant from Argentina. I was born in Germany. It was the day, the terrible day, *Kristallnacht,* when the Nazis started to destroy the synagogues. We all ran to our synagogue, to save some of the things that were dear to our community. I ran, too. When I was next to the Torah ark I saw this *rimon* lying there. I took it, then when we got home I kept it with my dolls. I was sent to a convent. The nuns took care of me. Then after the war my father came back and found me. We left for Argentina. Now I am here."

"Do you have any brothers or sisters?"

"Yes, I had a brother, but as far as I know he was killed in a concentration camp."

"How old was he?"

"He was three years older. . . . I was three years younger." She had tears in her eyes; me, too. I bought all the silver she had, and after she went away I compared one *rimon* with the other. Everything, every detail, was exact. There was no mistake. The two *rimonim* were born together.

After a few weeks of research I found the man through the Jewish Agency, and I asked the same questions again: "Do you have any brothers and sisters?"

"Yes, I had a sister. She must be dead now, because I never heard from her."

"How old was she?"

"She was three years younger, but why do you ask all these questions?"

Now I was sure: "I know where your sister is. She is here in Israel. The *rimon* that you saved and the *rimon* that she saved are identical. I think you can meet your sister now."

The man started shaking and sweating and did not know whether to laugh or cry. We went in my car to see his sister. It *was* his sister. A history of forty-four years passed in that room in seconds. You need two *rimonim* for the Torah. They are together now. Nothing can happen to them anymore. They are in Israel. Brother and sister—the two *rimonim* for the Torah.

Denny Pinkus

The Family Heirloom

The measure of one's success in life is not the money raised. It's the kind of family that is raised.

Joseph P. Kennedy

Every Friday evening for sixty years, Abe sang to Esther—sometimes low and soft, sometimes loud, almost boisterous, as if making a pronouncement to the world. Whether in the winter, when he had to rush back to synagogue for a late Friday evening service, or in summer, when there were no late services, he sang slowly and with lots of feeling. Right after Esther's stroke, Abe even sang to her in her hospital bed, stumbling over the words that he knew by heart, but which had become as well-worn and fragile as he in his seventy-nine years.

Now Esther was in the hospital again, another Sabbath amidst oxygen tubes and saline drips. Still, Abe sang. "A woman of valor," he whispered, leaning close to Esther's ear, beginning the familiar melody of *Ayshet Hayil* ("A Woman of Valor," a prayer praising the virtuous wife and mother), even though he was not sure she could hear him. As he sang softly, the crisp smell of the hospital linens took him back to the birth of their son, to their first apartment, so tiny there was no room for a crib.

However sparse their surroundings, Esther had always insisted they make room for the important things, what she called the family heirlooms. The Shabbat lamp, *Judenstern* in German, had belonged to her parents. It hung in their living room, its seven branches filled with oil and lit by wicks. On their single bookshelf they kept Abe's father's *mahzorim,* volumes of holiday prayerbooks that Abe chose from each *yomtov* (religious holiday) and took to *shul.* And on the fireplace mantel rested the *siddur,* the worn Sabbath prayerbook that had comforted Abe's great-aunt Sarah during her days of confinement in Theresienstadt. These gifts which had been so lovingly passed on to them were the only things of value they had, their son's only inheritance, Abe thought, still serenading Esther. He brushed a wisp of white hair from her forehead.

"Give her of the fruit of her hands; and let her own works praise her in the gates," Abe finished singing in Hebrew, bowing his head.

"Let's go, Pop," David said, gently placing a hand on his father's shoulder.

Abe started, having forgotten his son was in the room. David waited as Abe kissed Esther good-bye.

"It's already nine o'clock. You need some rest," David said. "Stay with me and Carol tonight. I'll bring you back in the morning."

Abe resisted, then agreed. "Let's stop by the apartment first. We'll walk?"

David bent down and kissed his mother, then sighed wearily. "No, Pop, we can't. I know it's important to you to walk on Shabbat, but it's too far."

"The world has gotten too big, Esther," Abe said absently, "and too fast. Important things get lost in the shuffle, traditions. . . ."

David was silent as he helped his father into the car. He knew Abe talked about lost traditions, because he couldn't bear to talk about losing Esther. Esther, and Shabbat rituals like *Ayshet Hayil,* had always been the glue. David recalled one Friday evening—it must have been even before he became a bar mitzvah—when Abe had invited a few students from *shul* to visit the apartment and discuss the meaning of "A Woman of Valor."

"*Ayshet Hayil,*" Abe began, "which closes the Book of Proverbs, refers back to the first chapter of Proverbs where we read, *'Shmah b'ni musar avikha; v-al tetosh Torat imekha:* Listen, my child, to the discipline of your father and do not abandon the teaching of your mother.' The teaching of the mother is embodied in *Ayshet Hayil.* The woman of this spiritual poem works tirelessly for her household and her community."

Abe knew he had a tough audience in these young students. It was the early seventies; everything traditional was suspect.

"I know what you're thinking, but read a little deeper," he persisted passionately. "This woman of valor is a homemaker and teacher, yes, and also a businesswoman, a politician! She is strong, caring and wise. She faces life with grace and kindness. And she loves the Lord. She embodies the very best of Jewish values. This is *Torat imekha,* the 'teachings of your mother' that you should internalize. This is. . . ."

"What is this, David—fire trucks?" The panic in Abe's voice brought David back to the present. They were about a block from the apartment building when they saw the flashing lights, then the smoke. The building where Esther and Abe had lived for forty years was engulfed in flames.

The newspapers would report that although no one perished in the fire, the building and its contents were a total loss. The Shabbat lamp, the *mahzor,* the *siddur,* all gone.

Abe was beside himself with grief, and neither Abe nor David knew how to break the news of the fire to Esther. At least she was doing better, the doctor had said the next day. Finally, it was Abe who spoke up while David went to get coffee from the hospital cafeteria.

"I can't believe it," Esther wept quietly.

"I'm sorry, Esther," Abe said, "but we have nothing of value left."

Esther suddenly stopped crying and struggled to sit up. Abe took her elbow and placed a second pillow to support her back.

Her speech was slurred from the stroke, but Esther spoke deliberately. "You mean the love songs you sang to me all those years meant nothing?"

"What?" Abe said, dazed. "What are you talking about, Esther?"

"'A Woman of Valor,' I'm talking about. Isn't that a worthy inheritance?"

Abe looked into Esther's eyes, still bright, clear and strong. For all his piety, he had not considered a spiritual heirloom.

"And you've taught David?" Esther continued, taking Abe's hand.

Abe frowned. "David never listened to my singing of *Ayshet Hayil.* He's not interested in this custom. David thinks 'A Woman of Valor' describes a servant, not a marriage partner."

"He told you this?" Esther pressed.

"No, he would never do that. I just know," Abe retorted stubbornly.

"Then love will have to be inheritance enough," Esther whispered and closed her eyes.

By the following Friday evening, Esther had been

released from the hospital, and she and Abe were staying with David and his wife, Carol.

David sat with his parents in the spare bedroom while downstairs, Carol prepared the Sabbath candles, the *challah* bread and the wine. "You can stay with us as long as you want, don't worry," David said.

"It may not be so long," Abe said very softly, then, raising his voice so Esther could hear, "I have something for you, David, even though I'm not sure you'll use it. Here." Abe pushed a sheet of paper into David's hand.

David looked over the paper and smiled, then laid it carefully at the foot of the bed and went to the bedroom doorway. "Carol? Can you come up for a minute?"

Abe took Esther's hand and began the ritual singing, his voice soft on the evening air, except for an occasional cracking on the high notes. Then for an instant Abe faltered, forgetting his place. Maybe it was the breeze or street noise from the open window, but in the silence he thought he heard another voice. He turned to see David, eyes closed, holding Carol's hand. David was singing, the paper with the words to *Ayshet Hayil* still laying at the foot of Esther's bed.

Linda Spiegler

"I like your style, Pablo, but maybe you should think about branching out and not just doing bar mitzvah portraits."

Reprinted by permission of Barricade Books.

Of Angels and Poinsettias

My father did not believe in angels. He could not be bothered with spiritual notions or metaphysical concepts. But when he died, and I stood beside his sheet-covered body in the mortuary's refrigerated room, I was overwhelmed by the sense that legions of angels were surrounding my father and escorting his soul to the next world. And I, his ardently spiritual daughter, stood there envying his place in the world to come.

According to Judaism, angels can be created by human beings. Every good thought, word and deed gives birth to a positive force in the universe, which is called an angel. These angels are eternal. They hover around us throughout our life and accompany us to our reward after our death. Conversely, every evil thought, word and deed creates a bad angel or demon. They also hover over us until, in the heavenly court, they become our accusers.

I could recognize the faces of many of the angels that filled that cold, white-tiled room in Bershler's Funeral Parlor. One whole contingent was born on those rainy mornings when my father, driving to work, would pull over to the bus stops along the way and offer a ride to anyone going to Camden.

And over there was the coal angel, born at the end of a cold winter day, when I was catching a ride home with my father from his drugstore. My father daily delivered prescriptions to the homes of people who were too sick to come in for them. I was in a hurry to get home that day, but my father assured me he had only one delivery to make. He drove up to a dilapidated house in the ghetto, which Camden, New Jersey, had become, and disappeared into the house. By the time he emerged fifteen minutes later, I was rabid.

"What took you so long?" I scolded him.

My father, who never explained himself, but who did not want to listen to my harangue, answered simply, "The house was ice cold. No wonder the woman is sick. So I tried to call the coal company to order her a load of coal, but their line was busy until a minute ago."

Hovering close to my father's body were the poinsettia angels. Christmas was a rare day off for my father, but instead of relaxing that day, my father would fill up the back of his station wagon with gift poinsettias. Most of these poinsettias he delivered to the poor black and Puerto Rican women who lived in the neighborhood of his store.

When my brother Joe was a teenager, he usually did the footwork of taking the poinsettias into the houses. Many of the women, without husbands and with a brood of children to tend to, told Joe that this poinsettia was the only thing of beauty they received all year long.

Among the regular poinsettia recipients was a woman suffering from MS (multiple sclerosis) who lived in a nursing home. Every year Joe would bring the poinsettia into her room, place it on the table and mumble, "Merry Christmas," while the paralyzed woman would follow him with her eyes, unable even to nod a thank-you. Finally one Christmas, Joe asked the nurses at the nursing station who this woman was. They told him that she had been a wealthy daughter of a fine family, engaged to be married, when she contracted MS. Her fiancé broke the engagement, her money was used up in doctor and care bills, and eventually even her family dropped all contact with her. In the course of a year, the nurses told Joe, the only card, letter or gift this woman received was this poinsettia from my father.

After Joe went away to college, my father did all the poinsettia deliveries by himself. Overweight, with varicose veins from standing in the drugstore since 1925, stricken with the arthritis that made it increasingly painful for him to move his legs, my father delivered these poinsettias until he retired from the drugstore at the age of seventy-five.

One corner of the mortuary room was filled with library angels. After my father retired, he volunteered for the local library to deliver books to shut-ins. Leaning on his cane and limping from his arthritis, he often had to climb flights of stairs to reach the desolate apartments of people, usually younger and sometimes less incapacitated than he, who had run out of reasons to get out of bed.

My father lived in a world without strangers. He could not stand in a supermarket line or sit at a restaurant table without striking up a conversation with the person next to him. I was always terribly embarrassed by his utter disregard for personal space. Didn't my father know that in the latter half of the twentieth century, alienation was the pervasive mind-set of society?

At college, I belonged to the radical leftist Students for a Democratic Society. I had taken my stand with minorities and oppressed Third World peasants against the bourgeoisie conservative establishment of America. Thus, I was mystified, on one of the occasional times I entered my father's drugstore during my college years, to see a black teenage girl whispering to my father that she wanted to see him privately.

When I later asked him what she had wanted, he answered that she thought she had a venereal disease and was asking him what to do. Why should a black teenager, in the age of the Black Panthers, be confiding in this middle-class, white, Republican, Jewish pharmacist? If I perceived him as the enemy, why didn't she?

Another time, I came into the store with him one summer morning. Five or six matronly black women, who were sitting at the soda fountain, greeted my father with catcalls and complaints: "We ain't talkin' to you no more, Mista Levinsky."

"You's in trouble in our book, Doc."

I wondered how my father's characteristic gruffness or fiery temper had hurt or insulted these women. He ignored them and went directly back to the prescription counter. I, however, was concerned with their plight. I approached and asked them what my father had done to them.

One of them replied, "Yesterday afternoon he done told de ice-cream man to give popsicles to all de kids on our block 'n he would pay for 'em. Us mamas had to spend all afternoon pickin' up popsicle wrappers. No, we ain't talkin' to him no more." And they all roared with laughter.

My father was not a rich man, but he gave and lent money as if he had it. During the Six-Day War, when the American Jewish community rallied to Israel's emergency need, my father, with two children in expensive private colleges, found he had no money to give to Israel. He went to the bank and borrowed four thousand dollars, which he donated to the Israel Emergency Fund. Later, when the local Jewish community was collecting money for a geriatric home, my father took out a second mortgage on his house in order to have a proper sum to contribute.

My father paid for his mother's two-bedroom apartment, plus full-time help. When he finished his ten- or twelve-hour workdays in the drugstore, almost daily he went to check on my grandmother to make sure she had everything she needed.

My father regularly lent money to any of the drugstore customers who asked him. Most of these loans were never repaid. When we were sitting shiva for my father, Carl, the Italian pharmacist who had bought the drugstore from him, told us how, when my father was transferring the store over to him, they came upon a one-inch-thick notebook filled with entries. Carl asked what it was. My father replied that this was his record of outstanding loans. Carl asked how much it was worth. Tossing the book into the wastebasket, my father shrugged, "It's priceless."

When Carl bought the drugstore, his lawyer and my father's lawyer drew up a purchase agreement. After it was signed, as Carl and his lawyer walked to his car, the lawyer said to Carl, "You just wasted your money."

Carl gulped. The lawyer continued, "With that man, a handshake would have been sufficient."

My father did not believe in life after death, nor in the world to come. He expected no rewards for giving people rides in the rain or for finding jobs for the sons of his ghetto clientele. How amazed, then, he must have been to find himself ascending to the next world, escorted by legions of familiar angels. Standing meditating over his body in that chilly mortuary room, I found myself saying, "Surprise, Dad!"

But there was also a revelation for me in that angel-thronged room. I saw that deeds are all that count—not good intentions, not beliefs, not convictions, not even spiritual consciousness, but deeds. Although I knew that Judaism is a religion less of faith than of action, I preferred to live in the ethereal realm of the mind and the spirit. Standing beside my father's body, gazing at his luminous face, I was shocked to realize who he had become by virtue of his deeds alone.

My father's road to heaven was paved with poinsettias and popsicle wrappers. And if there was a gap created by the faith he did not hold, I saw that it was spanned like an immense bridge by that book of loans he had tossed away.

I, who had spent my forty-two years wrestling with profound concepts and lofty aspirations, had nothing in my entourage as significant as my father's coal order for the sick lady. So, I could feel my father winking at me, his religious daughter, from his honored place in the next world, saying, "Surprise!"

Sara Levinsky Rigler

The Shawl

Nothing brings me more joy on earth than to see my children succeed.

Judah Benasher

Most children are put to bed with cozy bedtime stories, but not so for me. At bedtime, my grandmother Bea would tell me the story of how she, her mother and her five siblings had escaped the Russian pogroms. As told by my grandmother, the Russian Cossacks stormed into their town and killed many Jews.

When the Cossacks stormed into my grandmother's house, my great-grandmother screamed, "Run, *Kinder,* Run!" My grandmother and her sister fled and were hidden by a non-Jewish neighbor in a cold and dark potato cellar. They stayed there for over two days, with rats crawling on them while the neighbor risked her life by telling the soldiers that she had not seen any Jewish children. Later, the neighbor took them out of the potato cellar and told the soldiers that they were her own children, again risking her own life to save the lives of my grandmother and her sister. Eventually, the family was reunited and my great-grandmother, Sara, led her six children on a journey away from Russia. This journey took over two years, during which they traveled and hid.

On a bitter cold, blustery night in 1910, Sara and her six children arrived in Buffalo, New York. They were tired, cold and hungry. The only warm item of clothing they possessed was Sara's winter coat. Sara cut her coat into six pieces, so that each child would have some warmth. Sara had nothing to keep her warm.

A kind woman named Esther Mintz heard of Sara's plight, as the Jewish community was very small and supportive of the newly arriving immigrants. Esther stayed up an entire night and knit Sara a beautiful and warm black shawl. She gave Sara the shawl and a basket of freshly cooked food. The food was quickly eaten, and the shawl saw Sara through her first cold winter in America. Sara never forgot the kindness of this stranger.

Forty-six years later, Renee, the American-born grandchild of Sara, told her grandmother that she was engaged to be married. Renee was to marry a man named Joseph Mintz. Sara quickly realized that Joseph was the grandchild of the woman who had knit her a shawl so many years ago when she arrived in America, a cold and hungry immigrant. Sara had saved this shawl, and she took it from her attic and showed it to Renee. Holding the shawl to her heart, Sara spoke in Yiddish, telling her grandchild that this marriage was *beshert,* meaning that Renee and Joseph's marriage was planned in heaven before Renee's birth, and the shawl was a sign of this destiny.

Renee and Joseph are still married—they are my parents. Sara and Esther died years ago and I never knew them. My grandmother Bea, who told me the story of her escape from Russia, died when I was pregnant with my own daughter, Jennifer. While dying, she symbolically, but likely unconsciously, continued a family tradition:

She knit a blanket to give warmth to the great-grandchild she would never meet. Today, I am writing this story with Jennifer sitting beside me. The blanket, first knit for Jennifer, has since sheltered my youngest daughter Allison and my sister's son Steven. While the original shawl has unfortunately been lost, its story, and the new knitted blanket, keep us warm inside and connected to the pain, kindness, love and perhaps even the destiny of past generations.

Laurie Mintz

Missing the Boat

Coins are round: Sometimes they roll to you, sometimes to others.

Folk Saying

In 1910, Abraham Bank, my great-grandfather, was impressed into the Russian army. At the time, he was twenty-one years old and had lived near Vilna in Latvia for his entire life. He was a qualified rabbi, *shochet,* and *mohel.*

The prospect of twenty-five years of mandatory military service was unthinkable to Abraham. So he decided to pack a few clothes and personal belongings and leave his hometown during the night. He promised his girlfriend, Rebecca, that he would write.

Abraham traveled via Finland to Stockholm, Sweden, where he worked for a while as a stevedore. He earned his passage to London where he continued to work. His goal was to earn enough money to follow in the footsteps of his brother, who had already emigrated to America.

Two years after leaving his home in Latvia, Abraham was finally able to buy a ticket on a ship leaving from

Southampton that would take him from England to America.

Abraham ran into two difficulties. The first was the knowledge that he would not be able to get kosher food in the steerage class of the ship. The second was the trouble he would have in getting from London to Southampton over Passover, as the holiday ended on the night before the ship would be boarding.

Finally, Abraham decided not to use his ticket. He remained in London for a few months and then emigrated to South Africa, where eight years later Rebecca joined him. It was not until 1987 that Abraham's descendants—his grandson (my father) and his family—made the move to America that Abraham had come so close to making seventy-five years earlier.

I have good cause to be grateful to Zeida for deciding not to use that ticket all those years ago. In fact, it might well have been the best decision he ever made. The name of the ship that steamed into the Atlantic that day was the *Titanic.*

Tanya Bank

A Direct Line to Heaven

With the fearful strain on me night and day, if I did not laugh I should die.

Abraham Lincoln

When we were kids, I always admired Heshy Greenblatt. He was in my kindergarten class, and we stayed together until sixth grade. But he moved a few blocks away and eventually, after high school, we lost touch with one another.

Nu, so why do I mention Heshy all of a sudden? Last week, while riding downtown, who gets on the train and sits down next to me? Of course, Heshy Greenblatt! His face, I'll never forget.

We reminisced, and then he sighed, "*Oy,* if you only knew what I've been going through these past months, a literal nightmare!"

"*Nu,* so please tell me," I pleaded.

Heshy sighed and began, "I married a wonderful girl. Gave me four wonderful kids, three college graduates, and one drives a cab. Listen, it's a living. But, with a beautiful wife, you get a mother-in-law and a grandmother-in-law."

Heshy sighed. "*Nu,* so my wife's grandmother was in her late eighties. She was an avid reader and loved cheap adventure and mystery stories. So she gets it into her head that a great number of people, when they are legally declared dead, they sometimes really aren't dead. So she added a codicil to her will that said when she dies the family should put a telephone in the coffin with her just in case she was really alive and might wake up. She figured, at least she would be able to call someone.

"So, she checked with a rabbi and he humored her and said it was okay if it wasn't attached to the coffin and if they didn't use screws in the process."

I looked at him like he was crazy. "A telephone in the coffin?"

"Yeh, yeh." Heshy continued. "Listen, she was a sweet old lady, what could we do? So we went along with the gag. *Nu,* maybe she had a premonition or something, but she passed away six months ago. Don't laugh, when we went to the funeral home there was a telephone company truck in front of the place. Really! My mother-in-law had notified a lawyer; the lawyer notified the phone company, and they actually sent a man to the undertaker to place a phone in the casket and lead the wires out through a tiny hole at the side."

I looked at him like he was crazy, but he wasn't smiling. He shook his head soulfully, "It's the truth! So the phone man placed a small kitchen wall phone on the inside of the box, with a length of wire sticking out.

"Our rabbi was going out of his mind. There was a question of *Halakhah,* but he figured this was what she wanted, so let it be as long as the phone was not attached to the casket.

"We got to the cemetery," Heshy sighed, "they had to dig her grave near the road so it could be near a telephone pole. A telephone lineman was waiting for us. So the rabbi said the prayers and that was it. Everybody was crying, even the man from the telephone company.

"My wife wasn't feeling well so I sent her home in the funeral director's car, and I stayed behind with my cousin while the workmen filled the grave.

"Then suddenly one of the workmen bent down on one knee and put his ear to the ground. He shouted, 'It's ringing!' Sure enough, there was a ringing sound we all could hear. We all grabbed a shovel and began to dig like mad to reach the box. Maybe it was a sign. Who knew?

"The gravedigger attached some ropes to the coffin. As we helped to pull the coffin up, the phone continued ringing. The gravedigger pried open the lid of the casket, put his hand inside, near the old woman's mouth, but she was still very dead. He reached for the phone, put it to his ear, waited a minute then uttered a solemn 'No.' Then he put the phone back in the box and reset the lid.

"My cousin and I just stood there. 'Who was that?' I screamed. He looked at me vacantly and said, 'The phone company called to see if the phone was working.'"

I looked at Heshy, who said, "Yeh, yeh, it's the truth."

"So what else happened?" I begged.

"What else?" he screamed. "The old lady paid the phone company for phone service for a year in advance for basic service before she died. She even got a discount. Listen, that was her thing."

Heshy looked at me and sighed. "Two months ago, my mother-in-law got a call from the phone company. The phone was showing up with four out-of-town calls—to Florida and California!"

I gasped. "You have to be kidding."

"Really," Heshy sighed. "*Nu,* so I called the phone company and I told them, 'You have to be kidding!' So the guy starts getting nasty and says, 'Look, mister, we have three calls to Florida and one to California made from that number.'

"I talked myself deaf, dumb and blind but the guy wouldn't listen. I told him where he could go and hung up. The next day another guy from the phone company gets on the phone and says they are going to remove our service and take back their instrument. I told him, 'Lotsaluck!' I doubted whether they were legally allowed to touch the grave! So he says if they can't get the phone back we have to pay for it. Anyway he says they are canceling the service immediately.

"*Nu,* so now my wife's mother panics. She calls the lawyer, who's got a pretty penny from that old lady so naturally he's gung-ho to see that the old lady gets to keep her telephone six feet under for the full year she paid for.

"So he gives the phone company the old razzle-dazzle and threatens them with all kinds of legal stuff and the phone company finally agrees to continue the service. They said the out-of-town calls were because of a crossed wire and we weren't going to be charged."

I asked, "So everything with the phone company was worked out?"

Heshy smiled uneasily. The train roared into the Brooklyn Bridge station, and he started to get off the train.

"Look, it's like I told you—one nightmare after another. That old lady drove me crazy when she was alive and now, even when she's dead, I can't get away from her. Then last Sunday was a corker!"

The train came to a halt and Heshy started to say goodbye. But I had to hear the end of this saga so I got off the train with him.

Heshy continued, "Last week, the people who are working on the headstone asked if I could come out to Staten Island where they were making the monument. They seemed to be having a problem with the stone the old lady ordered before she died.

"'What's the hurry?' I asked. 'We have a few months yet before the unveiling.'

"The monument maker showed me a letter from the attorney. Would you believe the old lady wanted her phone number engraved on the stone over her name so her children could dial that number if they were ever in need of solace? Do you believe this!?!"

I looked at him in bewilderment. "*Nu,* so what did the monument man want?"

"He wanted to know if we wanted the area code engraved in the stone also! Honest! So I told him, just do what the note says and leave me out of the whole thing.

"'I can't,' the monument man said. 'The note says to check with you to see if the area code is necessary. *Nu,* so we're checking!'

"I told them to put the area code on the stone. The reason the monument man wanted to start on the stone so early was because he wanted to use it as a sample in front of his place so people should stop and see this thing. It's a curio! It could start a whole trend.

"So now I feel everything is over with," Heshy explained. "However, when I get home I get a call from the manager of the cemetery, and he wants me to come out there the following Sunday. He said it was something of a delicate nature.

"So I have to go *shlepping* out to Long Island. When I get there he tells me he has a great idea. The cemetery wants to take ads in the local papers, and he wanted to know if we would object to the slogan, 'The Only Cemetery with a Direct Line to Heaven' with a picture of my wife's grandmother's grave site with the phone wires coming from the ground!

"So I tell the guy, 'You're nuts! The old lady was crazy, but you take the cake! Let the old girl rest in peace!' So he tells me she really isn't. The workers in the cemetery can hear the phone ringing all day long. Apparently some guy at the phone company passed the number on to his friends and kids. The kids must have passed the number on to their friends for a big thrill, so they call that number night and day, especially before the Regents exams. They figure the old lady may have an 'in' with the Lord. It doesn't cost them anything, because no one picks up, so they call and call!"

"So," I joked, "what do you want them to do, change the number to an unlisted number?"

Heshy didn't laugh. "That's just it. The old number is engraved on the stone already and to have them change it will cost over two hundred dollars. I even refused to pay a penny when the phone company changed her area code."

I looked at him strangely. "*Nu,* so what are you going to do?"

"Nothing," he said softly. "By the end of the year the phone service will run out and the whole mess will end— I hope."

Arnold Fine

Reprinted by permission of Barricade Books.

Raisins and Almonds

The mother's heart is the child's schoolroom.

Henry Ward Beecher

When I was small, the neighborhood was big and Bubbe's lap was bigger. Bubbe was my grandmother. She had the kindest smile in the world. When I sat in her lap, she'd put her soft arms around me and kiss my neck.

Bubbe taught me to cook in her clean little kitchen. She made ruby-red soup—borsht—from beets and all the other vegetables I could carry from her garden. I'd help her stuff chicken necks with breading, then watch in wonder as she sewed them together with a needle and thread!

As she cooked, my bubbe would sing songs of her childhood. My favorite was a lullaby about raisins and almonds—*"Rozhinkes Mit Mandlen." "Shlof zhe,"* Bubbe would sing, "Sleep now, *Yidele,* sleep."

When she made chopped liver, Bubbe used an iron grinder from her grandmother, which clamped onto the table. As I turned the handle around and around, the meat would tumble into her big blue bowl. Then Bubbe would add chicken schmaltz, eggs, onions and secret spices.

I loved to watch my grandmother in the kitchen. She could make a steaming mountain out of mashed potatoes. She'd offer me a juicy slice of orange faster than I could crack the rind. And Bubbe could peel an apple in one long, shiny red ribbon.

Bubbe's yard was a beautiful garden of life. She loved to sing as we wandered among the fragrant flowers and fat vegetables. There were greedy squirrels, noisy birds, dragonflies with double-wings. Bees would settle on the peonies. The cherry tomatoes were as sweet as candy.

I'd watch the sunflowers grow until they towered over me. Then I'd stand under their giant petals and stretch. My grandmother would smile. *"Klayneh kinderlach,"* she'd say, "sweet child, you are such a bright flower." And she'd kiss the tip of my sunburned nose.

The garden held other wonders. Once, when I poked my stick in a bed of brown leaves, I found a shimmery snakeskin. When I showed my bubbe, she said I had found a memory of the snake, and that memories were precious. Of all the trees, I loved the slender birches best. I would gather bits of their papery bark and write parchment letters to Bubbe. Whenever she read one, she'd blow me a kiss. I didn't know until much later that my grandmother couldn't read.

We played dolls in the dining room. Bubbe called them all *dollinkeh* and sang to them in Yiddish. *"Rozhinkes mit mandlen;* sleep now, *babeleh,* sleep." When I was frightened or sad, she would stroke my hair and hum. Her voice was my rainbow.

I grew, and Bubbe aged. Each year, she measured me against the door of her kitchen, making my mark with her pencil. I measured my grandmother, too. The day my mark was higher than hers, I called her The Incredible Shrinking Bubbe. We laughed and laughed.

When Bubbe got tired, she'd sit on her glider and watch

me play. When we went to synagogue, I'd help her up the steps. But the day I became a bat mitzvah, a daughter of the covenant, Bubbe danced the special dance of celebration, the Hora, with me.

Now I am big. The neighborhood is small. My bubbe is gone; she's gone to the gardens of memory. But the gifts she left are more precious than any treasure.

Whenever I reach for the old blue bowl, I remember the smells of my bubbe's kitchen. When I run my palm against a paper-white birch, I recall the parchment of her skin. And on quiet nights, as I rock my drowsy daughter to sleep, I can hear my bubbe's lullabies.

Shlof zhe, bubbeleh, shlof. Sleep, my dear bubbe, sleep.

Elizabeth Sussman Nassau

The World's Greatest Stand-Up Comedian

A light heart lives long.

William Shakespeare

My bubbe, may she rest in peace, was one sharp lady. If she'd been born in a different time and place, she could have been president of the United States—or the world's greatest stand-up comedian.

Bubbe picked up the telephone one day to call my aunt. It was not a long-distance call, just an ordinary call from Chelsea to Wakefield, but something happened. This was back when Nixon had nominated Henry Kissinger to be his secretary of state, and the U.S. Senate was holding confirmation hearings. Bubbe's call got connected into somebody else's line. Two men were having a conversation about Kissinger: *Yes, he was from Germany, but still, he was a Jew, and you know those Jews, and wasn't it awful that we were going to have a Jew for Secretary of State?*

"So vat's wrong vit det?" said Bubbe into the telephone.

"WHO IS THIS?"

"Dis is Kissinger's mother!" And she hung up.

I always wonder what those guys must have thought.

Rabbi Joan S. Friedman

6

THE HOLOCAUST

Everything can be taken from a man but one thing; the last of the human freedoms—to choose one's attitude in any given set of circumstances, to choose one's own way.

Viktor E. Frankl

A Hill in Bergen Belsen

Without faith man becomes sterile, hopeless, and afraid to the very core of his being.

Erich Fromm

Anna was among the tens of thousands who succumbed to the typhus epidemic in Bergen Belsen. Her friends gave her up for dead and told her that her struggle with death was useless. But Anna was determined to live. She knew that if she lay down, the end would come soon and she would die like so many others around her. So, in a delirious state, she wandered around camp, stumbling over the dead and the dying. But her strength gave way. She felt that her feet were refusing to carry her any farther. As she was struggling to get up from the cold, wet ground, she noticed in the distance a hill shrouded in gray mist. Anna felt a strange sensation. Instantly, the hill in the distance became a symbol of life. She knew that if she reached the hill, she would survive, but it she failed, the typhus would triumph.

Anne attempted to walk toward the hill, which continually assumed the shape of a mound of earth, a huge grave. But the mound remained Anna's symbol of life, and she was determined to reach it. On her hands and knees, she crawled toward that strange mound of earth that now was the essence of her survival. After long hours passed, Anna reached her destination. With feverish hands she touched the cold mound of earth. With her last drop of strength, she crawled to the top of the mound and collapsed. Tears started to run down her cheeks, real human, warm tears, her first tears since her incarceration in concentration camps some four years ago. She began to call for her father. "Please, Papa, help me, for I cannot go on like this any longer."

Suddenly, she felt a warm hand on top of her head. It was her father stroking her, just as he used to place his hand over her head every Friday night and bless her. Anna recognized her father's warm, comforting hands. She began to sob even more and told him that she had no strength to live any longer. Her father listened and caressed her head as he used to. He did not recite the customary blessing but, instead, said, "Don't worry, my child. You will manage to survive for a few days, for liberation is very close."

This occurred on Wednesday night, April 11, 1945. On Sunday, April 15, the first British tank entered Bergen Belsen.

When Anna was well enough to leave the hospital in the British Zone where she was recovering from typhus, she returned to Bergen Belsen. Only then did she learn that the huge mound of earth in the big square where she spent the fateful night of April 11 in her combat with typhus was a huge mass grave. Among thousands of victims buried beneath the mound of earth was her father, who had perished months earlier in Bergen Belsen. On that night when she won her battle with death, Anna was weeping on her father's grave.

Hasidic tale retold by Yaffa Eliach
Based on an interview by Kalia Dingott with Anna, May 1976

Dreaming of Matzah

Courage is never to let your actions be influenced by your fears.

Arthur Koestler

"If all you have is lemons, make lemonade." But what if you could only dream of having a lemon, or a potato, or even a bowl of watery broth? Where would you find your strength? This was the situation twenty-eight-year-old Abraham Krotowski faced at Passover time in 1945 when he was dreaming of *matzah* while being held captive in Dachau, Germany.

To some Jews today, Passover is considered a difficult eight days during which you are not to nosh on your beloved bagel, not eat your favorite pasta, not indulge in your delicious pizza. But the commandments of Passover are not "nots." As a remembrance of the Exodus of the Jewish slaves from Egypt, we are commanded to eat unleavened bread. Out of respect for the sacrifices of those who have gone before, it is a *mitzvah* to eat *matzah.*

To a concentration-camp prisoner, however, any food is an impossible dream. Eating *matzah* would be considered crazy. Since being Jewish was the crime that you were being punished for, why flaunt that in the face of your captors? There was nowhere to get *matzah,* anyway. Or was there?

Call it crazy, but with the help of some friends, Abe set out to make *matzah* in Dachau. The resolve that he mustered to achieve his goal was the same determination that kept him alive through six difficult years in three ghettos and two concentration camps. He was, above all, a Jew, a survivor, sustained by the same belief that had kept the Jewish slaves in Egypt before him alive—that someday soon he would be free.

The recipe for making *matzah* in a concentration camp is an odd one. Start with a generous portion of determination, add a few packs of American cigarettes, throw in a German construction foreman with a fondness for schnapps, keep your faith, and say a *brakhah* (Hebrew blessing).

For some time, Abe had been sneaking out of the camp at night and had befriended some Russian and Italian officers who were prisoners working in the nearby building for a factory. Having cleverly fashioned woolen blankets into much-needed scarves to fend off the fiercely cold weather, Abe exchanged them for bread or potatoes, enough to sustain himself. He was an honest and clever barterer, aware that what one person doesn't need, another will pay dearly for. You just have to know your customer.

Thanks to the American Red Cross, that winter some prisoners in Dachau received relief packages—a small bar of soap, some sugar cubes, one can of sardines and two packages of Camel cigarettes. For those like Abe who did not smoke, the cigarettes became valuable bargaining tools. Abe offered his cigarettes to a lazy German construction foreman named Karl, who seemed to pay little attention to the prisoners at work. Karl asked Abe what he wanted in return, and Abe said food. The German told Abe how to get into his work shack where he could take some bread. It was risky business since Abe would have been shot if caught. But Abe got the bread and later came to Karl again saying that there were some sick people in his barracks and they needed flour for soup. Karl said he could get him flour, but Abe had to bring him some schnapps—a nearly impossible request. A few days later, after much trading and bartering, Abe had a small bottle of vodka for Karl. When Abe gave Karl the bottle, he was certain he would be killed on the spot. But Karl was a man of his word—and a man with a fondness for drink. His eyes lit up when he saw the bottle, and in exchange he helped Abe smuggle a five-kilo bag of flour into the camp.

For three nights, Abe and his brother-in-law Isaac Zelinski, a baker by trade, made *matzahs* in improvised tin ovens, under the cover of darkness. They made enough *matzah* to feed the entire barracks so that, on Passover 1945, each of the seventy-five prisoners had their own piece of *matzah* to eat during the short, secret Passover Seder. No bitter herbs were needed to remind this group of the harshness of slavery—or that miracles can happen anywhere.

Trish Krotowski

The Fire of Hope

Faith is the true force of life.

Leo Tolstoy

This is a story I heard Rabbi Hugo Gryn tell at an interfaith meeting held in the Jerusalem Chamber at Westminister Abbey:

When I was a young boy my family was sent to Auschwitz. For a while my father and I shared a barracks. In spite of the unspeakable horror, oppression and hardship, many Jews held onto what scraps of Jewish religious observance as they were able. One midwinter evening one of the inmates reminded us that tonight was the first night of Hanukkah, the festival of dedication, the feast of lights. My father constructed a little Hanukkah menorah out of scrap metal. For a wick, he took some threads from his prison uniform. For oil, he used some butter that he somehow procured from a guard.

Such observances were strictly "verboten," but we were used to taking risks. Rather, I protested at the "waste" of precious calories. Would it not be better to share the butter on a crust of bread than to burn it?

"Hugo," said my father, "both you and I know that a person can live a very long time without food. But Hugo, I tell you, a person cannot live a single day without hope. This is the fire of hope. Never let it go out. Not here. Not anywhere. Remember that, Hugo."

Rabbi Kenneth L. Cohen

The Making of a Physician

A great doctor works with an angel at her side.

Folk Saying

The last year of World War II was the year the war reached my family.

In March 1944 the Germans occupied Hungary, causing an endless series of earthquakes in Jewish lives all over the country. I was nineteen. Just two hours after the news of the occupation, my fifteen-year-old brother and I were turned back at the railway station: Jews were not permitted to use the train or leave the city by any means. We were living with family friends in Budapest, going to school. In this frightening situation, all we wanted was to go home to our parents to face whatever would come. It never happened. We exchanged letters full of love, anguish and hope, promising each other to survive and meet again "when it was all over." We never saw our parents again. They were killed in the gas chambers of Auschwitz.

My personal Holocaust started when all Jewish women between sixteen and forty were ordered to report to work. We were to bring sturdy shoes and warm clothes and food for three days. The huge crowd of young women looked like a summer camp gathering. As we set out for the march to our first destination, I felt tough, strong and determined to take any hardship and survive.

The awakening came in brutal shocks. Everything was a shock the first time. The first night, crowded in a building with a bombed-out roof, standing room only, the October rain pouring on our heads, running down our backs, collecting at our feet up to our knees. The first body, a girl beaten to death, paraded in front of us in a wheelbarrow for enlightenment. The first of thousands of lice in my clothes. The first shooting spree by the guards, just for fun.

The march toward Germany showed more and more evidence of its real purpose, and it was not to get workers. They did not want us to work. They wanted us dead. Some of us gave up. All you had to do was sit down by the roadside, and you were shot to death. We got no food, we all had dysentery; we were hopeless and confused. We spent our nights in the open in a softball field, in the hold of a cargo ship, in pigsties where the pigs had just been evicted. The inventiveness of our captors was inexhaustible.

Whenever we arrived at our night place, there was one solid semblance of normalcy, of purpose, order and hope: a Red Cross flag and a makeshift tent and two or three doctors with their bags. They were prisoners like the rest of us, they got here by the same painful marching, but somehow they still had the energy to help others. They cleaned wounds, gave advice, comforted. I felt they must know a secret hidden from us ordinary people that gave them strength in this desperation.

One day a young doctor was removing a bullet from a prisoner when the order came for a head count. The guards rounded everybody up, but the surgeon just kept operating. The commandant walked over to him and ordered him to join the roundup. "I am almost done," he replied. "I must stop the bleeding first." The commandant said jokingly, "I'll give you a choice. You can do as I say and I'll let you live, or you can finish and then I'll shoot you." The doctor finished the suturing, dressed the wound and was shot dead on the spot.

I didn't think I would ever have the courage to behave like that, but I made myself a promise: If I survive, I will become a doctor. This dream faded through the coming months. The starvation, the cold, the lice, the beatings and the shootings killed some two hundred people each day. My mind was reduced to a simple thought: to survive, one hour at a time.

And I did survive, one of sixty of the original five thousand women sent to "work" nine months earlier. I went to Budapest and found my brother, who had also survived; the rest of our family had been killed. Strangers were living in our home. We stayed in a shelter for returned prisoners. I was planning to find a job to support the two of us after I recovered from some wounds.

One day my brother brought home my papers for medical school. He had enrolled me secretly. After the war, everybody who wanted to study was accepted. My dear little brother beamed at me. "Isn't this what you wanted to do? We'll survive, don't worry. We've survived harder times!"

Five years later I received my medical degree. Did I learn the secret of the doctors in the camp? I don't know. I learned patience, curiosity, self-discipline and compassion. I have been a physician for forty years now.

Judita M. Hruza, M.D.

The Day Hitler Touched Me

The year was 1937 when I turned thirteen in my hometown of Dresden, Germany, often referred to as "The Florence of the North." My parents had expected great scholastic achievements from me, insisting every day that I follow in the footsteps of my older cousin, a celebrated honors student and admired athlete. Unfortunately, I was unable to live up to their expectations, disliking school and my cousin, an arrogant showoff!

My parents, who had me late in life, could not cope with an independent, unconventional, rambunctious teenager. I was difficult to control and grew ever more distant to them as they were seldom home to care for me. That job was handed to our maid, Erna, who became my confidante.

My father was a successful businessman. My mother was a rising opera star and accomplished pianist, appearing on opera and concert stages. The end of her performances was greeted with standing ovations.

Most of my longtime Christian friends enthusiastically joined the Hitler Youth, which I was not allowed to do because of my Jewish religion. I was shut out from taking part in exciting field trips, fighting phantom enemies under real battlefield conditions, and midnight torchlight parades ending up in gigantic political pageants resembling those of ancient Rome.

One day in June 1937, my friends of many years, who had never abandoned me and took great risk by socializing with a Jew, showed up unannounced at my house. They were bubbling over with excitement in their Hitler Youth uniforms and swastika armbands, to the dismay of our maid, Erna.

In a frenzy, talking all at once, they made a crazy offer to change me instantly into a Hitler Youth with an extra uniform they had brought along. They wanted to take me to see, close up, Hitler, who was scheduled to visit our town. It was an adventurous undertaking I could not refuse, to the misgivings of Erna, who felt it was a very risky scheme that, if uncovered by the Gestapo, could cost us all our lives.

My friend Werner and his pals were assigned by their group leader to perform crowd control, to become part of a human chain of boys and girls of the Hitler Youth, to hold back the masses and prevent a stampede around the Fuhrer by the thousands who wanted to touch their man-made god, feared by the world, who had lifted the German people from the ashes of defeat, defying the English and French by marching unopposed, illegally, into the Rheinland, a demilitarized zone according to the Versailles peace treaty.

For me, it was a chance of a lifetime; nothing could stop me from taking part in such a historic event.

It was a very satisfying feeling to be able to join my friends and be addressed as "comrade," to become part of my peer group, to try something dangerous and daring and not be caught. We were too young and stupid to realize the consequences.

Determined to look danger in the face, feeling free in my Nazi uniform, I did not obey Erna, who was frightened to death by my shenanigans. With a kiss on both cheeks, I departed with my friends, ready for the challenge: to see the Fuhrer on the big town plaza, across from the Jewish synagogue whose parishioners he wanted to eradicate from German soil, as forecast in his book *Mein Kampf*.

As the boys and girls in the youth group joined hands, the anticipation made my heart pound, aware that I had become part of an historic event to see one of the most powerful men in the world!

With German punctuality, Herr Hitler arrived on the dot of three that afternoon. Exiting from his classic, shiny black Cabriolet, surrounded by his SS staff and Gestapo agents, he examined the crowd, which went into a religious trance, accepting the Fuhrer as their "Savior"—shouting in unison their endless *"sieg heils"* with raised arms.

Hitler did not wander into the crowd, but shook hands over our shoulders; women cried hysterically, wanting to touch him or to be touched. Children held flower-filled baskets, tiny flags and hard candy, all bearing the swastika.

To our great shock, after accepting baskets from the little girls and boys behind me, Hitler suddenly stopped in front of my friend Werner—whose secret only I knew, namely that he was half-Jewish—complimenting him on his slick Aryan appearance. Then he turned to me, stroking my cheek, impressed by my Germanic features and asking my name.

Hitler had a yellow glow around his face. His dark, piercing eyes made me shudder, wondering if he could see through me and find out that I was everything but an Aryan.

I clicked my metal-lined heels in military fashion, standing in full attention and blaring the words, "At your service, my Fuhrer." He put his hands on my shoulders and turned to one of his SS officers, saying in his Austrian dialect that he considered me the perfect specimen of an

Aryan youth, upon which the Third Reich can fully rely to defend the Fatherland against its many enemies!

We all felt that our cover was blown when the Fuhrer asked a press photographer to take my picture with him; it could mean our end, a "Nazi Jew" seen in a Hitler Youth uniform lent to him by members of the Nazi Youth movement. Our pictures would appear in all the morning papers—many would be labeled "anti-Nazi conspirators." We all prayed to come out of this alive.

Erna was happy to see me back. I did not mention to her that a picture of me talking to Hitler would appear in the press. I lay awake all night with heart palpitations, my body drenched in sweat, seeing myself tortured at Gestapo headquarters.

The next day, I saw my prayers had been answered by a miracle; Hitler had cast a shadow over me, and no names had been printed.

My parents looked at the pictures of Hitler talking to me, and mother called Erna and me over. "That young boy talking to Hitler looks just like you," she said. "Is it?"

"Of course not, mother," I lied. "How could it be me?" But Erna knew!

I buried the picture of me and Hitler in our town's park in 1937, but when I returned to Dresden in 1990, it had disappeared.

I will never forget that day, glad that my foolish act did not cause serious harm to my family. But not long after that, all of us vanished, abducted to extermination camps. Of the ten members of our extended family, only I returned alive.

Norman W. Jaffe
Submitted by Leslie Riskin

The Last Four Digits

The long arm of coincidence.

Haddon Chambers

As a child growing up in the Bronx, the last four digits of Terry Noble's phone number were 7401. Coincidence: When Terry got a Social Security number, the last four digits were 7401. And years later when he found himself as a volunteer on a kibbutz in Israel, he now called himself Tuvia Ariel, he worked with a carpenter whom he respected. The carpenter was a wiry, solid man, dedicated, the silent type. Tuvia learned that he was one of the few who had escaped Auschwitz alive, that he then joined the Polish partisans, then the British Army. He was sent to Palestine, where he deserted to join the Palmach and help Israel win her independence in 1948.

Quite a history.

But more than awe piqued Tuvia Ariel's curiosity about this survivor's experiences in the Holocaust. Tuvia had read the number tattooed on his arm. Its last four digits were 7401.

"Don't talk about it!" Tuvia recalls the carpenter telling

him forcefully and painfully. "I lost my whole family, my mother, my father; there was a brother in back of me, a brother in front of me—I'm the only one left. Don't bring it up again!"

Tuvia didn't.

Except once.

Tuvia Ariel is a man with many stories. In fact he *is* a story: the man who was Bob Dylan's adviser for some time, who arranged *kaddish* to be recited for Abbie Hoffman, who put in a stint at Yale Law School, the man who, as a soldier in the U.S. Army, arrived in Israel during the 1956 Sinai war, tore the "USA" from his uniform and, looking just like an Israeli, hitched his way down to the Sinai Peninsula, ready to fight, only to find that the war had ended just two hours before.

I was told in advance how colorful Tuvia was, but nothing prepared me for the likes of a comment he made an hour after I met him last Friday afternoon. I knew he had a new leg. I knew it was a breakthrough for him. But who gives thought and thanks to such things? Who wonders what it's like without a leg or with a new one?

Praying in *shul,* I sensed nothing unusual as the afternoon service came to an end. Suddenly, Tuvia approached me, almost in tears. "This was the first time in my life I prayed *Shemoneh Esrei* standing up in a minyan. I have never been able to address the Almighty like any other Jew, standing up, three steps forward, three steps backward. . . ."

Tuvia was raised in a non-observant home, in which the *Shemoneh Esrei* was not recited. Then he went to Israel in 1963 to volunteer on *kibbutzim.* In 1967, on the fiftieth anniversary of the Russian Revolution, he saved his life by cutting his own leg off as it accidentally got caught in the machine he operated on a *kibbutz*—a machine that sucked his leg into its grinder and from which the rest of him escaped only by his quick and courageous self-amputation. A little over ten years later he became observant, but by then he was rotating between a wheelchair, crutches and artificial legs which, however, could never keep him aloft long enough to *daven Shemoneh Esrei* (Hebrew prayer which requires recitation while standing).

One Friday he did it.

After walking home (only three blocks), he choked up again, "That's the furthest I've walked in twenty-two years."

He was fitted with a new leg only shortly before the day the Berlin Wall crumbled.

Whence this living miracle?

It began innocently enough. Tuvia was in the United States at the beginning of 1989 on a business trip. He saw a television commercial by DuPont. It featured a new kind of plastic developed for spacecraft and also used for artificial limbs. The commercial featured amputees engaged in vigorous basketball, not from wheelchairs, but standing up, running, passing, even jump-shooting. A regular game.

And not with people amputated below the knee, but above the knee.

Tuvia thought to himself that seeing this was as if seeing your grandmother who had died years ago suddenly walking down the street. When he lost his leg twenty-two years ago he never thought he would see himself live normally again—and here were people just like him, playing basketball!

He called DuPont. They directed him to an advanced prosthetic clinic in Oklahoma City. He called immediately, "When can you make me a leg, how long does it take and how much does it cost?"

It seems that for above-the-knee amputees the old system had the stump rest on the prosthesis, which caused pain and circulatory problems and often didn't work well, sometimes not at all. Using DuPont's flexible, rubberlike plastic, the new system grips the stump, which not only relieves pain and circulatory problems, but also better channels the energy and movement of the stump in natural leglike movement.

Even in advance of receiving his leg, Tuvia Ariel was not satisfied to give himself new life. He wanted it for the above-the-knee amputees in Israel. So he had a long talk with an American expert in this field, John Sabolovitch, about the special merit of bringing this technology to the Holy Land. Sabolovitch agreed to do so in two ways. First, to train Israeli prosthesists in Oklahoma City (he has already trained his first); second, to travel to Israel with his staff to train Israeli prosthesists there. Tuvia only needed to provide the plane tickets.

A man whose history included the likes of trying to bring Bob Dylan to his Jewish heritage, not to mention saving his own life with supreme courage and pain, does not shy away from the innovative. But his goal reached even beyond making the technology available in Israel. He wanted to establish a "Hebrew Free Limb Society." This will provide a limb to the amputee as a loan, until, only an amputee like Tuvia has the right to make this pun, "the amputee gets back on his feet."

Strictly speaking, it is not idealism that motivates Tuvia. It is something more: his sense that he has been designated a messenger of the Almighty. He had reason to think this happened once before. The way he sees it, his years of suffering now make him a messenger again to help those whom the world forgets. Why is he certain he had been a messenger once before and thus able to be one again?

Tuvia volunteered on two *kibbutzim.* The one where he lost his leg preferred him to leave the country. He was an embarrassment. But Tuvia wouldn't leave Israel, no matter what. It took him about five years of various struggles to get into tourism school; somehow, between cars, crutches and artificial limbs, which kept him in pain and then went bad altogether, he remained a tour guide for fifteen years.

Toward the beginning of his career, when he was low man on the totem pole, he was assigned to pick up tourists at the airport in Lod and bring them to the main office, whereupon an experienced guide would take over.

One day he picked up an American, ostentatiously wealthy, ostentatiously dressed and mannered. Even crude. Tuvia could not bring himself to be friendly, so he was formal. Halfway from Lod to Jerusalem, the tourist, a perceptive man, yelled, "Pull over!" Tuvia pulled over. The man barked, "You think I'm just a materialistic, superficial American tourist, don't you? Well, I've paid my dues!" He yanked up his sleeve to show Tuvia the number tattooed on his arm. Tuvia looked, almost went into shock, and before he knew what was happening the tourist was saying, "I lost my whole family . . . a brother in front of me, a brother in back of me. . . ." Tuvia's mind burned.

The man's face was florid. Tuvia calmed himself, saying simply: "Was your brother's name Shimon?" The red face turned white. "We're turning around, I'm not taking you to Jerusalem."

Tuvia made a U-turn and drove one and a half hours to the kibbutz where he had worked with the wiry carpenter, near Afula. The psychic noise in the car was palpable. Tuvia finally reached the kibbutz, then the carpenter shed, saw his former supervisor for the first time in ten years. Without introduction, he said simply: "Was your brother's name Reuven?"

His face turned white.

Tuvia returned to the taxi, unloaded it, told his American tourist, "Come, I am bringing you to your brother."

He led him to the carpenter shed, did not enter, did not want to infringe on the privacy of the moment—then made a U-turn and drove to the entrance of the kibbutz. He stopped, he cried.

Why?

When he had looked at the number tattooed on the tourist's arm, the last four digits were 7-4-0-2.

Rabbi Hillel Goldberg

Owing a Debt of Gratitude

Stand by the roads, and look, and ask for the ancient paths: Where is the good way? Walk in it and find rest for your soul.

Jeremiah 6:16

It was the summer of 1996. My husband Joe and I, along with two other couples, were on a journey "tracing our roots" through Eastern Europe. Right before our trip to Annykst in Lithuania, the hometown of my husband's grandmother, we were joined by four more tourists. One of them, Miriam Libenson, was a witty, cultured woman who could recite reams of Hebrew and Yiddish poetry. She had left Annykst as a very young woman, and now she was returning for a nostalgic visit with her two sons, Michael, a psychologist, and Eli, an educator from Israel.

Before their trip, Michael had done some Internet research on Annykst. He had learned the story of Max Curtis, an Annykster who, in 1941, at the age of eighteen, had fallen victim to the Nazis. He had been stripped naked and taken to a pit in town. There, together with several other young men, he was shot and left for dead. By a miracle he had survived and had come to the United States after the war.

Michael got in touch with Max, who was living in Cleveland. They soon became close friends, and the Libensons invited Max to join them on their trip "home." So Max Curtis was the fourth person who joined us as we headed for Annykst.

As we traveled, Max told us his wartime story. After being shot three times, he had regained consciousness and climbed with great difficulty to the top of the pit. There, he discovered, to his horror, that he was the sole survivor of the massacre. Grief-stricken, he went down to a nearby river that night to wash his wounds. He then lay in a cornfield to hide. As dawn broke, he saw people walking by, and he recognized Verutke, a local gentile girl. He instinctively decided to trust her, even though most of the townspeople had demonstrated allegiance to the Nazis. He revealed his presence to her. Verutke brought Max clothes, and for several days, brought him water and a small amount of bread. One cannot imagine the great risk she took, but Max, who had seen his entire family and all his friends and their families taken away and shot, realized the danger in which Verutke had placed herself. Her brother-in-law, with whom she lived, was an active member of the Nazi Youth Movement.

After several days, Verutke told him that she had confided in the local priest, who had suggested that Max come to the church. Not knowing what would await him there, and very frightened, he fled.

Max endured many hardships after that. He fought with the partisans and later was caught by the Germans, who thought at first that he might be a Russian spy. They were about to shoot him, but upon discovering that he was a Jew, they decided to put him in the ghetto instead.

Through all the ensuing years, Max had remembered Verutke. She was gentle, pretty and young, and knew that she had to do what was right no matter what the personal cost to her might be.

When we reached Annykst, we all went to the pit where Max had been shot. At the site stands a monument dedicated to the memory of the people who died there. It was a very emotional occasion, and we all cried bitterly as Max told us that he actually knew some of the people who had rounded him up and shot him. He had played the trumpet in a band with them. This betrayal was as painful as the bullet wounds. Max had a special request of Joe. Would he please make a *El Malei Rachamim* (the traditional Hebrew memorial prayer) for his friends? Joe was honored to fulfill the request, as Max supplied the Hebrew names of his friends, one at a time. Then suddenly, Max added one last person to the list: his own Hebrew name. "So much of me died along with them the day we were all shot," he wept. And so a *El Malei Rachamim* was then recited for Max, the sole survivor.

Regina, our resourceful guide, was deeply touched by Max's story. She was determined that he should find Verutke since it was clear that the enormous debt he owed her had been on Max's mind for over fifty-five years.

The next day, a Lithuanian author who has written a book on the relationship between Jews and gentiles in Lithuania during World War II, accompanied Max Curtis and the Libensons to Annykst in search of Verutke. Max, demonstrating his usual sensitivity to others, repeatedly requested that if they should find her, they not immediately reveal his identity to her. He feared that the revelation of what she had done might still put her in jeopardy. He also prepared himself for the fact that she might no longer be alive. He said that in that case, he would repay whatever debt he could to her heirs if he could find them.

Together they walked through the town interviewing elderly people who might know of Verutke. With the help of local residents, they eventually found her. She was living with her daughter and son-in-law.

When they visited Verutke, they found a poor, elderly woman. Some of her teeth had gone and had not been replaced. Her skin was leathery and wrinkled. She was most curious about her visitors.

After they had exchanged pleasantries, the Lithuanian author asked Verutke about the war years, and whether she remembered the boy of eighteen she had saved. Verutke nodded vigorously. Yes, she remembered him clearly, and she went on to relate the entire incident, referring to Max as "Motke."

Max, who had been listening to Verutke with deep emotion, knew that the time had come to speak up. He stepped forward and announced in a firm voice, "I am Motke!" For a moment or two, Verutke looked at him, shocked, disbelieving. Then she began to smile, and her eyes, undimmed by time, sparkled once more. Max took another step forward and in a moment they were embracing, stiffly and awkwardly at first, but then with warmth and tenderness.

Max was overcome with joy, and the weight of the years seemed to fall away. For Max, the old woman to whom he owed so much was once more the pretty, young, vibrant, protective girl who had come to his aid when he had most needed it. When their embrace ended, Max spoke gently to Verutke. His words had a simple eloquence. "Your acts of kindness and concern encouraged me to continue and succeed in life," he said. "I owe you my life, but more than that, you confirm my faith in humanity. I can never repay you enough."

Verutke looked at Max and nodded her silent understanding. As they parted, Max promised to stay in touch.

Since that emotional reunion, Max has sent Verutke a monthly stipend that more than doubles her meager pension. Max is still visibly moved as he tells of those days in the fields, and he is forever in awe of Verutke's simple, generous spirit.

Erica S. Goldman-Brodie

It Should Once Again See Light

Kindness, I've discovered, is everything in life.

Isaac Bashevis Singer

Several years ago, a physician from southern France contacted me. His granddaughter had taken ill with a disease that baffled the physicians there. He called after reading several of my articles on disorders of the autonomic nervous system. His granddaughter's symptoms seemed to match those I had described, and he asked me if I could help. I readily agreed, and for many months, I collaborated with the child's French physicians by telephone and by fax, directing their diagnostic testing. At last we came to a diagnosis, and I prescribed a course of therapy. During the next several weeks, the child made a seemingly miraculous recovery. Her grandparents expressed their heartfelt thanks and told me to let them know should I ever come to France.

In the summer of 1996, I was invited to speak at a large international scientific meeting that was held in Nice, France. I sent word to the physician I had helped years before. Upon my arrival at the hotel, I received a message to contact him. I called him, and we arranged a night to meet for dinner.

On the appointed day, we met and then drove north to his home in the beautiful southern French countryside. It was humbling to learn his home was older than the United States. During the drive he told me that his wife had metastatic breast cancer and was not well, but she insisted upon meeting me. When introduced to her, I saw that despite her severe illness, she was still a beautiful woman with a noble bearing.

I was thereafter treated to one of the most wonderful meals I have ever eaten, complemented by the most exquisite of wines. After dinner, we sat in a seventeenth-century salon, sipping cognac and chatting. Our conversation must have seemed odd to the young man and woman who served us because it came out in a free-flowing mixture of English, French and Spanish. After a time the woman asked, "My husband tells me you are Jewish, no?"

"Yes," I said, "I am a Jew."

They asked me to tell them about Judaism, especially the holidays. I did my best to explain and was astounded by how little they knew of Judaism. She seemed to be particularly interested in Hannukah.

Once I had finished answering her questions, she suddenly looked me in the eye and said, "I have something I want to give to you." She disappeared and returned several moments later with a package wrapped in cloth. She sat, her tired eyes looking into mine, and she began to speak slowly.

"When I was a little girl of eight years, during the Second World War, the authorities came to our village to round up all the Jews. My best friend at that time was a girl of my age named Jeanette. One morning when I came to play, I saw her family being forced at gunpoint into a truck. I ran home and told my mother what had happened and asked where Jeanette was going. 'Don't worry,' she said, 'Jeanette will be back soon.' I ran back to Jeanette's house only to find that she was gone and that the other villagers were looting her home of valuables, except for the Judaic items, which were thrown into the street. As I approached, I saw an item from her house lying in the dirt. I picked it up and recognized it as an object that Jeanette and her family would light around Christmas time. In my little girl's mind I said, 'I will take this home and keep it for Jeanette until she comes back,' but she and her family never returned."

She paused and took a slow sip of brandy. "Since that time I have kept it. I hid it from my parents and didn't tell a soul of its existence. Indeed, over the last fifty years the only person who knew of it was my husband. When I found out what really happened to the Jews, and how many of the people I knew had collaborated with the Nazis, I could not bear to look at it. Yet I kept it, hidden, waiting for something, although I wasn't sure what. Now I know what I was waiting for. It was you, a Jew, who helped cure our granddaughter, and it is to you I entrust this."

Her trembling hands set the package on my lap. I slowly unwrapped the cloth from around it. Inside was a menorah, but one unlike any I had seen before. Made of solid brass, it had eight cups for holding oil and wicks and a ninth cup centered above the others. It had a ring attached to the top, and the woman mentioned that she remembered that Jeanette's family would hang it in the hallway of their home. It looked quite old to me; later, several people told me that it is probably at least one hundred years old. As I held it and thought about what it represented, I began to cry. All I could manage to say was a garbled *"merci."* As I left, her last words to me were *"Il faudra voir la lumière encore une fois"*—it should once again see light.

I later learned that she died less than one month after our meeting. This Hannukah, the menorah will once again see light. And as I and my family light it, we will say a special prayer in honor of those whose memories it represents. We will not let its lights go out again.

Blair P. Grubb, M.D.

Reprinted by permission of Benita Epstein.

A Shabbat Evening in Warsaw

There is something better than modernity, which is eternity.

Solomon Schechter

Poland. To a Jew, even the word sounds cold and forbidding, conjuring up images of peril. It was here, in Poland, that the Nazi war machine placed its camps of death, interlaced in the snow by endless miles of train tracks like so many spider webs of murderous intent. Their names call to mind the horror of the Holocaust: Chelmno, Treblinka, Sobibor, Belzec, Plaszow, Maidanek, and above all—Auschwitz.

Twenty-four of us, ranging in age from thirty-five to eighty-two and representing every part of the Jewish spectrum, had traveled from all over the United States on a pilgrimage to Eastern Europe. We came for many reasons: to pay tribute to family members who had perished here; to link ourselves to unknown Jews who were members of our extended family; or to exorcise persistent demons that tormented us with vague nightmares and wordless dreams.

And now here we were in Warsaw. The city itself is completely new, having been totally leveled by bombs during the war and then rebuilt. There is nothing left of the city as it had been—and only bittersweet remnants of Jewish life.

Gathering for a Shabbat dinner at a small kosher restaurant, we joined together in song and lingered in the glow of the Shabbat candles. Outside, the rain came down in torrents.

After dinner, our guide led us through black, rain-drenched streets to the beautifully restored Nozyck Synagogue, the only synagogue functioning in Warsaw today. Thanks to the Ronald Lauder Foundation, which has undertaken the renaissance of Jewish life in Poland, the Nozyck sparkles under fresh paint and polished brass—but does not play host to many Jews. The older generation is all gone, and what is left of the younger generation has intermarried. Those who attend services do so in an attempt to revive memories of a life that was but is no more. There is a large and gaping hole where a vibrant Jewish life once flourished.

We were late in arriving, and the *shammas* (the caretaker) bowed to us as he let us in.

"So sorry! Too late," translated our guide. "The rabbi has gone home. No one is here."

Our disappointment was palpable. I felt tears come to my eyes. To have come this far and not to be able to attend a service in this city brought a sharp stab of regret.

"At least, please, can we look at the sanctuary?" one of the older members of the group asked. "We won't stay long, but if we could just go inside, it would mean so much to us."

The aged caretaker led us down a few shallow and uneven steps into the foyer of the synagogue, and then left. The lights were still on in the sanctuary, and we could see that it was indeed beautiful, with a high ceiling and golden-white walls. We felt a mixed sense of wonder and heartache, for here in this Jewish place, there was no living Jewish presence of any kind, except for us.

"We don't really need a rabbi, you know," whispered someone in the group. "We don't need a rabbi to lead us in the services."

"No?" someone else asked.

"Of course not. Anyone can lead the service. Why don't we just do it ourselves?"

With a few more words, and whispered assent among the members, it was quickly decided: We would hold our own Shabbat service. We would lead the prayers, sing the songs, and say *Kaddish.*

I went to the front of the sanctuary, and there in a stack was a jumble of prayerbooks. Thankfully, they were in Hebrew, and many of them were legible. As we distributed them, I felt some trepidation.

"I don't know if you will all feel comfortable with this," I said in a quiet voice. "I know that some of you come from traditional Jewish backgrounds. Would one of you please lead the service?"

No one volunteered. They shook their heads and politely declined.

"We don't know quite how to do it—but could you?" one of the people asked.

I didn't want to presume, but with the group's approval, we began.

"Bar'khu et Adonai ha-m'vorakh. . . ."

And so it was that half a century after the fall of the Warsaw ghetto, we held a service in the historic Nozyck Synagogue. It was quite an unorthodox minyan, after all: It did not have separate seating for men and women. Some of the men wore yarmulkes, and some did not. The service was led by a woman and two gentlemen who shared the prayerbooks between them. The cantor was also a woman. There was no great choir, and there were no throngs of Jews there to respond to the prayers. Instead, there was a small and devoted group who had come to this far place to pray, to remember, and to pay tribute to those who had lived and died here. It was a simple service of great beauty and purity.

Yet we were not alone. All around us were those who had prayed here in years past. I could feel their eyes as I turned the pages of the prayerbook. I could hear their voices in my mind as I mouthed the ancient words of praise to God. Even though there were only two dozen of us in that sanctuary, the room seemed filled with the presence of hundreds, even thousands, of those who had come before us. Jewish life was rekindled for a moment, and as we all recited the *Kaddish* prayer, the demons were put to rest and the dreams were held at bay—for a little while. It was a Shabbat evening I will remember for the rest of my life.

When we left the synagogue afterward, the rain had stopped and there was a new moon.

Palli Moskovitz

Shoes and Hair

The least pain in our little finger gives us more concern and uneasiness than the destruction of millions of our fellow-beings.

William Hazlitt

I had read all the books. I had seen all the movies. I had been to all the memorial programs. I had lit our Yom *HaShoah* candle every year with my family. I had walked through the eerie halls of the Holocaust Museum and had cried with my sisters at *Yad Vashem.* So what aspect of this trip would be different? What would affect me in a way I had never been affected? What experience would bring out emotions I had never felt before?

It wasn't the brutal pictures. It wasn't having Polish teenagers spit on us as we stood in the train station. And it wasn't even having young children greet us on the streets with the "Heil Hitler" salute. It was actually something seemingly simplistic. Shoes . . . and hair. It was seeing over two million pairs of shoes and tons of hair on display in the barracks of Majdanek and Auschwitz. Shoes that had belonged to more than one million people. People just like me—some younger, some older. And hair that had once been beautiful and alive. Long, flowing hair that young girls had brushed and fussed over, just as I do every morning. Yet they were not like my shoes. For they had walked paths I had never walked. And it was not like my hair. For it had been cut not by beauticians, but by barbarians—not to beautify, but rather to humiliate and dehumanize.

When I walked into the first barrack at Majdanek and saw the floors covered with cages of shoes, the sheer numbers overwhelmed me. As I covered my mouth with my hand, I felt myself gasp. Then I walked into the next barrack and there were more shoes—over eight hundred thousand pairs altogether—on display in front of my eyes. Children's shoes thrown together with adults' shoes. As I reached out to touch them, some of the dirt came off on my hand. I felt the leather, I smelled the leather and the strong scent that overtook the room.

On the following day, we were in Auschwitz, and I entered another room displaying shoes. I had seen so many shoes at Majdanek that I couldn't imagine there being any more. But here there were more—many more. This time they were behind glass walls, so I could not touch them. Like the shoes at Majdanek, they were filthy and worn. All of these shoes had been lived in, and each pair told the story of a different life once lived. The graceful sandal of a woman who stayed at home to raise her children. The heavy boots of a working-class man lying on top of the dress shoes that another man wore to his office. The play shoes of a child who ran in the park. In life, these people were all unique. The young were different from the old. Their shoes told their stories—not only of life before the war, but also of the long, hard walk from the train station in the center of town to Majdanek or of the death march from Auschwitz to Birkenau.

As I continued on, in Auschwitz I came to a barrack where on one side of the room was a glass container filled with hair. It all looked the same. We couldn't see the blond, the red, the curly, the silky. Only the dark, dull, ash-gray of hair discolored by gas. Someone read a poem that touched all of us. It spoke the words of a lone strand of hair. A strand of hair crying out to be recognized as something once alive, once adorning the head of a beautiful eighteen-year-old girl. But the hair in that glass case had no life, it had no shine, no texture, no style. It was dead, just like the victims from whose heads it was savagely cut.

For the next few days, whenever I hugged someone who was crying or just walked with my arm around someone, I would feel the person's hair. I would put my fingers through it and feel its texture. I would notice its color and its shine. It was such a contrast to the dull dead hair I saw in that glass case.

How ironic, it seemed to me, that these victims' shoes—inanimate, impersonal possessions—could now tell us more about their lives than their own hair could. Though it was once living, once a part of the people whose heads it adorned, it can no longer tell us anything about the stories of their lives. It tells only the stories of their deaths. It speaks not of the memory of lives once lived, but only of the memory of gas chambers.

Every morning, before I leave for school, I spend an hour straightening my hair and a good twenty minutes looking for the shoes that match my outfit. Is that wrong? Should my experiences in Poland make me ashamed to focus on such things anymore? No, that is not the lesson of The March. I must go on and live my life. But I know that I will never be the same, and that the memories of those cages of shoes and cases of hair will stay with me for the rest of my life. That is the lesson of the March of the Living. That the living should remember the dead and live the lives they never were allowed to live.

Arielle Greenbaum

The Man Who Waited Forty-Five Years to Blow His Shofar

Once you have lived a moment at the Western Wall, you never go away.

Rabbi Abraham Joshua Heschel

At the end of World War II, after fighting the Germans for three years, Yasha returned home to Kiev. When he arrived there, he learned that the Germans had murdered all of his family. He went to his old house and found strangers living there. He searched the neighborhood seeking someone who could tell him anything about his family. Finally, he found a neighbor who told him that just before the Germans had rounded up all the Jews, Yasha's father had come to him and given him something for Yasha. The neighbor took him inside his house, down into the cellar. Yasha felt tears in his eyes. His father must have known that the Germans were going to kill all the Jews. What was it that he wanted Yasha to have?

The neighbor pulled out something from underneath a pile of boxes. It was a shofar, his father's shofar. The neighbor handed it to him and said: "Your father told me that you were to blow this when the Germans have been defeated and the Jews were safe and free."

In the year that followed, Yasha found a job and an apartment. A few thousand Jews who had escaped the German murderers or, like him, had been in the army, returned to Kiev. Yasha tried to determine when he should blow the shofar. The Germans had murdered thirty-five thousand Jews from Kiev in a ravine outside the city called Babi Yar. Yasha decided that on the anniversary of the two days when the slaughter was carried out, he would go to Babi Yar. Maybe he would even blow the shofar there.

It seems as though dozens of other Jews also had the same idea. When Yasha arrived at Babi Yar, people were there saying the *Kaddish.* Before he could blow his shofar, the Russian police suddenly appeared and told the people that they had to go home. They had no right to conduct a demonstration or a prayer service at this place. The people protested and the policemen beat several of them. Yasha decided that even if the Germans had been defeated, the Jews were still not safe or free. He could not blow the shofar.

Years went by. Many Jews wanted to build a monument at Babi Yar to commemorate the thousands of Jews who had been murdered there. The Russian government refused to allow them to do that. Finally, the government decided that it would build the monument. When it was finished, Yasha took his shofar and went to Babi Yar. He looked at the monument. It mentioned the different nationalities of the people who were killed there. It did not mention the Jews, though over half of those who died were Jewish. Yasha decided that he could not blow the shofar, for although the Jews were safe in Russia, they were not free to be Jews.

Then, in 1967, Israel won the Six-Day War. The Russian

government supported the Arabs and every day attacked Israel in the newspapers and on the radio. Yasha had become the manager of a large factory. Together with a number of other factory managers, Yasha was called to the mayor's office and told to sign a statement for the newspapers attacking Israel. He refused. In a few weeks, he was sent to another job, which was much harder and paid less. Yasha decided that the Jews would never be free in Russia. So he applied for a visa to go to Israel. It was refused, and a little later he lost his job. However, each year he applied again.

At long last, in the summer of 1973, Yasha received his visa. But his wife refused to go to Israel with him. She said, "It is too dangerous to live in Israel." Yasha pleaded with her, but she preferred the peace and safety of Kiev to the risk of living in a Jewish State.

So Yasha decided to go himself and send for her later. He left as soon as he could, arriving in Israel with only two suitcases and his father's shofar. It was just after Rosh Hashanah, so Yasha decided that he would wait until the end of Yom Kippur to blow his father's shofar. Yom Kippur afternoon, while he was in the synagogue praying, he suddenly noticed that all of the young men were leaving. A little later he heard the sound of air-raid sirens. The Arabs had attacked Israel in the middle of the holiest day of the year.

"Oy," said Yasha, "now that the Jews in the Land of Israel are free, they are not safe. I still can't blow my father's shofar."

After weeks of very difficult fighting, Israel defeated the Arab armies that had attacked it and the land was safe. But the Yom Kippur War had frightened Yasha's wife even more and for a few more years she refused to join him. When she was finally ready to move, the government stopped letting Jews leave Russia.

More years passed. Then Mr. Gorbachev came to power and he permitted Jews to go to Israel. Because a lot of Russian people blamed Jews for their troubles, many Jews became afraid to remain in Russia. Some came to America, but most went to Israel. Yasha's wife now realized that the risk of living in Israel was much less than the risk of living in Russia. In 1990, two hundred thousand Jews came to Israel. One of them was Yasha's wife.

On Rosh Hashanah in 1990, forty-five years after he had returned home and been given his father's shofar, Yasha was at last able to fulfill his father's last request. Now, indeed, the Germans had been defeated and the Jews were both free and safe in the Land of Israel. Yasha blew the shofar. It was the happiest moment of his life.

Rabbi Allen S. Maller

7

INSIGHTS AND LESSONS

Who is a wise person? One who learns from all people.

Talmud

Awakening

Listen and you will learn.

Shlomo Ibn Gabirol

There were so many admissions that night that I had begun to lose count—and my temper. A seasoned intern, I had learned well the art of the quick, efficient work-up. Short-cutting had become a way of life. Morning was coming and, with it, my day off. All I wanted was to be done. My beeper sounded. I answered it. I heard the tired voice of my resident say, "Another hit, some ninety-year-old 'gomer' with cancer." Swearing under my breath, I headed to the room. An elderly man sat quietly in his bed. Acting put upon, I abruptly launched into my programmed litany of questions, not really expecting much in the way of answers. To my surprise, his voice was clear and full, and his answers were articulate and concise. In the midst of my memorized review of systems, I asked if he had ever lived or worked outside the country.

"Yes," he replied. "I lived in Europe for seven years after the war." Surprised by his answer, I inquired if he had been a soldier there.

"No," he said. "I was a lawyer. I was one of the prosecuting attorneys at the Nuremberg trials."

My pen hit the floor. I blinked.

"The Nuremberg trials?" He nodded, stating that he later remained in Europe to help rebuild the German legal system

Right, I thought to myself, *some old man's delusion.* My beeper went off twice. I finished the examination quickly, hurried off to morning sign-out and handed over the beeper.

Officially free, I started out the door but suddenly paused, remembering the old man, his voice, his eyes. I walked over to the phone and called my brother, a law student, who was taking a course on legal history. I asked him if the man's name appeared in any of his books. After a few minutes, his voice returned.

"Actually, it says here that he was one of the prosecution's leading attorneys at the Nuremberg trials." I don't remember making my way back to his room, but I know I felt humbled, small and insignificant. I knocked. When he bid me enter, I sat in the very seat I had occupied a short time before and quietly said, "Sir, if you would not mind, I am off-duty now and would very much like to hear about Nuremberg and what you did there. And I apologize for having been so curt with you previously." He smiled, staring at me.

"No, I don't mind." Slowly, with great effort at times, he told me of the immense wreckage of Europe, the untold human suffering of the war. He spoke of the camps, those immense factories of death, the sight of the piles of bodies that made him retch. The trials, the bargaining, the punishments. He said that the war criminals themselves had been a sorry-looking bunch. Aside from the rude awakening of having lost the war, they could not quite understand the significance of the court's quiet and determined justice or of the prosecution's hard work and thorough attention to detail. The Nazis had never done things that way. So moved had he been by the suffering he encountered there that he had stayed on to help build a system of laws that would prevent such atrocities from happening again. Like a child I sat, silent, drinking in every word. This was history before me. Four hours passed. I thanked him and shook his hand, and went home to sleep.

The next morning began early, and as usual I was busy. It was late before I could return to see the old man. When I did, his room was empty. He had died during the night.

I walked outside into the evening air and caught the smell of the spring flowers. I thought of the man and felt despair mixed with joy. Suddenly my life seemed richer and more meaningful, my patients more complex and mysterious than before. I realized that the beauty and horror of this world were mixed in a way that is sometimes beyond understanding. The man's effect on me did not end there. Despite the grueling call schedule, the overwhelming workload and the emotional stress of internship, something had changed within me. I began to notice colors, shapes and smells that added magic to everyday life. I learned that the gray-haired patients that I had once called "gomers" were people with stories to tell and things to teach. After nearly two decades I still look to the night, remember that man, and reflect on the chance and privilege we have to share in the lives of others, if only we take the time to listen.

Blair P. Grubb, M.D.

Reprinted by permission of Benita Epstein.

The Two Eyes

By emphasizing that which is good in people and in the world, and by bringing the positive to the fore, the evil is superseded by the good, until it eventually disappears.

Rabbi Menachem Shneerson

My son, one of triplets, was playing with his brothers in their room a few days before the Jewish Holiday of Scholars, *Lag B'Omer.* The triplets were almost eight years old at the time. They had made bows and arrows out of twigs for *Lag B'Omer,* and I decided to let them play with them a few minutes before getting them into bed.

One of the boys was showing his brothers how to shoot the bow in a safe manner, with the bow pointing downward. As he was about to demonstrate this, one of the other boys banged into him, lifting his arm up and causing him to shoot the arrow. The arrow flew across the room at the very moment that the third boy, Elishama, happened to turn around to face his brothers. The arrow struck him in the eye.

Filled with horror at this freak accident, we rushed

Elishama to the hospital. He was immediately sent into emergency surgery to try to save his eye. But when the surgery was over and the surgeon came to tell us the news, it was not good. Elishama's vision in his left eye was destroyed.

The next day, as Elishama was recovering from surgery, he asked me from his hospital bed, "What am I going to do now?"

I had been thinking carefully about what I could tell him, how I could comfort him.

I took his hand and said to him very gently, "God created everyone with two eyes—one to see the world with a good eye and one to see the world with a bad eye. Right now God has given you the privilege to be able to see the world with only a good eye."

Elishama considered this for a moment. Then he said, "Boy, I'm sure glad the arrow didn't hit my other eye!"

Leah Golomb

My Five-Year-Old Spiritual Teacher

Out of the mouths of babes you have founded strength. . . .

Psalm 8:2

Most mornings I have trouble getting out of bed. It's an old bad habit. I used to lie awake and brood. I've progressed to the point where I now lie awake and meditate. It's very joyful, actually. But it still doesn't help me get out of bed.

Often my son, Lior, wakes up during my morning inertia. His general routine is to climb out of his bed (he's learned better than to expect a parent to attend to him at such an early hour) and mount the stairs to the third floor where our bedroom is. He peeks into the doorway expectantly. I lift up my head. "Hey Lior," I whisper. "Come to Mommy." He bounds over and then, with unsuppressible exuberance, he bursts out, "Mommy, Mommy!" I lift him up and tuck him under the covers, feeling the blessing of this very special soul cuddled beside me. My cheeks are soon soaking wet. "I love kisses," he whispers with serious big brown eyes.

"Lior, let's not wake up Daddy. Let's go downstairs."

Lior slides out from under the covers. I follow him, grabbing my early-morning stretched-out sweater and my tattered Israeli slippers from ten years ago.

He leads the way with a purposeful step, down two flights of stairs to the front room. He grabs two prayer-books from the shelf and hands me one. We cuddle under Grandma's crocheted blanket.

Lior's *davening* is mesmerizing. His little body naturally moves in the way of the ancient *zaydes*. His eyes are half shut. A serious look is on his face. He vocalizes sounds reminiscent of *Kabbalat Shabbat,* Friday night *z'mirot, Shabbos* morning *P'sukei D'zimra,* and various Yiddish melodies. His voice is clear and very strong.

I remember the winter after Lior was diagnosed. The entire family participated in a statewide conference for families with young children in early-intervention programs. Another participant approached me after a workshop we had both attended, with great earnestness on her face. "I heard what you said in there. You're so lucky. You have a child with Down's syndrome. He's a real person. My young daughter may someday be able to turn over herself, but that's all I can hope for. Your son is going to have a life."

I think about that woman a lot. I am lucky. I suppose most people don't think so. But when I sit beside Lior at sunrise and he pours his heart out to God, using every technique four years of speech therapy have given him, raising his little arm to emphasize his earnestness, I feel deeply, deeply blessed.

I'm not sure why he loves to pray so much. Most typical kids his age would much rather be playing with Tinkertoys. But the big question Lior asks every morning is, "Is it *Shabbos?*" And when the answer is, "Yes, Lior, tonight is *Shabbos,* and tomorrow we go to *shul,*" he jumps up and down with unbounded joy and shouts, "Yay, *Shabbos!*"

His sense of time reflects a deep understanding of the process of Jewish time. There's "everyday," profane time, and then there's *Shabbos,* holy time. Each day of the week brings us that much closer to holy time, to *Shabbos.* I think Lior's weekday *davening* is a way of borrowing from *Shabbos*'s holiness. It helps keep him on track. Great Jewish philosophers have written deep and powerful essays on this phenomenon. Lior gets it naturally.

My family has the blessing of living in a neighborhood that houses several wonderful *davening* communities. Our community, Minyan Dorshei Derech, is part of the Germantown Jewish Center. For Lior it is a second home.

There are those Saturday mornings when I admit I would love to lie in bed—it's just too much trouble to get four children out to *shul,* I'm tired from the previous week's chemotherapy, there's a lot of great excuses. But most of the time I can't. I get there on time because I don't want to miss *davening* with Lior. My husband feels the same way. We're responsible for providing Lior with this weekly opportunity to do what he loves to do best and to be where he loves to be most in the whole world.

Lior's relationship to Dorshei Derech is really quite amazing. He is a very important and vibrant member of the community, even though he's only five and a half years old. When he enters the room he nods to people, gets his *siddur,* puts on his *Tallis* specially made for him by several women in the neighborhood and takes his regular seat in the front. He shyly looks around, out of the corners of his eyes, and checks out if his beloved regulars are sitting in their usual spots. He then has me help him find the correct page, according to where my *siddur* is turned, and begins to quietly *daven.* Periodically, the group breaks out in song. Lior listens for a minute. And then he closes his eyes, and with that same serious look on his face I saw during our private weekday *davening,* he lets go his voice.

Lior's *davening* has a profound effect on the community. I used to think people were so aware of him because they loved him so much. I now realize it's a much deeper relationship than that. Lior's *Kavannah* serves as an inspiration to every adult in that room. When he lifts his voice with unwavering clarity, "Ya, ya, ya," and puts it inside the cacophony of voices around him, he gives everyone in the room permission to do the same. People measure where they are in their inner prayer experience against the authenticity of his.

The Torah service is a very important time for Lior. He deeply loves the Torah. He needs to show this love in very physical ways. And so each week Lior helps to open the ark. And then, upon seeing the Torah sitting inside, he stands on his very tiptoes and gives the Torah a huge hug and kiss. He smiles to himself. "Torah," I hear him murmur to himself, "Torah." I am in awe of such a moment of *Kedusha,* of pure holiness. What Lior is experiencing at that moment is a true connection with the Divine.

Lior then proceeds to walk through the entire congregation, shaking everyone's hand. He greets his special adult friends at this time. "Hi, Mitch," he whispers. "Michael, Good *Shabbos.*" A collective smile flows from one end of the room to the other as Lior continues on his rotation. He manages to connect with every single member of his prayer community.

"Can you imagine what his bar mitzvah is going to be like?" I hear someone whisper. I feel a surprisingly strong emotional reaction to that statement. I pray that God will grant me the blessing to live to be part of that day. I also wonder about what it will be like. Will Lior continue to be able to create a place for himself in this community? Will his charming, childlike innocence be able to evolve into more mature forms of expression?

And then I hear our communal introductions at the end of the service. It's Lior's turn. "Lior Liebling," he says clearly (except for the *l*'s, which still give him trouble). And, I think, he's doing just fine. He's figuring it out himself. It's my job to sit back and trust him. I don't know where he's going with all this. But our communal tradition is powerful enough to guide him. And he's wise enough to listen.

Lior has opened up so many people to the multidimensionality of human nature. What does it mean that he is "retarded"? He speaks to God in a way that eludes most of us. He is one of my most important spiritual teachers.

And he gives great kisses.

Rabbi Devora Bartnoff

The Presence of God

A person should always be flexible like a reed, and not rigid like a cedar.

Talmud, Tractate Taanit

My grandfather and I had many discussions about the teachings and principles of Judaism, but I can remember only one disagreement. It had to do with the nature of the *minyan.* The idea of the *minyan* is central to the spiritual life of Jewish people. When anyone can pray at any time, before an official prayer service can be held there must be at least ten men present. This group of ten men is called a *minyan.*

"Why, Grandpa?" I asked, puzzled. Patiently he explained the law to me. It is believed that whenever ten adult men are gathered together in the name of God, God Himself is actually present in the room with them. "Immanent," my grandfather said. Any room then became consecrated ground, a holy place where the sacraments of the religion could be performed. After five thousand years of persecution and homelessness, nothing could be taken for granted. Holy ground had to be portable.

I was fascinated by this. My grandfather told me that this law was so important that often men were called from their homes to come to the synagogue because there were fewer than ten men present to pray for the dead, inscribe a baby into the book of life, or conduct one of the many rituals that acknowledged that life is holy and bound people to God. Once or twice in Prussia, he had even gone out into the streets and collared a passing Jew, a total stranger, to complete the circle of ten. One did not refuse such an invitation, said my grandfather. It was considered to be a duty.

"But why only men, Grandpa?" I asked. He hesitated. "The law says ten men," he responded slowly. I waited for a further explanation, but he said nothing.

"Isn't God present when ten women gather together?" I asked. Thinking back on it, I imagine this to have been a difficult moment for him.

"The law says nothing about this, Neshume-le. It has always been ten men, since the beginning." I was astounded. "If something is old, does it have to be true?"

"Certainly not," he responded.

"Well, then I think that God is there in the room when ten women gather, too," I stated flatly.

He nodded. "This is not what the law says," he told me.

We had never disagreed about anything before and I was shaken, but my grandfather seemed quite comfortable with the distance between our beliefs. We never discussed the matter again, and I thought that he had forgotten it. A few years later, he became very sick. In the months before he died, I was allowed to visit with him only briefly so as not to tire him. I was almost seven years old and terribly proud of my reading, and so I would read to him from one of his books or we would simply sit quietly together. Sometimes I would hold his hand while he slept. Once after a nap he opened his eyes and looked at me lovingly for a long while. "You are a *minyan,* all by yourself, Neshume-le," he told me.

Rachel Naomi Remen, M.D.

Diamonds Polished Here

Life will either grind you down or polish you up, and which it does is your choice.

Roger Walsh

Although I gave up my rabbinic pulpit in 1959 to practice psychiatry, the lore, wisdom and ethical beliefs that imbue my family mythology and formed my growing years have never left me.

As a psychiatrist, I specialize in treating addiction. Twenty-five years ago I founded The Gateway Rehabilitation System in Pittsburgh. I am often asked whether any particular treatment modality is employed at Gateway. I always answer that our strength lies in our belief in the inherent goodness of every client. This quality is not always easy to recognize in a person who has led a destructive lifestyle for decades, someone whose use of alcohol or drugs has caused great suffering for others. But in all my years of treating illnesses of the heart and soul, this belief has never failed me; each individual's integrity is always there, lurking right beneath the surface, eager to emerge.

A story occurs to me of a man named Avi. I first met him while I was in Tel Aviv speaking before a group of ex-convicts in recovery who were coming into our Israeli rehabilitation program, a sister home to Gateway. When I began to speak of self-esteem, this man interrupted me. "How can you talk to us of this? I've been a thief since I was eight. When I'm out of prison I can't find work, and my family doesn't want to see me."

I stopped him and asked if he'd passed by a jewelry store lately. "Consider the diamonds in the window," I said. "Try and think what they look like when they come out of the mine—lumps of dirty stone. It takes a person who understands the diamond to take the shapeless mound and bring out its intrinsic beauty. That's what we do here; we look for the diamond in everyone. We help the soul's beauty come to the surface, we polish it until it gleams." I looked at Avi, all disheveled and hunched over, nearly hiding in his seat, and said, "You're like that dirt-covered stone, and our business is to find the diamond within and polish it until it glows."

Two years passed. Avi had graduated from the treatment center, and when the following event took place he had already completed his stay in the halfway house and was integrated into the community, working in construction. One day Annette, who manages the halfway house, received a call from a family whose elderly matriarch had died. They wanted to donate her furniture to the halfway house. Annette called Avi and asked him to pick up the furniture, which he willingly agreed to do. When he went to pick it up, he saw that it wasn't worth saving but not wanting to insult the family, he hauled it anyway.

While Avi was laboring to carry the shabby sofa up the stairs to the halfway house, an envelope fell from the cushions. After getting the couch inside, Avi retrieved the envelope, in which he found five thousand shekels (about seventeen hundred dollars). Now Avi, remember, had served time in prison for burglary. When he was doing drugs he would have broken into a home for twenty dollars. But now Avi called Annette and told her about the envelope. Annette said it must be reported to the family.

The family was so gratified by Annette's and Avi's honesty that they told her to keep the money for the halfway house. As a result, the halfway house was able to buy one more bed and provide room for one more guest, creating another opportunity for recovery. And Avi wasn't a crook anymore.

Avi relayed this story to me in a letter. He wrote, "When I used drugs I would get a high for a very short time, and when the high wore off I felt terrible, worse than before. It's been three months since I found that money and every time I think of what I did, I feel good all over again. How different a feeling than a temporary fix."

Another year went by and I returned to that halfway house where Avi's good deed had set off a chain of events, which led to, among other things, an extra bed. There was a sign hanging above the entry. It read: DIAMONDS POLISHED HERE.

Rabbi Abraham J. Twerski, M.D.

Lost and Found

Teach us to number our days that we may acquire a heart of wisdom.

Psalm 90:12

This past summer for the third year in a row, I was the camp "Mom" at Camp Moshava in Wild Rose, Wisconsin. It's a job I love. I get to see things in the kids who go there that their parents generally don't. The reason for this is that children, once they are away from home, have the opportunity to reinvent themselves. They can present themselves to others any way they want. And most often, I've found, the best they have to offer comes out. As parents, we work hard to give our kids what they need to make it on their own without us. Occasionally, we get a little glimpse that we have been successful.

One of the boys at camp this summer was the kind of kid who makes you wonder if anything you say penetrates. He spent a lot of his time being brash and swaggering, impressing his friends. He was at the age where it's considered cool to act self-assured, a little obnoxious, and to court trouble. It's not that he had ever done anything seriously bad, but the staff at camp tended to keep a special eye on him. He was very good friends with another boy, a quieter type, more of a follower. The two of them lived in different cities and saw each other at camp each summer.

Partly because of this one young man's reputation, I happened to be close by these two on one of the trips out of camp. We were in a crowded and popular arcade. The boys had been playing the games, taking turns cheering each other on as others watched. I noticed how easily they both blended into the crowd. The clothes they wore were unremarkable—typical shorts and T-shirts. They both wore baseball caps, like most of the other boys there in rural Wisconsin.

What happened next was so quick, I almost couldn't be sure of what I'd seen. A child, about ten, there with his father, reached into his back pocket for something. As he pulled his hand out, a twenty-dollar bill floated to the floor. Just as quickly, one of these two Moshava boys—the quieter one—picked it up and put it into his own pocket. I was so shocked that, for a moment, I couldn't think how to react. In any case, I was far enough away and the room was so crowded that by the time I did move, the child and his father had moved away, unaware of their loss.

But I wasn't the only one who noticed. The boy's friend—the one we staff members thought we had to keep an eye on—had also seen. Without a word, he reached into his own pocket, took out a twenty and ran after the child and his father. I watched as he stopped them and handed over the money. I couldn't hear the exchange, but from the pleased expression on the face of the father and the relief on the face of his son, I could imagine what was being said.

I moved over to where our two campers were playing, expecting to overhear an animated conversation. But there was none. The two of them just continued playing as if nothing had happened. The only difference was that now, both of them were quiet.

I thought about what had happened on the long bus ride home. I wasn't sure how to or even if I should intervene. Being a camp "Mom" is tricky. I would know what to say to my own child if she were either of the players in this scenario, but I didn't know these boys well. And I wanted them both to understand the ramifications of what had transpired. I wanted to understand, also.

As we reached camp, I asked the boy who had given his own money to the child at the arcade to wait for me a moment when he got off the bus. The others in his group kind of nudged him and said good-naturedly, "Okay, what did you do now?" It seemed the expected thing to say.

"I saw what happened at the arcade," I said when we were alone. He said nothing.

"Why did you do it? Give your own money to that little boy? You weren't responsible for making up to him what your friend did."

He looked at me anxiously. "Of course I was!" He said it almost angrily.

I was surprised by his reaction. He was quiet for a long moment. Then he said, "Look, don't do anything to my friend. Just let me handle it, okay?"

I thought about his request for a minute. I decided he'd earned the right to try to handle it. I asked him to tell me later what happened.

That evening as the boys were on their way back to their cabins, I heard a knock at my door. It was my young hero.

"I want to tell you something," he said. "You wanted to know why I did what I did? I saw someone else do almost the same thing once. It was my grandfather, and it was in his tobacco store in Brooklyn. I used to visit him there.

One day, a customer came into the store. He bought something and when he reached into his pocket to pay, he dropped some money on the floor. A kid picked it up and put it into his own pocket."

He stopped and seemed to be thinking hard. I waited for him to continue. "My grandfather finished waiting on the man and waited for him to get almost to the door. Then he called out, 'Oh Mister, did you lose something?' My grandfather had reached into the cash register and taken out a bill. But he pretended to come around the counter, bend over and pick it up off the floor. The man thanked my grandfather and left."

There was a long pause before my friend said, "I was the kid who put the money in his pocket."

"What happened next?" I asked.

"My grandfather didn't say anything at all to me. He didn't tell me to put the money in the cash register or give it to him. I felt awful. The rest of the day, he didn't speak to me except if I asked him something. Finally, I put it back. As we were closing up, I told him I was sorry. I knew it was wrong. I don't know why I did it. It just seemed okay to do at that moment. And the man dropped it. It wasn't as if I stole it or anything. But my grandfather just shook his head.

"That night, I was still feeling terrible. We went out for a soda and my grandfather told me something. He said other people could get away with that kind of thing but not me. He expected more from me because he knew what kind of person I am."

A lot of thoughts ran through my mind as I listened. We often try to give kids positive reinforcement for good behavior as opposed to punishing them for bad behavior. It's really true that children rise—or sink—to the level of expectation. Here was a child who had been identified, and he probably knew it, as someone we had to watch.

Well, I still felt we should watch him, but now it was for other reasons.

"Did you tell your friend this?" I asked.

"Not yet," he answered. "But I will." He seemed sad, reluctant.

"Your grandfather is going to be pretty proud of you when you tell him. He'll know how much you love him and that you really took to heart what he told you!" I was trying to cheer him up.

"Yeah, that'd be great, wouldn't it?" the boy said glumly. "But I can't. He died last year, suddenly, right after my bar mitzvah."

I took a breath, looking at this child in front of me. I wanted to convey what I felt to him, wanted him to know just exactly how his stature had changed. I was thinking how I could convey to him that the connection he had with his grandfather was forever and that he was living his grandfather's example. Most of all, I guess I just wanted him to understand that he had done something of merit, had learned something of value, and could have a positive effect on someone else. I thought if I could just find the right words, he would be comforted. Then they came to me:

"Your grandfather died *after* your bar mitzvah?" I asked. "Well, then he got to see what I saw today—a boy, one who loved his grandpa a lot, become a man."

Marsha Arons

KUDZU

SMITE MINE
ENEMIES, LORD!

SMITE MY WORST
ENEMY WITH A
PLAGUE OF *LOCUSTS!*

LET ME
REPHRASE
THAT!
8/11
© 1995 Creators Syndicate, Inc.

To an Audience Yet Unborn

Much have I learned from my teachers, more from my colleagues, but most from my students.

Talmud

There is a delightful story about a Rosh Yeshiva, the head of a rabbinical seminary. His name was Rabbi Shlomo Heiman, the first dean of Yeshiva Torah Voda'ath, who had a most amazing way of teaching his students. Unlike the dry lectures given by many brilliant scholars, he would shout with almost breathless rapture as he explained the Talmud and its commentaries. His eyes would sparkle, and his arms would wave as he expounded Talmudic theory. After the class, he would almost collapse from the exertion.

On one particular snowy day back in the early 1940s, only four boys came to class. Nevertheless, Rabbi Heiman delivered his lecture as if the room was packed with hundreds of students. Beads of sweat rolled down his face as he passionately argued points of law to the incredulous four boys. As he paused to catch his breath, one of the boys mustered his courage and beseeched the Torah Giant.

"Rebbe, please—there are only four of us."

The rabbi's eyes widened. "You think I'm giving this class for four boys? I am giving this class to hundreds of boys. I'm giving this class to you, your students, their students and their students!"

Rabbi Mordecai Kamenetzky
Adapted by permission from Parsha Parables
©1998 Bentch Press

Here I Am

Like the grasses showing tender faces to each other, thus should we do, for this was the wish of the Grandfathers of the world.

Black Elk

There were two special synagogues in my childhood. Congregation Beth El was a huge synagogue in my hometown of Cherry Hill, New Jersey. Another Beth El in Gloucester, New Jersey, was as tiny as the other was large. It was there that I met Cantor Charles Goldhirsh. Wanting to increase my Jewish knowledge and ritual skills, I asked Cantor Goldhirsh to be my teacher. "Okay," he said in his heavily accented voice, "I'll teach you. But if you start, you have to finish."

So Cantor Goldhirsh and I began our relationship as teacher and student. It turned out that Cantor Goldhirsh was also a member of my other Beth El, so we attended services and studied together. He taught me to lead the prayers and to chant the melodies for weekdays and *Shabbat.* A fast friendship soon developed between us.

At the same time, my relationship with my beloved rabbi, Howard Kahn, deepened as well. In my early twenties, because of Rabbi Kahn's influence, I decided to study for the rabbinate. When Cantor Goldhirsh said to me, "If you start, you have to finish," neither of us knew how far I would eventually take my studies.

I think of Cantor Goldhirsh every Rosh Hashanah. Not only was it when I met him, but it was also when I lost my teacher and friend. Cantor Goldhirsh died between Rosh Hashanah and Yom Kippur while I was in rabbinical school. In his eulogy, Rabbi Kahn mentioned the cantor's profound influence on a young rabbinical student. And even though Cantor Goldhirsh did not live to see me ordained, we did get to share the pulpit together as student rabbi and cantor in a Jewish home for the aged in Philadelphia. He knew I was going to finish what I—we—had started.

Many years later, I decided to write about him for the Rosh Hashanah issue of the bulletin published by the synagogue I serve as rabbi. My congregants had heard me speak of Rabbi Kahn, but I wanted them to know about the other special friend and teacher in my life. So I reminisced and wrote about Cantor Goldhirsh, never imagining the role he was about to play in my life that year.

It began when the cantor of my synagogue had a medical procedure before the High Holidays. He expected to be ready for the holidays, but with less than a week to go before Rosh Hashanah, our cantor announced that he would not be able to sing on Rosh Hashanah or Yom Kippur.

All of a sudden, we were plunged into turmoil. What should we do? Try to bring a substitute at the last minute? Let the rabbi (me!) take over for him? Just in case, I began to prepare to substitute for the cantor.

Many of the prayers were simple enough, but others

really needed a cantorial setting. Perhaps the most important of these was a prayer called *Hineni. Hineni* is the very first prayer the cantor sings after taking over the leading of the service. It is a powerful and dramatic prayer in which the cantor begs God to accept his prayers on behalf of the congregation, despite the fact that his human failings make him unequal to the enormous task of praying on behalf of so many other persons. As one of the highlights of the holiday liturgy, *Hineni* could not simply be chanted. *Hineni* had to be sung the way a real cantor would sing it. *No problem,* I thought. *I'll learn it from a tape.*

I went to my set of prayer tapes. No *Hineni.* I went to the tapes from cantorial class in rabbinical school. No *Hineni.* Of course not. Rabbis might have to help out leading the prayers from time to time, but the rabbi never has to do *Hineni.* That's always the cantor's job. But this year, it was mine.

I began to contact friends. Did anyone have a tape of *Hineni*? No one did. What was I going to do? Was I even going to need to do *Hineni*? Maybe the synagogue was going to bring in someone else to substitute for the cantor. Did I want them to do that? I didn't know. Which was worse, the pressure of preparing to do something I was not really trained to do, or the pressure of working with a stranger without adequate time to prepare together? I didn't know. All I knew was I was starting to feel pretty panicky about Rosh Hashanah that year.

I sat down to think. I decided I wanted the success or failure of our services to be in my own hands, not in a stranger's. I called my president, Paula Harris, and told her I did not want a substitute cantor. "Okay," she said, "let me talk to the board, and I'll call you back." She went off to talk to her board, and I went on searching for that elusive tape of *Hineni.* No luck.

Later that night, the phone rang in my study. It was Paula. We would do it the way I wanted, she said. No substitute cantor. I listened to her as I stood behind my desk. And as I thanked her for listening to me, my eye fell on an old, wooden box in a bookcase.

To this day, I don't know what pulled me to that box, but something did. I looked inside. Tapes. Old tapes from fifteen years ago or more. One of the tapes had a small label on it. The label read "Goldhirsh." I put the tape in a player and hit the play button. There was my old teacher's voice, saying, "Now this is the prayer for the cantor to sing before *Musaf*." And Cantor Goldhirsh began to sing *Hineni*.

I stopped the tape and started to cry. Then I listened to Cantor Goldhirsh's *Hineni*. When had he made this tape? I had never studied High Holiday prayers with him. But there it was. And then, as the tape came to an end, my dear, late friend had one more thing to say, one last, precious gift for his student. "This is Cantor Goldhirsh. Ben, I hope you'll do a good job. I know you will."

Was this just a coincidence? Maybe, but if you believe that, you have more faith than I do, even if it is faith in coincidence. Rabbi Kahn always taught me that there are no coincidences, and I am not a big believer in coincidence. But I do believe in God, and I believe in the *neshamah*, the human soul. I believe that there are bonds between loved ones that death cannot destroy. And I know that after being without him for more than ten years, my dear, old teacher was still teaching me.

All of a sudden, my panic was gone. Everything would be all right. I would not be alone this Rosh Hashanah. Cantor Goldhirsh would be with me on the pulpit. After all, what does the word *Hineni* mean? "Here I am!" And there he was.

Rabbi Benjamin Sendrow

8

ECLECTIC WISDOM

A wise person learns from every source.

Ethics of the Sages

The Jewish Mayor and Mother Teresa

Laughter is the shortest distance between two people.

Victor Borge

On a strictly personal level, there were other third-term distractions to divert me from the persistent charges of corruption. Chiefly, there was my stroke, on August 6, 1987. . . . I was speaking at the Sheraton Center Hotel at a *New York Post* forum on AIDS. Afterward I went off to visit a welfare facility in Harlem. When we got to Seventy-third Street and Third Avenue, I realized that I wasn't listening to the commissioner of the Human Resources Agency, Bill Grinker, who was sitting beside me. That wasn't like me. When I tried to speak, the words didn't come out right. That wasn't like me, either. I knew instinctively that I was having a stroke.

I tapped the detective, Eddie Martinez, sitting in the front passenger seat and said, "Eddie, I'm having a stroke. Take me to Lenox Hill Hospital," which was about six blocks away. Then for some reason, it occurred to me that the press would undoubtedly interview everyone in the car and ask, "What did he say before he died?" I didn't want the public to think I had no confidence in the municipal hospitals, so I added, "And if you can't get to Lenox quickly, take me to Bellevue." (This was hardly likely, since Bellevue was at least forty blocks away.)

When I got to Lenox Hill about two minutes later, there were several doctors waiting for me in the emergency room, and the press, I was later told, started arriving in droves. The stroke's grip came and went several times, affecting my eyesight and distorting my face. I was then placed in the intensive-care unit. My sister and brother and their families were the first to come and see me.

The next visitor was Rabbi Arthur Schneier of Park East Synagogue, of which I am a member. He said, "Ed, I'm not going to stay very long, you have to sleep, but I want you to say with me in Hebrew and English the prayer asking for God's intercession." The prayer is simple: "Heal me and I shall be healed, save me and I shall be saved." I repeated the prayer with the rabbi, and he left.

Ten minutes later, Cardinal John O'Connor came. The cardinal and I are friends. I have requested that when I die he participate in the funeral ceremony. He has agreed to do so. He said, when he entered the room, "Ed, I'm not going to stay very long. You have to sleep." Apparently, that's what everyone says when they enter the room of someone they think is dying. He went on: "I want you to know you are in my prayers, and if you would like, I'll pray for you in Hebrew."

"Your Eminence," I responded, "I've taken care of the Hebrew. Would you try a little Latin?" Four days later, I left the hospital without any diminution in motor function or cerebral faculties. Most people agreed with the first premise, although the second was contested by some of my critics. The doctor said that I had to take a week off and rest. That's not so difficult to agree with when you're living at Gracie Mansion. I went home. The next Sunday, while I was sitting on the porch, the cop at the gate called on the telephone and said, "Mr. Mayor, a car just pulled up and there are four nuns in it, and one says she's Mother Teresa." It was about three o'clock on a hot August afternoon.

"That's hardly likely," I said. "I know Mother Teresa, so keep them there, and I'll be right down." When I approached the car, sure enough, it was Mother Teresa. "Mother," I said, "what are you doing here?"

"I knew you were ill, Ed," she said. "You are in my prayers, and I came to see how you're doing."

"Mother," I told her happily, "your prayers are working. I'm doing fine." I asked her to stay and sit with me awhile, so she got out of the car with the sisters. I took her by the hand, and we skipped up the path toward the porch overlooking the East River. The three nuns followed behind us, and I remember thinking it was just like a movie.

"Mother," I asked, as we sat on the porch, passing the time, "is the city providing you with any money for your work?"

"We don't take money from any government," she said.

"How do you raise the money you need to provide for the poor?"

"The Lord will always provide," she said.

"Mother, you do so much for all of us, is there anything I can do for you?"

"Yes," she responded, without hesitation. "I need two parking permits."

"Mother," I allowed, "that may be harder than getting money for you, but I'll see what I can do." Of course, I was able to arrange quickly for the two permits she needed, to park in front of the AIDS hospice she runs in Greenwich Village, where she cares for fourteen terminal patients. Even a saint has to park.

At that point, my chef came out with a pitcher of ice-cold lemonade and freshly baked chocolate-chip cookies. I poured the lemonade for Mother and the sisters, as well as for me. I thought mine was delicious, but Mother and the nuns did not drink.

"Mother," I said, "the lemonade is really good, and it's so hot outside. Why don't you drink it?"

"Ed," she explained, "my sisters and I work primarily in India, and if a poor family were to offer us the same there, it would cost them a week's wages. So we have a rule: We never eat or drink in the homes of the rich and powerful, so when we go into the homes of the poor and the homeless, they are not insulted because they know our rule."

How charming, I thought, and went on to say, "But Mother, these chocolate-chip cookies are the best ever baked."

"Wrap 'em up," she said. She is, after all, a practical saint.

Mayor Edward I. Koch

To Make a Minyan

Marriage is an edifice that must be rebuilt every day.

André Maurois

Danny was a runner. He'd fly out of bed at 5:30, throw on his running clothes and bound out the door, leaving his wife Marti asleep. Danny had once resented Marti's not joining him on his run, sharing what was so important to him. But after twelve years, she had her things, and he had his.

He'd run out of the comfortable suburb toward the city, a world of broken glass and shuttered storefronts. When his watch beeped he'd turn around and thread his way back through the maze of industrial buildings until he found a familiar route home. Then he'd shower and dress, grab a cup of coffee, and drive to his counseling appointments at the Veteran's Administration hospital.

On Monday and Thursday mornings, he'd finish jogging early so he could go to minyan at synagogue—a quick, businesslike minyan populated mostly by old men, but also by a few women and several middle-aged guys.

His *shul* hadn't gone without a minyan in two years thanks, in part, to himself.

One Thursday morning Danny jogged as usual into the deteriorating streets of the city. Turning a corner, Danny faced a long block of old tenements and small stores. Out of the shadows stepped the figure of a man. Danny jogged into the street as the figure came slowly into focus. The old man, wearing a black, wide-brimmed hat and a long black coat, his beard grizzled and shaggy, waved his arms like a policeman stopping traffic. He jumped into the street to block Danny's way.

The old man shouted as if Danny were deaf. "We need a tenth! For the minyan, we need a tenth! It's a *mitzvah* to be the tenth! You maybe need a *mitzvah?*"

Jogging in place to keep his rhythm, Danny mumbled breathlessly, "I can't, this is my run! I'll be late for *shul!*" And with that he zipped around the old man and shot down the street.

Back home, Danny thought about the incident, wondering if the stranger had even been real. "If so, why did he need a minyan? What could I have been thinking? Why didn't I stop?"

At *shul,* Danny greeted the others inside the small sanctuary and began putting on his *tefillin,* methodically wrapping the worn leather straps around his arm the prescribed number of times, making the blessings at each appropriate moment. The beautiful chanting of prayers began, the melody laid down over millennia. *Davening* rose and fell in a counterpoint of different voices. The Torah Scroll was taken out of the Holy Ark, and paraded around the congregation. Each person touched it reverently with the strings of their prayer shawls or with their prayer books, then kissed the strings or book. Suddenly, Danny wished Marti were there.

The selection for the day was read. As the service came

to an end, the rabbi looked up and spoke. This took Danny by surprise; the minyan was usually in too much of a hurry for sermons. But this morning was different. The rabbi seemed to look directly at Danny.

"I was reading this morning a passage from an old sage who said that each of us will have an opportunity to receive a message from On High. And that most of us do not recognize that message and go on unheedingly. Perhaps, today, my friends, you could be on the lookout for such a message and try not to miss it if it should arrive."

All day these words bothered Danny. He canceled his afternoon appointments and drove home. He drove the path of his morning run, looking for the spot where the old man had confronted him. But nothing looked the same. He even tried running the path he'd taken that morning, without luck. At home, Marti noticed his mood. "Hey, honey, what's up?" she asked.

Danny was having difficulty explaining this story to himself, let alone to someone else. Especially Marti. The stresses in their marriage had been rising in the last six months and their closeness was waning; sometimes they were like strangers. Danny the psychotherapist, the religious Jew, the Vietnam veteran, felt vulnerable enough without looking like he was having a breakdown.

"It's nothing," he said abruptly. "Just things from work." He watched Marti look away, wounded.

For weeks after that, Danny jogged up the hilly streets into town searching for that lost place, the Street of The Old Man. He bought a map and tried to puzzle it out with highlighter again and again, until the overlapping colors became a mass of confusion. Danny knew he had to stop.

"Rabbi," he said very softly, "I need your time. Are you free now?"

They sat in the rabbi's tiny study, facing each other across the cluttered desk. "*Nu,* Danny?"

Danny struggled to begin, but finally the story poured out, ending in a long silence. The rabbi nodded. "Perhaps it's all a great parable. Let's also say this old man was not a figment of your imagination. Perhaps there was a death in a family and they needed a tenth for the minyan. It would have been a real *mitzvah* to make the tenth. Maybe you feel guilty because you refused."

Danny bristled.

"But," continued the rabbi quietly, "let's pretend that the old man's appearance was actually a message from On High. What do you think the message was?"

Danny felt annoyed at hearing the kind of question he had so often asked his own therapy patients. But the rabbi's words hit home.

"The message . . ." Danny said slowly. "The old man was telling me, 'I see you're in the middle of your run on the way to your minyan. But right now I need your help.' And I ran right past his words."

"Yes," the rabbi said, "but maybe you just have to run to the right place to hear such a message. Here." The rabbi smiled, tapping his chest. "Maybe it isn't a stranger who needs you, Danny."

Danny didn't remember the drive back home from *shul*. He didn't remember parking the car or running through the house to Marti's ceramic studio. He found himself standing before her open door.

Marti looked up from her wheel and smiled, clay dripping from her fingers and caked on her nose. Danny saw the sweet vulnerability he'd fallen in love with years ago, and felt a lump rise in his throat.

"Marti, could you do me a favor?"

"Sure, honey. Is everything okay?" She stopped the pottery wheel.

"Would you come with me?" Danny hesitated, then stepped inside her doorway.

"What about the hospital, your patients? What's going on?"

"I'm not sure, but I think I've been running too much."

"You're not hurt?" Marti asked, alarmed.

"Only from running away from my heart," Danny said. "And from you. Is there a chance we could try again? Not running, just walking." Danny reached out his hand.

"A *mitzvah* worth waiting for," Marti said, with warmth. She rose from the potting wheel, tears starting down her face, and threw her arms around Danny, dripping wet clay everywhere. "I've been waiting to take that walk for a long time."

Hanoch McCarty

Reprinted by permission of Rabbi Henry Rabin.

Harry's Blessings

Help your brother's boat across, and your own has reached the shore.

Hindu Proverb

On a cold January morning, Harry entered my office where I worked as the volunteer director in a hospital. Unbeknownst to me, in his Yiddish-accented English, he asked the guard for the outpatient department, the name of which is almost identical to mine. The guard had difficulty understanding him. Hence, Harry was ushered into my office. In my outgoing manner, I welcomed him and discussed volunteer possibilities. Harry was elderly. I assumed that he would want an easy job.

"No!" Harry declared in a boisterous voice. "I do not want to do a sissy job. I want a real job." He had worked in a kitchen and asked to do the same for one or two days a week.

I informed the dietary department that a new volunteer was on his way. I explained how frail he appeared and asked that they treat him with "kid gloves." Harry was welcomed into the hospital's dietary department.

With each hour, I anticipated Harry returning to my office or receiving a phone call saying that Harry could not handle the job. The next morning, Harry appeared in my office bright and early. I invited him to sit down and talk, expecting him to complain about his job assignment. Harry stated that there was nothing to talk about. He had a job to perform. They needed him in the kitchen. He returned to my office several hours later. I now expected complaints and a request for a softer job more fitting an elderly person. Was I wrong! Harry took his free volunteer meal pass, and in his unique English said to me, "May God bless you for placing me as a volunteer." Daily, Harry came to my office and bestowed God's blessings upon me. Harry's original two days of volunteering turned into five, six and sometimes seven days a week.

I called the dietary department about Harry's performance. I expected to hear that they did not want to hurt an old man's feelings and, therefore, kept him on board. Again, was I wrong! Harry was a real asset to the kitchen crew and a team player. Rather than sit and relax, he found other areas where he could assist: cooking at the grill, serving food or placing trays and silverware in bins. Yes, Harry was one of the best workers in the department!

Weeks later, I received three phone calls concerning him: one from a psychiatrist and two from social workers. The psychiatrist informed me that Harry had recently been an inpatient. My stomach turned. The hospital has a policy prohibiting recent patients to become volunteers. I expected a reprimand. Instead, in the sweetest of tones, this doctor said to me, "I don't know what you did to Harry, but he is a new man and is no longer a patient." Two phone calls from social workers produced similar comments. These calls made me reflect upon my original meeting with Harry.

In his heavily accented English, he had asked for the outpatient department. However, in error, he was directed to my office. That was the beginning of his experience as a volunteer rather than being a hospital patient. Days turned into weeks and weeks turned into months. Harry could be found daily in the kitchen. Late each morning, Harry would appear in my office to bless me. With each passing day, he appeared younger, more spritely and zestful.

Summer came. One day, I received a call from the dietary department asking me if I knew where Harry was. He had not appeared in two days. We were not too concerned. After all, it was summertime, and he certainly was entitled to a vacation. I called his home. No answer. I tried for several days. Still no answer and still no Harry. I called Harry's son. His son's secretary said that her boss was unavailable for the week. I explained the situation. The secretary gasped. She continued that her boss's father had died several days ago. Her boss, Harry's son, was at home in mourning for the week. I ran to the dietary department to share this. We hugged. We cried. What a loss we felt. Harry's bright demeanor and helpful attitude were now only memories.

I wrote to Harry's son. I expected no further contact. One week later, I received a moving letter from him. "I want to thank you and the wonderful staff who were so kind to my father. Dad often spoke of the nice people with whom he had volunteered. Working in the kitchen helped him feel important and worthwhile. His volunteering became an important part of his life and helped him overcome the loneliness, grief and depression he felt after the death of my mother. He lived a productive, active and busy life until the very day of his death. A special thanks to all the lovely people in the kitchen. God bless all of you."

One week later, an elderly man with a heavy Yiddish accent appeared at my office stating, "I am here to replace Harry in the kitchen." I gave a start. Could I be receiving another one of Harry's blessings? I welcomed this gentleman and sent him directly to the kitchen. One question still remains with me. Who gained more from this experience—Harry or the hospital?

Carole Goldstein

The Hanukkah Party

Who is truly rich? One who is content with his lot.

Sayings of the Sages

Hanukkah was finally here. After the doldrums of school, homework and report cards, my kids and I (being a teacher, I suffer from many of the same school ailments that my kids do) were looking forward to a real "Hanukkah" treat . . . a meal out in our favorite Chinese restaurant. As my family and I opened the door and entered the restaurant, we anticipated a real treat. After all, it was Hanukkah, a time for celebration, joy and oily foods. Besides, China Palace was our favorite restaurant. We had been coming here for almost fifteen years.

Once inside, and sitting at our favorite table, we were in for a shock. First of all, after waiting for at least twenty minutes, and after waving wildly at every waiter (and being totally ignored), we were all cranky and starving. This was a celebration! Soon my kids would want me to go home and start frying up a storm. (Heaven forbid!)

Second, all the action seemed to be centered at the opposite end of the restaurant, in the party room.

"I'm going over there," I said to my husband. "I want to see why they are getting served, and having their party, while we're waiting here, dying of starvation."

My husband, who knows how much I hate waiting for service, said, "No, let's just leave. Obviously Hanukkah is the wrong time to go out." He grabbed my arm to restrain me. "After all, we can always go home, and you can make latkes. . . ."

I knew it! Desperation motivated me to say, "I don't want to leave yet. Let me at least go to check it out," I protested, loosening his grip.

With a sigh, he let me go.

I walked to the other side of the room . . . and what a sight met my eyes! Balloons, gold *dreidels,* and sparkling *menorahs* were festooned everywhere . . . at least fifty people sat at various tables. There was a big sign, with a picture of an elderly, smiling couple, propped up on a table, with the words "Happy Hanukkah . . . Celebrate the Miracle" written in gold pen, which each guest had signed. The thing that made the deepest impression on me was how happy these people seemed. The love was palpable in the air. I knew Hanukkah was a time of joy, but they were really excessive . . . smiling, and hugging, especially over in the corner, where the celebratory couple (whom I recognized from the picture on the table) sat. I remained standing there, all hunger forgotten, as guest after guest went up to this couple, hugged and kissed the woman, and left beautifully wrapped presents on a side table, already piled high with previous gifts.

Suddenly, a feeling of terrible black envy filled my heart. I thought, *You know, it's not fair. . . . I will never have a Hanukkah party like this, with that many people.* You see, my extended family is very dysfunctional, and I would have given anything to be part of such a family gathering. Sure, I always celebrated with my husband and kids, but never grandparents, uncles, cousins. . . . *Why her and not me?* I wondered darkly.

The black, cold feelings enveloped me, and I literally had to sit down as I felt self-pity overcome me. I could at least watch the party, even if I'd never have one like it, I thought. Then, a wild impulse entered my mind. Why not go over and wish this woman Happy Hanukkah? After all, I could sort of be a part of the celebration that way. I got up and walked over to the table, which was still a beehive of activity.

"Uh . . . You don't know me," I began awkwardly . . . feeling like a fool. "But, I saw how lovely your party is, and I felt I just had to go over to you and wish you a happy Hanukkah."

The woman looked at me and smiled, but I could see by the way she was gazing into my eyes, she sensed that something was awry.

"One minute, Sy," she turned to an elegant-looking man seated at her left. "I want to talk to this young woman." She took my hand and began walking away from her table. "Oh, no," I protested. "I didn't mean to disturb your party. Please, go back and sit down . . . please . . ."

"In a moment," she said in a quiet voice. "But first, I need to tell you something. . . ." She placed her arm around my shoulders and led me to a quieter corner of the restaurant.

"You see, I saw you staring at the party, and I knew that you were wondering what was going on. Maybe you even wished it was yours. Isn't that right?" she asked.

How could she possibly know that? I wondered. Hot shame, like a high tide, filled me. I could feel my cheeks burning red hot. I nodded, looking at the ground.

She reached out her hand and lifted my face, her kind eyes gazing into mine.

"I want to explain to you what this party is all about, and then you'll see that you have nothing, nothing at all, to envy."

I looked at her in disbelief. Not envy the attention . . . presents, people who obviously loved this woman. I truly doubted that anything she'd say would make any difference to me.

"First, do you know what this party is for?" she asked me.

"I assumed . . . a Hanukkah party," I stammered.

"The reason all these people are here is because this is a very special Hanukkah for me. So you are correct, this Hanukkah is special because a few months ago the doctors told me that I'd never live to see it. . . ."

I gasped in shock, my mouth gaping open.

"Yes," she continued, "I have no family left either. . . . The 'guests' you see here are the nurses and doctors who saved me from my heart attack. Over there," she pointed, "is my private nurse, whom I have to have with me at all times, and there," she pointed to the corner table, "is my husband. He was my teenage sweetheart, do you know that? I never would have made it back without him. He's the only family I have." She held my hand as she resumed her sad tale. "There is also a dietitian at the table, to make sure I eat only what is on my special diet. . . . No latkes for me, I'm afraid." Then, she smiled sadly at me.

"Another reason my husband is giving this party is because I probably won't make it to next Hanukkah. But he doesn't know that I found out, and that's such a heavy burden to carry alone, all the pretending. For his sake . . . that's why I had to tell someone." She gave me a fierce look.

"Do you have a family, dear?" she questioned then. Speechless, I raised a very shaky finger, and pointed to my husband and kids, patiently waiting at our table.

"Oh yes," she nodded. "So sweet, so young and healthy. You see, my dear," she said, "it is you who are the lucky one."

She gave me a tremulous smile, straightened out her shoulders, and walked slowly and with great dignity back to her party.

I turned away, my eyes blurred with tears . . . choking sobs rose up in my throat.

I felt so mortified, so low. How could I have forgotten what was really important? Health, a wonderful husband, great kids, a wonderful home. Now I understood everything, the solicitous attention her "family" was giving this woman, the waiters' attentiveness. How could I have envied her, even for a moment?

I returned to my table, a much wiser woman.

"You were gone so long," my husband said. "So when are we going to have some service?"

"You know what?" I said, reaching for his hand and covering it with my own. "We can wait a while, it's okay," I smiled, my heart aching, remembering. "After all, it's Hanukkah, right? A time for families to be together."

"Right," he affirmed, gripping my hand and squeezing. I regarded him with new love in my eyes, then turned to gaze at my children. *Having them in my life is a miracle, indeed,* I thought. *I truly am blessed. Truly blessed . . .*

As I looked around the table, there was only one thing I could say, and this time, I finally understood its true meaning. "Happy Hanukkah, everyone . . . ," I said.

Rina Friedman

"All those in favor say 'Oy.'"

Reprinted by permission of Barricade Books.

Glossary of Hebrew and Yiddish Terms

Aliyah—move to Israel (literally—"go up"); also, an honor at the Torah at worship
Aron HaKodesh—the Holy Ark
Ashkenazi—a Jew from Eastern European descent
Ayshet Hayil—a woman of valor (Proverbs 31)
Bar Mitzvah—male ritual ceremony of adulthood at age thirteen
Bat Mitzvah—same as above, for a female
Beshert—predestined (Yiddish)
Brit Milah—ritual circumcision ceremony
Bubbie (or *Bubbe*)—grandmother (Yiddish)
Challah—braided egg bread for Shabbat and holidays
Chasid—see *Hasid*
Daven, Davening—praying
Dayanu—popular Passover song, part of the Seder
Dreidel (or *Draydel*)—spinning top, game for Hanukkah
Goyim—gentiles
Grogger—noisemaker used on holiday of Purim
Habad—orthodox religious sect
Haggadah—book of Passover Seder rituals and prayers
Halachah (or *Halakhah*)—Jewish law
Hanukkah—Jewish holiday in December
Haroset—chopped nuts and apples with cinnamon and wine, used at Passover *Seder*
Hasid (or *Chasid*) (pl. *Hasidim*)—one in a pious sect
Kaddish—memorial prayer
Kashrut—Jewish dietary laws
Kavannah—sincerity and intentionality during prayer
Kiddush—blessing over wine on *Shabbat* and festivals
Kippah—head covering for religious purposes
Kol Nidre—opening prayer Yom Kippur eve, considered to be one of most sacred prayers
Kosher (adjective; noun: *Kashrut*)—acceptable food made according to Jewish dietary laws
Kugel—traditional Jewish dish of potato pie (yiddish)
Lag B'Omer—Festival of Scholars
L'chaim—Yiddish toast meaning "To Life!" (sometimes accompanied with a drink)
Ma-ariv—evening worship service
Mahzor—Jewish holiday prayerbook
Matzah—unleavened bread eaten at Passover
Menorah—ritual candelabrum used at Hanukkah

Mensch—decent, honorable person (Yiddish)
Meshugah—crazy
Mezuzah—Scriptural passages in box placed on doorposts
Midrash—ancient and medieval collections of homiletical biblical commentary
Mikveh—ritual bath
Minchah (or *Minhah*)—afternoon liturgy
Minyan—quorum of ten adults for Jewish prayer
Mitzvah—biblical commandment; or a good deed
Mohel—one who performs circumcisions
Motzi—blessing over the bread or meal
Musaf—"additional" prayers chanted on Sabbath and festivals
Oneg Shabbat—festive food and celebration on Sabbath
Pesach (or *Pesah*)—Passover
Purim—Jewish holiday on which biblical Book of Esther is read; joyous festival of celebration of defeat of Persian threat of Jewish persecution
Pushke—charity box (Yiddish)
Rosh Hashanah—Jewish New Year
Saba—grandfather
Sabra—native Israeli
Seder (pl. *Sedarim*)—Passover ritual feast
Shabbos (pl. *Shabbosim*) or *Shabbat*—Sabbath
Shema—prayer from Deuteronomy 6:4–9
Shemoneh Esrei—central Jewish prayer
Shivah—seven days of mourning
Shochet—ritual slaughterer for kosher meat
Shofar—musical instrument played during High Holiday period
Shpiel—play, usually for Festival of Purim
Shtetl—village (Yiddish)
Shul—synagogue (Yiddish)
Siddur—Jewish prayerbook
Sufganiyot—donuts eaten on Hanukkah
Takeh—really! (Yiddish)
Tallit—prayer shawl
Tatte—Daddy (Yiddish)
Tefillin—Scriptural passages in small boxes worn on forehead and arm during worship (sometimes translated as "phylacteries")
Torah—the five books of Moses
Tzedakah—charity
Yad Vashem—Holocaust museum and archives in Jerusalem
Yahrzeit—anniversary of date of death (Yiddish)
Yeshivah (or *Yeshiva*)—academy of study
Yom HaShoah—Holocaust Memorial Day
Yom Kippur—Day of Atonement
Zeida (also *Zayda* and *Zaydie*)—grandfather (Yiddish)
Z'mirot—Sabbath hymns

More Chicken Soup?

Many of the stories you have read in this book were submitted by readers like you who had read earlier *Chicken Soup for the Soul* books. We publish at least five or six *Chicken Soup for the Soul* books every year. We invite you to contribute a story to one of these future volumes.

Stories may be up to 1,200 words and must uplift or inspire. You may submit an original piece, something you have read or your favorite quotation on your refrigerator door.

To obtain a copy of our submission guidelines and a listing of upcoming *Chicken Soup* books, please write, fax or check our Web site.

Please send your submissions to:

Chicken Soup for the Soul
P.O. Box 30880, Santa Barbara, CA 93130
fax: 805-563-2945
Web site: *www.chickensoup.com*

Just send a copy of your stories and other pieces to the above address.

We will be sure that both you and the author are credited for your submission.

For information about speaking engagements, other books, audiotapes, workshops and training programs, please contact any of our authors directly.

נאַציאָנאַלע ייִדישע ביכער-צענטראַלע

NATIONAL YIDDISH BOOK CENTER

The authors of *Chicken Soup for the Jewish Soul* and Health Communications, Inc. invite you to help rescue Yiddish books and re-energize Jewish culture for future generations.

The National Yiddish Book Center in Amherst, Massachusetts, a young nonprofit organization, has collected 1.5 million endangered Yiddish books and distributed them to readers and libraries worldwide.

Our exciting English-language programs, designed to open up Jewish books to new generations, include:

- ✦ *a beautiful Visitors Center, open to the public and free of charge*
- ✦ *imaginative museum exhibits*
- ✦ Pakn Treger, *our popular English-language magazine*
- ✦ *conferences, performances, readings*
- ✦ *publications and translations*

The Center's most recent initiative is the historic Steven Spielberg Digital Yiddish Library, which will preserve in electronic form the entirety of modern Yiddish literature and make every book available for reprinting on demand. Visit *www.yiddishbookcenter.org* for a complete online catalog.

Join Us!

The Center depends on members to help us continue our critical work. Please join us today by calling 413-256-4900 or mailing the form on the opposite page. You'll enjoy the many benefits of Book Center membership, including a free subscription to *Pakn Treger;* invitations to events; and discounts on the purchase of Yiddish and English books, gifts, audiotapes and videos.

NATIONAL YIDDISH BOOK CENTER

Amherst, Massachusetts

www.yiddishbookcenter.org

Join Us!

YES, I want to help rescue Yiddish books and re-energize Jewish culture for future generations. Enclosed is my tax-deductible membership check, made payable to the National Yiddish Book Center.

☐ $36 Member (U.S. and Canada) ☐ $360 President's Circle
☐ $54 Special Gift ☐ ___ Other
☐ $180 Benefactor

Please charge my

☐ MasterCard ☐ Visa ☐ AmEx ________________________
CARD #

____
SIGNATURE EXP. DATE

With a contribution of $54 or more, you'll get a free copy of *Say It in Yiddish*, a fascinating Yiddish-English phrase book. All members receive *Pakn Treger*, our English-language magazine, plus invitations to our programs and special events. Members also receive discounts on the purchase of Yiddish and English books, music and gift shop items.

____
NAME

____
ADDRESS

____
CITY STATE ZIP

____
PHONE E-MAIL

☐ I read Yiddish. Please send me a catalog of Yiddish books available for purchase.

נאַציאָנאַלע ייִדישע ביכער-צענטראַלע

NATIONAL YIDDISH BOOK CENTER

Harry and Jeanette Weinberg Building
1021 West Street, Amherst, MA 01002-3375
phone: 413-256-4900 *fax:* 413-256-4700
www.yiddishbookcenter.org *e-mail:* yiddish@bikher.org

Who Is Jack Canfield?

Jack Canfield is one of America's leading experts in the development of human potential and personal effectiveness. He is both a dynamic, entertaining speaker and a highly sought-after trainer. Jack has a wonderful ability to inform and inspire audiences toward increased levels of self-esteem and peak performance.

He is the author and narrator of several bestselling audio- and videocassette programs, including *Self-Esteem and Peak Performance, How to Build High Self-Esteem, Self-Esteem in the Classroom* and *Chicken Soup for the Soul—Live.* He is regularly seen on television shows such as *Good Morning America, 20/20* and *NBC Nightly News.* Jack has co-authored numerous books, including the *Chicken Soup for the Soul* series, *Dare to Win, The Aladdin Factor, 100 Ways to Build Self-Concept in the Classroom, Heart at Work* and *The Power of Focus.*

Jack is a regularly featured speaker for professional associations, school districts, government agencies, churches, hospitals, sales organizations and corporations. His clients have included the American Dental Association, the American Management Association, AT&T, Campbell's Soup, Clairol, Domino's Pizza, GE, ITT, Hartford Insurance, Johnson & Johnson, the Million Dollar Roundtable, NCR, New England Telephone, Re/Max, Scott Paper, TRW and Virgin Records.

Jack conducts an annual eight-day Training of Trainers program in the areas of self-esteem and peak performance. It attracts educators, counselors, parenting trainers, corporate trainers, professional speakers, ministers and others interested in developing their speaking and seminar-leading skills.

For further information about Jack's books, tapes and training programs, or to schedule him for a presentation, please contact:

Self-Esteem Seminars
P.O. Box 30880
Santa Barbara, CA 93130
phone: 805-563-2935 • fax: 805-563-2945
Web site: *www.chickensoup.com*

Who Is Mark Victor Hansen?

Mark Victor Hansen is a professional speaker who in the last twenty years has made over 4,000 presentations to more than 2 million people in thirty-two countries. His presentations cover sales excellence and strategies; personal empowerment and development; and how to triple your income and double your time off.

Mark has spent a lifetime dedicated to his mission of making a profound and positive difference in people's lives. Throughout his career, he has inspired hundreds of thousands of people to create a more powerful and purposeful future for themselves while stimulating the sale of billions of dollars worth of goods and services.

Mark is a prolific writer and has authored *Future Diary, How to Achieve Total Prosperity* and *The Miracle of Tithing.* He is coauthor of the *Chicken Soup for the Soul* series, *Dare to Win* and *The Aladdin Factor* (all with Jack Canfield), and *The Master Motivator* (with Joe Batten).

Mark has also produced a complete library of personal-empowerment audio and videocassette programs that have enabled his listeners to recognize and use their innate abilities in their business and personal lives. His message has made him a popular television and radio personality, with appearances on ABC, NBC, CBS, HBO, PBS and CNN. He has also appeared on the cover of numerous magazines, including *Success, Entrepreneur* and *Changes.*

Mark is a big man with a heart and spirit to match—an inspiration to all who seek to better themselves.

For further information about Mark, write:

MVH & Associates
P.O. Box 7665
Newport Beach, CA 92658
phone: 714-759-9304 or 800-433-2314
fax: 714-722-6912
Web site: *www.chickensoup.com*

Who Is Dov Peretz Elkins?

Dov Peretz Elkins is one of the world's best-known rabbis. His books and other writings are used by rabbis, educators, teachers and communal leaders through North and South America, Israel, Europe, Africa and Asia. His unique blend of Judaism, Eastern religions, psychology and education has enabled him to pioneer internationally known programs in spirituality and interactive education. His popular lectures and workshops have been attended by thousands of students all over the world.

Rabbi Elkins holds degrees from Temple University, The Jewish Theological Seminary and Colgate Rochester Divinity School. He was the first rabbi to win a doctoral degree from Colgate Rochester. His thesis, *Teaching People to Love Themselves: A Handbook of Theory and Technique for Self-Esteem Training* is used as a text in universities throughout the world. Dr. Elkins's work in self-esteem brought him into contact with Jack Canfield in the 1970s, when the pair led widely attended human development workshops throughout the United States. Spin-off books from his doctoral thesis include the bestselling, still-in-print books, *Glad to Be Me: Building Self-Esteem in Yourself and Others; Twelve Pathways to Feeling Better About Yourself,* and *Self Concept Sourcebook.*

After serving two years as military chaplain at Fort Gordon, Georgia, Dov Peretz Elkins became spiritual leader of several of North America's largest and most prestigious synagogues, in Rochester, Cleveland and Philadelphia. He currently serves as rabbi of The Jewish Center, Princeton, New Jersey.

Dr. Elkins's most recent books include *Moments of Transcendence: Inspirational Readings for the High Holidays, Prescription for a Long and Happy Life, Hasidic Wisdom, Jewish Guided Imagery, Forty Days of Transformation, Meditations for the High Holy Days,* and *New and Old Prayers and Readings for the High Holy Days, Shabbat and Festive Occasions.*

For further information about Rabbi Elkins's books and lectures, contact:

Growth Associates Publishers and Consultants
212 Stuart Road East
Princeton, NJ 08540-1946
phone: 609-497-7375 • fax: 609-497-0325
e-mail: *DPE@DPElkins.com*
Web site: *www.DPElkins.com*

Contributors

Several of the stories in this book were taken from previously published sources, such as books, magazines and newspapers. These sources are acknowledged in the permissions section. If you would like to contact any of the contributors for information about their writing, or would like to invite them to speak in your community, look for their contact information included in their biography.

The remainder of the stories were submitted by readers of our previous *Chicken Soup for the Soul* books who responded to our requests for stories. We have also included information about them.

Rabbi Scott Aaron is the Director of Education for the Brandeis-Bardin Institute in Simi Valley, California. Ordained by the Hebrew Union College—Jewish Institute of Religion, he is formally the rabbi of the Hillels at the Ohio State University and New York University. He is thankful every day that he is married to Rabbi Donni Aaron and is the proud father of their son, Meitav. Their second child was born in June 2001 and named after Grandma. He can be reached by e-mail at *aaron.15@ohio-state.edu.*

Rabbi Harvey Abramowitz is a computer specialist in the graphic-arts industry and serves as associate rabbi at Kehillath Shalom Synagogue in Cold Spring Harbour, New York, a Reconstructionist Congregation. Growing up in Brooklyn, his parents taught him the love of Zionism and Israel. Educated in the Orthodox tradition, he has found his spiritual home in Reconstructionism.

Rabbi Mona Alfi was ordained in 1998 at HUC-JIR in New York. She is the Associate Rabbi of Congregation B'nai Israel in Sacramento, California, and is currently serving her second term as the chaplain for the California State Assembly. Mona and her husband, Glenn Hammel, make their home in Davis, California.

Rabbi Robert A. Alper is "the world's only practicing clergyman doing stand-up comedy . . . intentionally," performing throughout North America and England. Bob is the author of the humorous, spiritually uplifting *Life Doesn't Get Any Better Than This: The Holiness of Little Daily Dramas* (Liguori Publications, 1996). Bob resides in Vermont with his wife, Sherri. They are empty-nest parents of Zack and Jessica. His Web site is *www.bobalper.com,* e-mail address is *Guffaw@compuserve.com,* and phone number is 888-483-3297.

Marsha Arons is a writer and lecturer in Skokie, Illinois. She is thrilled to be associated with the *Chicken Soup* series, and her stories appear in *Woman's Soul,*

Mother's Soul and *A 5th Portion*. She also contributes to national magazines such as *Good Housekeeping, Reader's Digest* and *Redbook*. She has authored a book for young adults and is currently at work on a collection of short stories dealing with mother-daughter relationships. You can contact her via e-mail for speaking or other assignments at *RA8737@aol.com*.

Bryan Aubrey is a former professor of English and is the author of two books, as well as numerous articles and reviews. He can be contacted at 1100 E. Madison Ave., Fairfield, IA 52556, or by phone at 515-472-2224.

Tanya Bank is a senior at Columbia University, majoring in anthropology and concentrating in psychology. She plans to pursue a career in education. Tanya tutors at the East Harlem Tutorial Program and sings with Pizmon, Columbia's Jewish a capella group. Tanya can be reached by e-mail at *Tanya@stny.rr.com*.

Rabbi Devora Bartnoff graduated from the Reconstructionist Rabbinical College in 1984. She served the Jewish community as a pulpit rabbi, education director, chaplain and family educator. Devora was the mother of four children with her husband, Rabbi Mordechai Liebling. She died of breast cancer in 1997 at age forty-four.

Miriam Newell Biskin is a retired English teacher and hobbyist writer. The author of many children's stories, a biography of Rebecca Gratz, *Pattern for a Heroine,* and an essay collection, *My Life Among the Gentiles,* she is inspired by her family.

Dr. Naomi Bluestone, now deceased, was a psychiatrist, accomplished writer and speaker. At her mother's funeral, she spoke for over an hour to the tears and laughter of those present. "Mary the Maid" was one of the many tales she told during that afternoon.

Elayne Clift is an award-winning writer, author and journalist. Her work has appeared in *The Washington Post, The Chicago Sun Times* and *The Christian Science Monitor*. She received the Award for Excellence in Journalism from the New Jersey Education Association. She can be reached via e-mail at *elayneclift@worldnet.att.net*.

Rabbi Kenneth L. Cohen is Executive Director of the United Synagogue of Conservative Judaism, Seaboard Region. He is a popular writer and lecturer. Ken lives in Bethesda, Maryland, with his wife, journalist Joanne L. Kenen, and their two boys, Zachary and Ilan. He enjoys bicycling and studying traditional Jewish texts. Please reach him at *Ken@RabbiCohen.com*.

Aryeh ben David (formerly Andrew Nemlich) moved to Israel in 1979 where he received Rabbinic ordination. He teaches at the Pardes Institute and Livnot U'Lehibanot in Jerusalem. His first book is *Around the Shabbat Table: A Guide to Fulfilling and Meaningful Shabbat Table Conversations*. He can be reached at *aryehbd@netvision.net.il*.

Yaffa Eliach is a pioneering scholar in Holocaust studies and creator of the exhibit, "The Tower of Life," at the United States Holocaust Memorial Museum. Her book, *There Once Was a World,* a National Book Award finalist, recounts the history of the *shtetl* protrayed in the "Tower." Among her earlier books is the classic *Hasidic Tales of the Holocaust,* which won a Christopher Award. Dr. Eliach is a professor at Brooklyn College. She is the president and founder of the Shtetl Foundation, which is building a full-size replica of a *shtetl* in Israel.

Jonathan Elkins is a TV news correspondent for Israel Television and currently resides in Tel Aviv. He translated a book of Hasidic sayings into English with his father, and is currently at work on a novel set on the backdrop of the Middle East peace process. Jonathan is also an avid Ultimate Frisbee player, and plays bass guitar in a rock and roll band. He can be reached at *JElkins@attglobal.net.*

Benita Epstein is a cartoonist whose work appears in hundreds of publications such as *The New Yorker, Reader's Digest* and *Better Homes & Gardens.* She has three cartoon collections: *Suture Self, Interlibrary Loan Sharks and Seedy Roms,* and *Science of Little Round Things.* She can be reached at *BenitaE@aol.com* or on her Web site at *www.reuben.org/benitaepstein/.*

Arnold Fine is senior editor of *The Jewish Press.* His column, "I Remember When," has been continually published in *The Jewish Press* for forty-nine years. His story, "The Wallet," appeared in the 1998 edition of *Chicken Soup for the Woman's Soul.* He was coordinator of special education at Samuel J. Tilden High School in Brooklyn, teaching handicapped and brain-injured children. Since retiring, he has become an adjunct instructor in the Behavioral Science Department at Kingsborough College (CUNY). He has been honored by The National Committee for the Furtherance of Jewish Education and The Jewish Teachers Association of New York State. He is married and has three sons and six grandchildren.

Rabbi Joan S. Friedman was ordained at HUC-JIR in New York in 1980. She serves as Jewish Chaplain and Instructor in Religion at Colgate University. She is a doctoral candidate in Jewish history at Columbia University and is completing a doctoral dissertation on Solomon Freehof and his influence on American Reform Judaism.

Rina Friedman is a wife, mother and educator. She enjoys writing stories about her Jewish life experiences. Rina also likes to write, cook, travel, play her guitar and teach children of all ages, especially her own! You can reach her at: Friedman, P.O. Box 2748, Briarcliff Manor, NY 10510.

Irene Frisch was born Irene Bienstock in Drohobycz (Poland, now Ukraine). She survived the Holocaust in hiding, and after liberation she finished high school in Poland. Irene later emigrated to Israel where she served in the Israeli Army and attended law school. She arrived in the U.S. in 1960, and married Eugene Frisch. They had two children, and she is now the grandmother of two. She graduated from Columbia University School of Library Science and later worked as the head of the medical library. She resides with her husband in Teaneck, New Jersey.

Bronia Galmitz Gallon was born in Russia, grew up in Poland and pioneered in Israel. She married and moved to the United States in 1946, where she raised two children and taught special education. She has lectured for the Israeli Consulate and freelanced on Israel and the history of Islam.

Hanna Bandes Geshelin's involvement in Jewish causes began when she collated Hadassah newsletters at age four, two years after Israel's independence. She has taught, worked with the elderly, and been a professional storyteller. Many of her articles, essays, stories and books are on Jewish themes. Reach her at *info@geshelin.com*.

Rabbi Michael Gold is spiritual leader of Temple Beth Torah in Florida. He has written three books and lectured around the country on infertility and adoption, sexual ethics and family relationships. His book *The Ten Journeys of Life* was recently published. Rabbi Gold can be reached at *www.rabbigold.com*.

Rabbi Hillel Goldberg, Ph.D. is executive editor of the *Intermountain Jewish News*, an independent scholar, and winner of the Academic Book of the Year award from Choice. A human-rights activist, he and his wife, Elaine, are the parents of six and grandparents. He can be reached at *ijn@rmii.com*.

Miriam Goldbrenner is a married mother of two. Her writing has opened up many doors. "It is both therapeutic and thought-provoking, which I believe is a perfect combination." She works part-time with a local magazine, does volunteer work and is president of the PTA in her son's school.

Erica S. Goldman-Brodie was born in England and grew up in Australia. Her grandparents and ten of her parents' siblings were killed during the Holocaust. She earned a B.A. from Yeshiva University and an M.S. from Hunter College. She is married and has two grandchildren, Sophia Judith and Ariella Granum Brodie-Weisberg. She teaches in New Jersey. Her e-mail address is *jobrodie@jtsa.edu*.

Carole Goldstein lives in Florida with her husband, Rabbi Nason Goldstein, where she is a full-time *rebbetzin*. She considers her three adult children, Deena, Arnon and Hana, her and her husband's greatest achievement in life.

Leah Golomb made aliyah twenty-three years ago. She is a mikve lady and swim teacher who also lectures widely on Chassidut. Leah is the mother of six and lives on Moshav Modi'in, which was established by Rabbi Shlomo Carlbach. She may be reached at *mamaleah@zahav.net.il*.

Arielle Greenbaum participated in the March of the Living as a sophomore in high school in 1996, as a representative of the Metrowest New Jersey delegation. Since then, she has spent a great deal of time writing and speaking publicly about her experience in Poland and Israel. Arielle lives in Livingston, New Jersey, and is presently a history and political science major at the

University of Pennsylvania in Philadelphia. Her potential career plans include Jewish activism and communal work.

Blair P. Grubb, M.D., was born in Baltimore, received his B.A. from the University of Maryland-Baltimore and his M.D. from Universidad Central del Este San Pedro de Macoris, in the Dominican Republic. He specializes in cardiology and electrophysiology. He is married and the father of a son and daughter.

Rebecca Heisler is a writer, psychotherapist and student of Judaism and the mystical experience. She is completing several children's stories and a Jewish mystical fantasy novel titled *Moonlight.* She gives presentations and conducts groups on psycho-spiritual development and finding new meaning in Judaism. She can be reached at 619-515-4622.

Judita M. Hruza, M.D., is a retired pediatrician and psychiatrist. Her husband, both her children and their spouses are physicians. Dr. Hruza has published several stories about her Holocaust experiences. She speaks in schools and participated in a documentary film on the death marches. Her e-mail address is *zdyhruza@hotmail.com.*

Beth Huppin enjoys teaching Judaics to children and adults. She currently teaches children at the Seattle Jewish Community School and adults at the Florence Melton Adult Mini-School. Beth is active in the Seattle Jewish community, where she lives with her husband and three daughters.

Norman W. Jaffe was born in Germany and survived forced labor, extermination camps and the Death March of 1945. He was brought back to life by American Army medics. He sailed to the United States in 1946, studied commercial art and opened an advertising studio. He authored a book, and wrote commentaries and nonfiction stories about his experiences as a boy under the Nazi regime. He can be reached by fax or telephone at 805-962-9252.

Rabbi Mordecai Kamenetzky is the scion of rabbinical dynasties and a student of some of the world's most prestigious Yeshivos. Author of the three-volume *Parsha Parables* series, in which he explains difficult Torah passages through stories and historical anecdotes, Rabbi Kamenetzky is a noted lecturer on issues of Torah thoughts and concepts. He shares his keen insights via fax and e-mail with thousands of subscribers to *FaxHomily,* a weekly inspirational newsletter. Rabbi Kamenetzky is the Associate Dean of Yeshiva South Shore in Woodmere, Long Island, where he resides with his family. He can be reached by e-mail at *rmk@torah.org.*

Bel Kaufman came from Russia at age twelve, received her B.A. degree, Magna Cum Laude, from Hunter College; her Master's Degree, First Honors, from Columbia University, and earned Ph.D.s from Nasson College and Hunter College. She taught high-school English and was an assistant professor at City College of New York. She is the author of the #1 bestseller, *Up the Down Staircase* and *Love, Etc.,* as well as numerous stories and articles. Winner of many awards for writing and public speaking, Bel Kaufman is the only surviving granddaughter of the famous Yiddish author, Sholom Aleicheim.

Gina Klonoff received a B.A. in English from the University of Washington, and an M.A. in linguistics from San Francisco State University. She taught English in California for twenty-five years and, after moving with her husband to Las Vegas, became chairperson of the Speakers Bureau of the Holocaust Survivors Group. A freelance writer, she is presently working on a novel. Please e-mail her at *ginanew104@aol.com.*

Trish Krotowski is a freelance writer and novelist in Princeton, New Jersey. As president of Quantum Communications Group, she has written, edited and produced books, reports and articles on health care and technology. She recently completed a contemporary suspense novel.

Harold Kushner is a retired Conservative rabbi living in Natick, Massachusetts. He is the author of *When Bad Things Happen to Good People* and five other bestselling books on religion as a resource for coping with life's problems.

Lawrence Kushner, a leading teacher of Jewish mysticism, is among America's most creative spiritual writers. Author of ten inspiring books, Kushner is Rabbi-in-Residence at Hebrew Union College. He teaches and lectures widely to audiences of all faiths and backgrounds. His books are published by Jewish Lights Publishing, 800-962-4544, *www.jewishlights.com.*

Rabbi Steven Z. Leder has served the Wilshire Boulevard Temple in Los Angeles since 1986. A graduate of Northwestern University, he received his rabbinic ordination from Hebrew Union College. His weekly column for the *Los Angeles Times,* "Jewish Journal," received the American Jewish Press Association's Rapoport Award for Excellence in Commentary.

Amy Hirshberg Lederman is an attorney, freelance writer, professional Jewish educator and educational consultant. After practicing real-estate law for more than fourteen years, she served as the director of the Florence Melton Adult Mini-School of Tucson and as the director of the Department of Jewish Education and Identity of the Jewish Federation of Southern Arizona. She has presented at numerous conferences, board retreats and Jewish organizational events throughout the United States. Lederman is a member of the National Speaker's Bureau for the United Jewish Communities and is available for consultation and presentations. She can be reached by phone at 520-747-8180, faxed at 520-571-7674 or via e-mail at *amyleder@aol.com.*

Rabbi Benji Levene received his rabbinic ordination from the Chief Rabbi of Israel in 1973. Like his grandfather Reb Arye Levin, The Zaddik of Jerusalem, Benji has earned the love and respect of Jews throughout the world. He resides today in Jerusalem with his wife Edna and their ten children. You can contact Rabbi Levene at *eaton@gesher.co.il,* or at his home address: 14 Chai-Taib St., Jerusalem, Israel 95405.

Michael Levy, author, poet, philosopher and inspirational speaker, has penned three books: *What Is the Point?; Minds of Blue Souls of Gold; Enjoy Yourself: It's Later Than You Think.* After a very successful business career, Michael now lives in Florida. Retiring early gave him time to reflect on the meaning of life. Michael has now become an author, poet, philosopher and inspirational speaker on finance, health and happiness. His articles and poems now grace over a thousand Web sites, magazines and journals. He can be contacted at *mikmikl@aol.com, http://www.pointoflife.com* and Point of Life, Inc., P.O. Box 3507, Boynton Beach, FL 33424.

Lisa Lipkin has been entertaining audiences for years with her lively storytelling performances. Combining her own personal experiences with her boundless imagination, her stories are unique. She has toured across America and internationally, appearing at festivals, theaters, museums and schools. She is the author of *Bringing the Story Home: The Complete Guide to Storytelling for Parents* (W. W. Norton, August 2000). Lisa 's original performances, workshops and weekend residencies are geared for adults, children, families and teachers. She can be reached at *Lip2@aol.com.*

Allen S. Maller has been the rabbi of Temple Akiba in Culver City, California, since 1967. He is the author of *God, Sex and Kabbalah,* and the chief editor of The Tikkun Series of Inspirational High Holy Days prayer books.

Yitta Halberstam Mandelbaum is the great-great-granddaughter of the Sanzer Rebbe, a nineteenth-century Hasidic master whose teachings were brought to the American Jewish public and popularized by Shlomo Carlebach. She pursued graduate studies in American literature at New York University. She can be reached at *YMYE@aol.com.*

Hanoch McCarty, Ed.D., is a highly sought-after motivational speaker whose corporate training programs focus on strategies that build employee and customer loyalty, as well as freeing creativity and maximizing personal productivity. His work uses the bottom-line power of kindness and integrity. He can be reached at Learning Resources, P.O. Box 66, Galt, CA 95632, via e-mail at *kindness@bigfoot.com,* or by phone at 209-745-2212.

Cynthia Mercati is a playwright with over thirty published scripts. She has had productions of her plays in every state, and has won several playwriting awards. Cynthia also writes children's books. She often writes about growing up in Chicago and baseball. As a White Sox fan, she's learned to wait for next year! Cynthia can be reached at 696 18th St., #2, Des Moines, IA 50314.

Laurie B. Mintz, Ph.D., is a mother, wife, practicing psychologist and college professor. She has published numerous academic works and is now focusing on creative and inspirational writing. She lives in Columbia, Missouri, with her loving and supportive husband, Glenn, and their two delightful daughters, Jennifer and Allison. Laurie continues to pass the knitted blanket to newborn family members, in hopes it will keep them warm and connected to their ancestors. She can be reached by phone at 573-882-4947 or via e-mail at *MintzL@missouri.edu.*

Patti Moskovitz has been a Jewish educator for more than forty years, teaching all levels of religious education in Reform and Conservative congregations in the San Francisco Bay area. For nearly twenty years, she has served as a conversion tutor for rabbis throughout Northern California. Patti is coauthor of *Embracing the Covenant: Converts to Judaism Tell How and Why* with Rabbi Allan Berkowitz. She is presently working on another book about conversion. Patti has lectured for the B'nai B'rith Youth Organization in the U.S. and Canada and conducts ongoing workshops and classes for interfaith couples, Jews-by-choice and born-Jews who wish to know more about their Jewish heritage. She is a member of the National Advisory Board to the Conversion of Judaism Resource Center. Patti lives in Foster City with her husband, Larry. They have three married children and two grandchildren. She can be reached at 269 Avocet Ct., Foster City, CA 94402 or at 650-349-1222/fax: 650-349-1254.

Elizabeth Sussman Nassau, a freelance writer, lives in Philadelphia with her husband and four children. "There is nothing like the unequivocal love of a Bubbe," she says. "My children no longer have a grandmother, either. But their memories will bring them joy, as have mine."

Rabbi Richard Plavin was ordained a rabbi by the Jewish Theological Seminary and earned his Ed.D. from Teachers College, Columbia University. He is the rabbi of Temple Beth Sholom in Manchester, Connecticut. He is married and has three daughters and one granddaughter. He can be reached at *rabbi@templebethsholom.net.*

Rabbi Henry Rabin is a graduate of Brown University and Hebrew Union College. For thirty-five years he was a Hillel counselor to hundreds of students in Southern California. He has coauthored four books of *Dayenu* cartoons and two counseling books, *Don't Salt the Peanuts: Sayings of the 5-Cent Psychiatrist* and *Simple Guides for the Perplexed.* His favorite hobby is tennis.

Jack Riemer is the founder of the National Rabbinic Network and the editor of *Torah Fax,* both of which are support systems for rabbis across the lines. He is the coeditor of *So That Your Values Live On,* and editor of *Wrestling with the Angel.* Happily married to Susan, they are the proud grandparents of Nathan, Naomi and Sterling. He can be reached at *jackriemer@aol.com.*

Sara Levinsky Rigler is a writer who lives in the Old City of Jerusalem. After a year in India in the 1960s and her graduation *magna cum laude* from Brandeis University, she spent fifteen years living in an ashram where she practiced and taught meditation and Vedanta Philosophy. At the age of thirty-seven, she moved to Jersusalem and began practicing Torah Judaism. She is married with two children. Sara is a featured writer on *www.aish.com,* Aish HaTorah's award-winning Web site on Jewish wisdom and inspiration. She is presently writing her autobiography.

Lottie Robins is a freelance writer who has authored over seven hundred columns, stories and articles. She has written for newspapers in Canada, Pennsylvania and New Jersey, and her articles have appeared in *The Writer, Writer's Digest, The New York Times, Saturday Evening Post, Moment Magazine, Ort Reporter, Catholic Digest* and many others. She was executive editor of Rodale

Press's *Yiddish Lingo*. In addition to teaching nonfiction, she has been conducting workshops in "Writing Your Memoirs" at Elderhostels and adult communities. She lives with her husband, Jack, a retired Ph.D. chemist, and her only claim to a degree is a Ph.T., Putting Hubby Through. Write to her at 223 Meryl Dr., West Palm Beach, FL 33411; e-mail: *jack223@msn.com*.

Rabbi Jack Segal has Bachelor's degrees from New York University and the University of Pittsburgh, two Master's degrees from Oregon State University, a doctorate from Hebrew Union College and a doctorate (in Counseling) from the University of Houston. For thirty-two years, he was rabbi of Beth Yeshurun Congregation in Houston. He speaks throughout the country as an inspirational speaker and on Jewish subjects. Rabbi Segal can be reached for speaking engagements at 4039 Falkirk, Houston, TX 77025, via e-mail at *rabsegal@aol.com* or by phone at 713-664-9989.

Benjamin Sendrow is a Conservative rabbi serving Temple Judea in Fort Myers, Florida. He and his wife, Arlene, have three children: Evan, Sammy and Rachel. Rabbi Sendrow grew up outside of Philadelphia in Cherry Hill, New Jersey. After almost ten years as a Floridian, Rabbi Sendrow still loves his hometown Philadelphia Phillies. He can be reached at *Rab eye@olsusa.com*.

Rabbi Hillel E. Silverman received his B.A. from Yale University in 1945 and was ordained a rabbi by the Jewish Theological Seminary in 1949. He received his Ph.D. in 1952. He is rabbi emeritus of Temple Sholom in Greenwich, Connecticut. He was a naval chaplain and is the coauthor of five books.

Barbara Sofer is a Connecticut-born journalist, novelist and lecturer, who lives in Jerusalem with her husband scientist/writer Gerald Schroeder and their five children. A graduate of the University of Pennsylvania and the Hebrew University of Jerusalem, Barbara is always learning and seeking the transcendence that elevates our ordinary lives. She can be reached at *BSofer@netvision.net.il*.

Linda Spiegler lives in Boulder, Colorado, where she writes and makes art. She also works at the University of Colorado School of Law and is affiliated with the Jewish renewal community in Boulder. Linda is interested in writing/editing projects that focus on spirituality, women, art and related topics. Her e-mail address is *linda.spiegler@colorado.edu*.

Corinne Stavish of Southfield, Michigan, has been a professional storyteller and workshop leader for almost twenty years, who enjoys traveling great distances to tell stories. She has produced three highly acclaimed audiocassette tapes and edited a book of Jewish folktales, *Seeds from Our Past: Planting for the Future*. She teaches full-time in the Department of Humanities, Social Science and Communication at Lawrence Technological University.

Roy Tanenbaum is rabbi of Congregation Beth Tzedec in Toronto, Canada. He is the author of *Prisoner 88: The Man in Stripes*, and *Rinat Dodim—A Commentary on the Prayerbook*. He and his wife, Loretta, have five children and eleven grandchildren. He can be contacted at *rabtenenbaum@cpol.com*.

Abraham J. Twerski is a psychiatrist, rabbi and medical director emeritus of Gateway Rehabilitation Center in Pittsburgh, Pennsylvania. Dr. Twerksi has written thirty-two books on self-esteem, spirituality and chemical dependency. He collaborated with the late Charles Schulz to produce four books utilizing the Peanuts characters to illustrate his points.

Tom Veres was asked by Raoul Wallenberg to document how two Swedes made an extraordinary rescue of thousands of Hungarian Jews from Adolph Eichmann's Einsatzkommando in 1944. Tom did so, often at the risk of his own life. Two of his photos form the basis of the 1997 U.S. stamp honoring Wallenberg. He works as a commercial photographer in New York City. More of his story is told in the young adult biography *Raoul Wallenberg: The Man Who Stopped Death,* which can be ordered from JPS at 800-234-3151. Veres is currently working on his own autobiography.

Kathryn Watterson, award-winning author, teaches writing at Princeton University. Her books, three of which have been chosen by the New York Times as Notable Books of the Year, include *Not by the Sword* (which won a 1996 Christopher Award); *You Must Be Dreaming* (basis of the NBC movie, *Betrayal of Trust*); *Growing into Love* and *Women in Prison* (the seminal book on the subject and basis of the ABC documentary, "Women in Prison"). Her short stories, essays and articles have been published in a variety of national journals, magazines and newspapers, including *The New York Times.* She frequently gives readings and workshops at colleges and universities around the country.

Mike Williams was born in Liverpool, England. He trained as an illustrator and became a cartoonist in 1968. His works have been included in *Playboy, Punch, Private Eye Spectator,* TV animation advertising and greeting cards. He has been a cartoon editor for *Punch* magazine and has produced three books and a large series of greeting cards/interest-sponsored inertia.

Rabbi Gerald I. Wolpe is a native of Boston, Massachusetts. He and his wife, Elaine, have four sons: Stephen, Paul, David and Daniel. Two sons are doctors and two are rabbis. He received his Bachelor's and Master's degrees from New York University, Master's in Hebrew Letters from the Jewish Theological Seminary and his Doctor of Divinity from the Jewish Theological Seminary. He has served congregations in Charleston, South Carolina; Harrisburg, Pennsylvania; and at Har Zion Temple since 1969, where he is now Rabbi Emeritus. He is director of Finkelstein Institute at the Jewish Theological Seminary of America, where he is on the Chancellor's Council. Rabbi Wolpe is on the Administrative Council of the Rabbinical Assembly of America where he also serves on the Executive Committee, and as Chairman of the Committee on Caregiving. He is currently Chairman of the Advisory Committee, Center to Bioethics, University of Pennsylvania, and is a member of the National Coordinating Group on Bioethics and the Law, American Bar Association.

Permissions *(continued from page vi)*

The Story of Mary the Maid. Reprinted by permission of Robert Press, the Estate holder of Naomi Bluestone. ©1999 Robert Press, the Estate holder of Naomi Bluestone.

My Son the Rabbi. Reprinted by permission of Rabbi Michael Gold. ©2000 Rabbi Michael Gold.

The Pretzel Lady's Hanukkah and *A Direct Line to Heaven.* Reprinted by permission of Arnold Fine, The Jewish Press. ©2001 Arnold Fine, The Jewish Press.

The Rebbe Said Thank You. Reprinted by permission of Yosef Jacobson. ©1999 Yosef Jacobson. (Originally appeared in *The Jewish Spark* magazine, September 1999, Vol. 5, Issue 3.)

A Hug in Prison. By Yitta Halberstam Mandelbaum from *Holy Brother: Inspiring Stories and Enchanted Tales About Rabbi Shlomo Carlebach* ©1997. Reprinted by permission of the publisher, Jason Aronson, Inc., Northvale, NJ ©1997. *www.aronson.com.*

A Ray of Peace. Reprinted by permission of Rabbi Harvey Abramowitz. ©1999 Rabbi Harvey Abramowitz.

Rosa. Reprinted by permission of Barbara Sofer. ©1998 Barbara Sofer. Originally appeared as *Mother Daughter's Story* in *Hadassah Magazine,* December 1998.

Stranger than Fiction. Reprinted by permission of Rabbi Hillel E. Silverman. ©1987 Rabbi Hillel E. Silverman.

My Ideals. From *The Diary of a Young Girl, The Definitive Edition* by Anne Frank. Otto H. Frank & Mirjam Pressler, Editors, translated by Susan Massotty, ©1995 by Doubleday, a division of Bantam Doubleday Dell Publishing Group, Inc. Used by permission of Doubleday, a division of Random House, Inc.

Choosing Life. "L'Chaim!" from *My Grandfather's Blessings* by Rachel Naomi Remen, M.D., ©2000 by Rachel Naomi Remen, M.D. Used by permission of Riverhead Books, a division of Penguin Putnam, Inc.

Welcome Home and *A Shabbat Evening in Warsaw.* Reprinted by permission of Patricia Moskovitz. ©2000, 1998 Patricia Moskovitz.

A Surprise in Jerusalem. Reprinted by permission of Rebecca Heisler. ©1999 Rebecca Heisler.

Climbing the Mountain and *Honors at the Kennedy Center.* Reprinted with the permission of Simon & Schuster from *Climbing the Mountain* by Kirk Douglas. ©1997 by The Byrna Company.

An Old Woman's Warmth. From *My Life* by Golda Meir, ©1975 Golda Meir. Used by permission of Putnam Berkley, a division of Penguin Putnam, Inc.

Hanukkah in a Soviet Prison. Reprinted by permission of Yosef Begun. ©1998 Yosef Begun.

How Do You Talk to God? Reprinted by permission of Rabbi Scott Aaron. ©1999 Rabbi Scott Aaron.

It's Only a Matter of Time. Reprinted by permission of Lisa Lipkin. ©1996 Lisa Lipkin.

The Power of a Blue Box. Reprinted by permission of Hanna Bandes Geshelin. ©1992 Hanna Bandes Geshelin.

Four Jewish Boys in the Presbyterian Choir. From *100 Years, 100 Stories* by George Burns, ©1996 by the Estate of George Burns. Used by permission of Putnam Berkley, a division of Penguin Putnam, Inc.

What It Means to Be a Mensch. Reprinted by permission of Rabbi Benjamin Levene and Rabbi Jack Riemer. ©1994 Rabbi Benjamin Levene and Rabbi Jack Riemer.

Standing by His Word. Reprinted by permission of Rabbi Roy D. Tanenbaum. ©1999 Rabbi Roy D. Tanenbaum.

Aaron Feuerstein. Reprinted by permission of Rabbi Jack Segal. ©1996 Rabbi Jack Segal.

Avital. From *Fear No Evil* by Natan Sharansky. ©1988 by Random House, Inc. Reprinted by permission of Random House, Inc.

The Power of Holding Hands. Reprinted by permission of Rabbi Harold E. Kushner. ©1986 Rabbi Harold E. Kushner.

The Letter. Reprinted by permission of Michael Levy. ©2000 Michael Levy.

Lovers . . . Still. Used by permission from *Life Doesn't Get Any Better Than This* by Rabbi Robert A. Alper, ©1996, Liguori Publications, Liguori, MO 63057, USA, *www.Liguori.org.*

I Married Her Sunshine. Reprinted by permission of Miriam Goldbrenner. ©1997 Miriam Goldbrenner.

Unspoken Blessings. "Blessings" [Reprinted here as "Unspoken Blessings"] from *My Grandfather's Blessings* by Rachel Naomi Remen, M.D., ©2000 by Rachel Naomi Remen, M.D. Used by permission of Riverhead Books, a division of Penguin Putnam, Inc.

With Faith, Back into Life. Reprinted by permission of Rabbi Gerald I. Wolpe. ©2001 Rabbi Gerald I. Wolpe.

The Laundry Bag. Reprinted by permission of Chava Weiss. ©2001 Chava Weiss.

The First Media Fundraiser. Reprinted by permission of Miriam Biskin. ©1999 Miriam Biskin.

Stranger on the Bus. Excerpt from *Invisible Lines of Connection: Sacred Stories of the Ordinary* ©1996 Lawrence Kushner (Woodstock, VT; Jewish Lights Publishing), $15.95pb + $3.50/h. Order by mail or call 800-962-4544 or on-line at *www.jewishlights.com*. Permission granted by Jewish Lights Publishing, P.O. Box 237, Woodstock, VT 05091.

The Merit of a Young Priest and *A Hill in Bergen Belsen.* Excerpted from *Hasidic Tales of the Holocaust* by Yaffa Eliach. Published by Oxford University Press. Reprinted by permission of Miriam Altshuler Literary Agency, on behalf of Yaffa Eliach. ©1982 Yaffa Eliach.

By Might or Spirit? Reprinted by permission of Jonathan Elkins. ©1999 Jonathan Elkins.

A Simple Blessing. Excerpted from *The Extraordinary of Ordinary Things,* ©1999. Reprinted with permission of the publisher, Behrman House, Inc., *www.behrmanhouse.com.*

We Are All Jews Now. Reprinted by permission of Bryan Aubrey. ©1999 Bryan Aubrey.

The Temples Are Burning. Reprinted by permission of Bryan Aubrey and Rabbi Mona Alfi. ©1999 Bryan Aubrey and Rabbi Mona Alfi.

Let Freedom Ring in Iowa City. Reprinted by permission of Corinne Stavish. ©1997 Corinne Stavish. Appeared in the *Century Village West* newspaper, "The Reporter."

Cardinal Bernardin and *Lost and Found.* Reprinted by permission of Marsha Arons. ©1998, 2000 Marsha Arons.

A Jewish Christmas Story. Reprinted by permission of Irene Frisch. ©1991 Irene Frisch.

Go in Good Health. Reprinted by permission of Lottie Robins. ©1965 Lottie Robins.

Upstairs at the Rialto. Reprinted by permission of Elayne Clift. Excerpted from *To New Jersey, with Love and Apologies* ©1999 Elayne Clift.

The Story of Raoul Wallenberg. Reprinted by permission of Thomas Veres. ©2001 Thomas Veres.

The Compassion of a King. Reprinted by permission of Beth Huppin. ©1997 Beth Huppin.

Jerusalem Encounter. Reprinted by permission of Bronia Galmitz Gallon. ©1970 Bronia Galmitz Gallon.

A Shabbat Miracle. Reprinted by permission of Aryeh ben David. ©2000 Aryeh ben David.

Grandmother's Candlesticks. Reprinted by permission of Amy Hirshberg Lederman. ©1995 Amy Hirshberg Lederman.

Connecting the Generations. Reprinted by permission of Gina Klonoff. ©2000 Gina Klonoff. Originally appeared in *Women's League Outlook Magazine,* Winter 2000.

The Rimonim. ©1989 by Denny Pinkus from *A Vase for a Flower: Tales of an Antique Dealer* by Denny Pinkus. Reprinted by permission of St. Martin's Press, LLC.

The Family Heirloom. Reprinted by permission of Linda Spiegler. ©1998 Linda Spiegler.

Of Angels and Poinsettias. Reprinted by permission of Aish HaTorah's Web site, *www.aish.com,* an award-winning Web site on Jewish wisdom and inspiration. ©2001 aish.com.

The Shawl. Reprinted by permission of Laurie Mintz. ©1998 Laurie Mintz.

Missing the Boat. Reprinted by permission of Tanya Susan Bank. ©2001 Tanya Susan Bank.

Raisins and Almonds. Reprinted by permission of Elizabeth Sussman Nassau. ©1998 Elizabeth Sussman Nassau.

The World's Greatest Stand-Up Comedian. Reprinted by permission of Rabbi Joan S. Friedman. ©1998 Rabbi Joan S. Friedman.

Dreaming of Matzah. Reprinted by permission of Trish Krotowski. ©2000 Trish Krotowski.

The Fire of Hope. Reprinted by permission of Rabbi Kenneth L. Cohen. ©2000 Rabbi Kenneth L. Cohen.

The Making of a Physician. Reprinted by permission of Judita M. Hruza, M.D. ©1992 Judita M. Hruza, M.D.

The Day Hitler Touched Me. Reprinted by permission of Norman W. Jaffe. ©2000 Norman W. Jaffe. Originally appeared in *The Santa Barbara Independent* (Issue 11-9-2000; p. 71).

The Last Four Digits. Reprinted by permission of Rabbi Harold J. Goldberg. ©1989 Rabbi Harold J. Goldberg.

Owing a Debt of Gratitude. Reprinted by permission of Erica S. Goldman-Brodie. ©1997 Erica S. Goldman-Brodie.

It Should Once Again See Light and *Awakening.* Reprinted by permission of Blair P. Grubb, M.D. ©2001 Blair P. Grubb, M.D.

Shoes and Hair. Reprinted by permission of Arielle Greenbaum. ©1996 Arielle Greenbaum.

The Man Who Waited Forty-Five Years to Blow His Shofar. Reprinted by permission of Rabbi Allen S. Maller. ©1990 Rabbi Allen S. Maller.

The Two Eyes. Reprinted by permission of Leah Golomb. ©2000 Leah Golomb.

My Five-Year-Old Spiritual Teacher. Reprinted by permission of Rabbi Mordechai Liebling, the Estate holder of Rabbi Devora Bartnoff. ©2001 Rabbi Mordechai Liebling, the Estate holder of Rabbi Devora Bartnoff.

The Presence of God. From *My Grandfather's Blessings* by Rachel Naomi Remen, M.D., ©2000 by Rachel Naomi Remen, M.D. Used by permission of Riverhead Books, a division of Penguin Putnam, Inc.

Diamonds Polished Here. Reprinted by permission of Rabbi Abraham J. Twerski, M.D. ©1997 Rabbi Abraham J. Twerski, M.D.

To an Audience Yet Unborn. Adapted by permission from *Parsha Parables* by Rabbi Mordecai Kamenetzky. ©1998 Bentch Press.

Here I Am. Reprinted by permission of Rabbi Benjamin Sendrow. ©2000 Rabbi Benjamin Sendrow.

The Jewish Mayor and Mother Teresa. ©1992 by Edward I. Koch with Daniel Paisner from *Citizen Koch: An Autobiography* by Edward I. Koch with Daniel Paisner. Reprinted by permission of St. Martin's Press, LLC.

To Make a Minyan. Reprinted by permission of Hanoch McCarty. ©1999 Hanoch McCarty.

Harry's Blessings. Reprinted by permission of Carole Goldstein. ©1991 Carole Goldstein.

The Hanukkah Party. Reprinted by permission of Rina Friedman. ©1998 Rina Friedman.

Also Available in Quality Paperback

A Cup of Chicken Soup for the Soul
Chicken Soup for the Cat & Dog Lover's Soul
Chicken Soup for the Christian Family Soul
Chicken Soup for the Christian Soul
Chicken Soup for the College Soul
Chicken Soup for the Country Soul
Chicken Soup for the Couple's Soul
Chicken Soup for the Expectant Mother's Soul
Chicken Soup for the Father's Soul
Chicken Soup for the Gardener's Soul
Chicken Soup for the Golden Soul
Chicken Soup for the Golfer's Soul
Chicken Soup for the Jewish Soul
Chicken Soup for the Kid's Soul
Chicken Soup for the Little Souls
Chicken Soup for the Mother's Soul, Vol. I, II
Chicken Soup for the Nurse's Soul
Chicken Soup for the Parent's Soul
Chicken Soup for the Pet Lover's Soul
Chicken Soup for the Preteen Soul
Chicken Soup for the Single's Soul
Chicken Soup for the Soul, Vol. I-VI
Chicken Soup for the Soul at Work
Chicken Soup for the Soul Cookbook
Chicken Soup for the Sports Fan's Soul
Chicken Soup for the Surviving Soul
Chicken Soup for the Teenage Soul, Vol. I, II, III
Chicken Soup for the Teenage Soul Journal
Chicken Soup for the Teenage Soul Letters
Chicken Soup for the Teenage Soul on Tough Stuff
Chicken Soup for the Unsinkable Soul
Chicken Soup for the Veteran's Soul
Chicken Soup for the Woman's Soul, Vol. I, II
Chicken Soup for the Writer's Soul
Condensed Chicken Soup for the Soul
Sopa de Pollo para el Alma, Vol. I, II, III
Sopa de Pollo para el Alma de la Madre
Sopa de Pollo para el Alma de la Mujer
Sopa de Pollo para el Alma del Adolescente
Sopa de Pollo para el Alma del Trabajador
Sopa de Pollo para el Alma del Cristiano